A Conversation with Fear

Mermer Blakeslee

for my teachers
especially the mountains

~

in memory of Otto Frei

I am grateful to:

Randlett Walster, co-worker in the dark from beginning to end;
Carol Levine, for her clarity;
Maggie Loring, for her tenacious idealism;
Joyce Weston, for her care and carefulness;
Cal Cantrell, for breaking all rules;
Jean Naggar, for her hope;
James Hillman and Margot Mc Lean, for their love of the world;
My mother, for her wildness;
Hansen, for his questions;
and Eric, always.

Contents

The minstrel now struck up a lively song
of Ares' lust for fair-haired Aphrodite
who bore to him, the piercer of shields, two sons,
dread Fear and Flight, and daughter Harmony.

— Homer and Hesiod, translated
by Herbert Jordan

A Note to the Reader

Fear is a four-letter word, an F-word. And like the other word with that label, it resonates far, spreads across many boundaries, sinks to the lowest levels, becomes very big very quickly.

As a professional skier and teacher, I have kept close company with fear, tracking its path in both my life and the lives of my students. In this book, I offer you ideas, stories, strategies, as well as a few flights of imagination distilled from twenty-five years of working with frightened students. I use skiing as a metaphor but it should remain just that—to clarify our intricate relationship with fear and invite into our lives the power of surrender. So for all those who do not ski, welcome. I hope the metaphor stays transparent, and that through fear's straightforward, often obvious expression in skiing, we can discern its more subtle turns when it sneaks closer to the core of our lives.

One of my first entanglements with fear occurred not on a mountain at all but in the tame environment of a local pool where I worked at seventeen as a swim teacher. There, standing in the shallow end, I held Tommy, a 250-pound man with hair all over his body, trembling in my arms as he tried to lower his head back to reach the water. He could not do it. As soon as his vision left the security of his surroundings—the table where his wife sat shaded by an umbrella, the dry aquamarine above the water line, the white coping at the pool's edge—as soon as matter gave way to only sky above him, his fists flailed in the air. He grabbed at my shoulders as he struggled to right himself again. My arms soon tired but my mind continued to race: how to get Tommy to do what he was paying me for, to help him achieve his one goal, to float on his back. And behind my mind's frenetic pace emerged what was to become a familiar question in my life, "What is this fear about?"

"Can you teach my Tommy?" the woman on the phone had asked, responding to my ad for private lessons. "He's so frightened of water, he can't even take a bath." I said yes immediately, revealing both my audacity and my ignorance. I was so sure Tommy was her son that I never bothered to ask his age. And I never doubted I could entice the small boy I imagined into the water. I gathered every toy I could find, some to float, some to sink.

When a couple with an infant approached the pool, it slowly dawned on me: the large man wearing a bathing suit was "my Tommy." I followed his eyes down to the pile of toys. Using a teenager's facility with quick lies, I scrambled to explain, "So you can learn how to play with your new baby in the water!" But that did not help me face the real issue: I had no clue what I was going to do. I had jumped headlong into the sink or swim cliché.

By the side of the pool, we touched the water with one hand, one foot, then the other. After half an hour, we were up to our waists, softening the knees, bouncing, again and again, deeper, feeling the water slip up to our chests. Too far! Tommy grabbed me, breathing so fast I thought he was about to cry. We stood straight, the water back down at our waists, safe. Very slowly, we began again. Tommy's huge biceps would involuntarily contract, making his hands and fingers clench into distorted, odd-shaped fists.

This is fear, I remember thinking. *Real fear. Not just being afraid.*

Just being afraid meant to me a feeling *Tommy* felt, a feeling inside him that I could only sense. This fear seemed larger than that. I supported him with my arms as he leaned farther back, his eyes squeezed shut, his face pained. Carefully, I softened my hold so his body stretched deeper into the water. He tightened. I responded, strengthening my support. Back and forth, we danced—leading, following, resisting, softening—both of us entangled and wet *within* the fear. The fear no longer belonged only to him; I could touch it, but even more importantly, I was being touched by it.

Recalling this event now is like recognizing the face of an adult in their baby picture. I could not know then that I would be working with frightened students for much of my life, or how this event would register a small but seminal shift in my perception of fear. Although I could not articulate it at the time, I had veered from the modern, Western perception that we own our emotions, that we can and should control them, and that they exist solely inside of us. As I perceived love to be real, with its own volition and power and sudden movements, so I perceived fear. And like love, fear could catch us, body, mind, heart and soul.

I have been afraid many times. As a kid, that fear lived on the back side of thrill. I grew up in Windham, a small town in New York's Catskill Mountains, and began skiing at age three. I remember at ten rolling into an aerodynamic tuck behind my older brother to schuss a steep, roughly packed trail from the top of the mountain to the bottom yelling "shi-i-it!" the whole way. Through my teenage years, training as a ski racer at Burke Mountain Academy, my relationship with fear grew more refined. I began to call it *the black door*. I knew that if I stepped through that door, there was no going back. I had to trust my body to respond and act on its own. The real trick in racing seemed to be getting through that door, leaving behind what was known, controllable, and therefore, safe.

After college, I began to teach skiing. I didn't draw a distinction between what I had felt as a racer and what my beginners were experiencing. In fact, I was drawn to those skiers who had the greatest sensitivity to fear. They understood, viscerally, the inherent tension skiing offered: the pull between control and surrender, technique and freedom, fear and thrill. And they displayed unusual emotional courage. I experimented with strategies I had used in racing, tweaking them to serve each student.

I began asking for students who were frightened, much to my supervisor's surprise because no other instructor wanted them. In 1987, Leila Brown, Howard Savin and I started Windham's first "fear workshop." Four students were courageous enough to sign up.

Vomiting, hyperventilating, uncontrollable trembling can all happen to frightened skiers on a hill and non-skiers often ask me, "Why would anyone do that to themselves? Why not just stay indoors?" I wondered the same thing until one student said to me, "I have tried to ski every winter for fifteen years and I've never been able to go downhill without holding onto the instructor. You're my last chance."

She predicted my question.

"I don't want to be a *skier*," she explained. "I just want to let myself go down the hill. Once. Feel my body just do it. I haven't been able to trust that it could. Just for a second, I want to feel that trust." She wanted to pass through the black door.

In 1984, I started competing again, this time to qualify as an examiner for the Professional Ski Instructors of America (PSIA). Once qualified, I could conduct clinics and examine teachers around the eastern United States. With my nerves inflaming regularly, I could now study fear from the perspective of performer and athlete as well as teacher. Conventional sport psychology was no help, with its emphasis on behavioral conditioning, its obsession with control, and its sterile, scientific language.

As a writer as well as skier, I knew how fear arose whenever I had to let go of control so a story or poem could emerge. I felt the same fear when I had to give up the tendency to micromanage my body during an athletic feat. So why, I wondered, would we approach fear by grasping for more control? Wouldn't we then lose the power of surrender? The possibility for innovation? As an instruction manual would be to an artist, behavioral sport psychology was to me as an athlete, arriving after the fact, prescribing step-by-step programs where originality should be the rule.

When my personal investigation into fear changed its context from racing to PSIA's competitions, my understanding broadened. The one god of racing is and always will be speed, with the supremely elegant efficiency that requires. Now I needed to recognize other qualities as well, like accuracy, finesse, freedom and flair. I found that each part of the competition—from skiing in bumps, powder, slush and ice to slow, controlled demonstrations, from charismatic teaching and public speaking to technical knowledge—each challenge wore its own face of fear which in turn required a different response. Fear of speed is easy to imagine but what about fear of slowness, fear of silence, fear of the initial anarchy of a group when a genuine synergy is about to emerge...

Each time I expanded the context for competition or the forum for teaching, my ideas about fear broke down, sometimes irreparably. This kept my engagement both vital and scary. I was becoming known in the ski industry for my "fear work" and yet I rarely stood on firm ground. The only thing I could be sure of was that fear would continue to offer me something I had never dealt with before. Not only did I *not* have a degree in psychology, I could actually guarantee my ignorance. I was usually my first guinea-pig, but every student was one as well, and each challenge, difficult at the time, demanded a deeper look, an opening previously concealed.

In 1992, I tried out for the Alpine Demonstration Team (called in the industry the national demo team). Every four years, PSIA holds a six-day competition at Snowbird, Utah. Each of the country's nine regions chooses its candidates who will compete. From that pool, the judges select thirteen team members.

I arrived at Snowbird well-prepared and with a lot of support, but I choked. I could not, even while skiing on my own, feel anything from my waist down. As if I were trapped in a bubble, I felt cut off from the undulations of the mountain, oblivious to what lay ahead or even beneath me. As a teacher, this was an important response to study, but even more important was accepting the failure that followed. I had lectured about the fertility of failure. I had empathized with many worthy teachers who had failed exams. I had quoted Churchill and Gurdjieff on the subject, but I had never failed a PSIA exam before. I was stunned by its effect. I felt like a rejected lover, even though I had always pretended my involvement in skiing and PSIA was a peripheral passion. But we can never anticipate what will tear the soul open. I felt the winds blow through, and those winds kept me reflective, raw, smarting, and still fascinated with fear.

Four years later when I went back to Snowbird to try out for the team again, I had none of my previous innocence. I was no longer under the illusion that being well-prepared would protect me. And I was immune to the bumper sticker slogans around me, especially the best-will-prevail or give-it-all-you-got varieties our culture spouts so prolifically. I knew I could step through a hole at any moment and be dragged down by the fear that lurked nearby. But for the previous four years, I had grappled with that fear. Our relationship, though still lively and unpredictable, had grown increasingly complex and substantial. That complexity helped me succeed on the second try. As a national demo team member, I expanded my work beyond the East. I traveled from Maine to Alaska, lecturing, training teachers, and giving fear workshops. All across the country, I found instructors familiar with frightened students. Their years of experience as well as their finely chiseled questions helped clarify the ideas that form the core of this book.

Training teachers kept my work balanced between practical techniques on the one hand and ideas that directed and strengthened intuition on the other. This book reflects both that balance and that tension. The sight of a student stuck halfway down a slope trembling and crying while five others are waiting at the bottom can terrify even veteran instructors. They needed nuts-and-bolts strategies. But I also found that what fear demanded was a flexible, resourceful intuition. I tried to offer stories and ideas that helped teachers respond to their students intuitively rather than programmatically. If they were to help people ski on the edge, I wanted to encourage them to teach on the edge.

We all pack different ideas and feelings into the word *fear*: fear of the unknown, fear of failure, of losing control, of aging, of falling down, of being carried up in a chair lift, fear of the body reacting and fear of the body not reacting, even the fear of saying the word *fear*. This book does not attempt to define fear or to explain why a frightened person experiences certain physiological responses. It does not separate students into categories or classify symptoms. Others have done a good job at that.

What this book does attempt is to offer you both audacity and comfort. Although comfort feels quiet, it arrives through a bold move: accepting the presence of fear. To do this, we must pick our way between two powerful tendencies, to control and to cure, the Scylla and Charybdis of our culture. These tendencies show themselves constantly in words like *manage, handle, overcome, conquer, dispel, banish, fix…* By regarding fear as a pathology to control or cure, we assume that life without its presence is possible, normal, or even desirable. But once we accept fear as a habitual acquaintance in an imaginative, meaningful life, we can begin to cultivate a conversation with it rather than engage it in a fight.

The word *conversation* contains many verbs—pause, respond, yell, sigh, reflect. But in our conversation with fear, to listen might be the most difficult and the most important action we do. "Now when my hands start to shake and my mouth goes dry," one man said to me, "I think, here it is again. Fear. Keep going but keep listening. I'm slowly learning how to listen without falling to pieces." Luckily, we have our entire lives to learn.

This book emerged from the convoluted give-and-take between student and teacher—a potluck of fear, pressure, humor, generosity, empathy, resourcefulness, and love. Although I have now broadened my work beyond the ski world, I still feel grateful to the collective insight and response skiing has generated. In the spirit of that gratitude, may this book help you take heart, a word once synonymous with courage.

The Moment of Fear

CHAPTER 1

Meeting the Moment

It is a tremendous act of violence to begin anything.
— Rainer Maria Rilke

The time has come to jump. I must leave the slow-paced, easy busyness of the garden and walk through the door into my study and face the blank page. Suddenly, I want only to putter among my plants—pink against red, gray, shades of green, deep pine to iridescent—a sanctuary of beauty and memory and what is too deep and inchoate to articulate. But I turn away to sit at my desk. The pivotal moment has come. I recognize it. I hate and love it. My body droops with fatigue, my hands shake as I look out from the edge of a cliff. I want the words to leap down onto the page. But do I dare push off? Like J. Alfred Prufrock, I brew myself one more cup of tea.

What *is* this moment that comes before every small or large leap? Whether it is time to begin a performance, or walk into the boss's office and say "I quit," or sit down in protest in the town square, there is a moment of passage, a push off, after which we cannot go back. It can seem like a quick flash of time, the tiniest of rooms, but it is packed with a magnetism that attracts and repels us in seemingly equal amounts.

What is comforting and mundane starts to beckon with a happy familiarity—the clean tabletop, the dish drainer stacked with dishes, the laundry basket waiting. I could vacuum the living room, it really *needs* it, I say to myself, and soon a list floods my mind: food to buy, that insurance company to call, the endless number of weeds to pull. I am tricky. I pick the most valid, must-do jobs that I could even wax self-righteous about, jobs that sustain and maintain the sturdy fiber of our lives: food and shelter. But I know this dilemma. If I keep retreating from that vital moment, those mundane acts of maintenance will stack up one after the other and turn living into a chronic support system for life.

What then do we want to avoid? What huge tension vibrates inside that miniscule moment that we do not want to face? Is it all the possibility inherent in the push-off? In that moment, we decide to leave behind firm ground and surrender ourselves into air. We willingly suspend the control that comforts us, and give ourselves over to the possibility rather than the certainty of landing. The moment carries a gravity not only for the body but for the soul. We become electrified, tense, engaged along our entire lengths: we are entering a mystery, a question. To do this, we must welcome, as in sex, a tiny death. This moment is an infinitesimal microcosm of life, packed with a pulsing larger than ourselves. And our proximity to this energy—electric, magnetic, divine— infuses a beauty into the homey comforts of our lives. What else can make the dish drainer shine so?

I remember the first time this moment took on a life of its own and I became aware of its force, a puppet of its push and pull. When I was a teenager, I loved to jump off rocky ledges into small pools of water along with my older brother and his friends. Then I fell in love and following my sweetheart, I made all sorts of unprotected leaps, across a deep chasm onto another outcropping, or across rushing water to grab an overhang. Though I was aware that I could not make a mistake, I never told myself that. If I had articulated my focus, it would have been, *Do this. Exactly this. Now.* The first time was the only time. My awareness squeezed itself down into that *one* jump. There was nothing left over, no thoughts leaking out the edges, no anticipation or fear of what was farther ahead.

Then it changed. I was nineteen, still in love. Four of us went to Huntington Gorge in the northwestern part of Vermont. Rocky cliffs rose on each side of the stream. We hiked to a flat ledge that jutted high above a narrow, deep pool where the water gathered itself up for a moment. It had been a couple of years since I had jumped. Scott, my sweetheart, took off his clothes and stood at the edge, comfortable in his nakedness. I watched him look down— for longer than a moment—before he leapt. A long silence and then a splash. We heard him surface, sputtering, hooting and hollering. The fall was long and the water was cold! He shot out of the pool and scrambled onto the rocks below, dancing the cold away. Then he crooked his neck up, waiting for us. He looked tiny down there, his skin a bright, fragile white against the shades of gray. Henry then followed his path out to the edge and jumped. My friend, Cece, also once fearless, was now scared. I told her I would go first. I took off my clothes and stood where rock and air met. The pool looked far away, black and small, the size of a puddle, of a quarter. There were rocky outcroppings everywhere, and huge upturned slabs of granite. Across from me, a small maple clung by its roots to a rock face, no more than three feet high with just a few leaves hanging. I had the thought, *What if I miss?* My feet got hot on the ledge. I backed up. Then I tried again. The boys yelled from below. Words of encouragement, words of instruction, words. I backed up again. Back and forth, back and forth. I stood at the edge, I even said yes! and went—or almost went, but even within that instant, I pulled myself back.

That moment of push-off had changed. It was no longer just a flash of time that I could rush through unconsciously. That day, it introduced itself to me; it revealed its nature. I was pushed, I was pulled. *The moment was energized.* I kept banging against a wall inside of it. *Three-dimensional.* I held my stomach feeling sick, both viscerally and emotionally under its power. *Grips body AND soul, makes them indistinguishable.* With my feet, I reached again for the edge of the rock... air. To leave the safety of the ledge meant to lose control, there was no going back. *A finality.* On the far side of this moment was an impenetrable darkness I could not see beyond. *Shadowed in mystery.* This was no ordinary moment.

A few minutes later, I jumped. I said yes! with enough intensity to make it over the wall. Shaky and elated, I crawled out of the water onto the rocks. Then Cece stood on the ledge alone. The three of us looked up knowing how small we must appear. We yelled. More words. Back and forth, back and forth till finally, she jumped.

We didn't know it at the time but the ambivalence that Cece and I experienced that day was far more valuable than the ease of jumping freely and unconsciously as we both had before. We had sparked a relationship with that enigmatic moment and had begun to glimpse its nature. How could we know what possibilities it held in store?

The Thrill-Freedom Continuum

We all reside on a continuum in relation to fear. On one extreme are those who want or need some thrill, crave some physical exhilaration. Their lives mirror that of the outward-facing hero who leaves his own city to conquer the dragon and capture a boon to bring back home. They want and choose the challenge of an adventure—somewhat risky, somewhat unpredictable—to bring back into their lives a spark of joy and vitality. Even though they flirt with this measure of thrill, they often want the accompanying fear to be erased. Look at all the other heroes on the quest—they look free and easy, why not me? But once someone is conscious of the push and pull within that moment, fear becomes the flip side of thrill and remains a permanent part of leaving the "home city."

Some thrill-seekers are accustomed to taking risks in the

court room, dealing with their teenagers, creating a painting. They know how to face that moment intellectually, emotionally, artistically, or psychologically but they want to translate that risk-taking into sport, experiencing fear in one of its most physical manifestations. "I want to feel it in every muscle," a student said to me. Conversely, others who barely blink at physical risk want to learn how to take more ethereal leaps, like a ski racer I know who deliberated for months before deciding to audition for a play.

At the other extreme of the continuum are those that do not want thrill at all. Fear haunts them. They want to be free of it. They want relief, some ease. They have often survived a trauma that has overwhelmed their lives, invading their home city. What was once comfortable and familiar is now often a challenge. Everywhere, even home, is a new place, with new rules, new pressures, new limits contracting their feelings of comfort and freedom. For them, the edge of a cliff can pop up anywhere. Just to live, they must constantly pass through the moment. Outsiders, especially thrill-seekers often can't see those moments. Getting in the car to drive three hours to see the grandchildren for the first time after her husband died. Returning, brain-injured, to golf where he golfed and socialized for twenty years. Walking alone out to the barn on a cold, winter night. These are the freedom-seekers. They want to return to some semblance of being free: safe and "at home." But like thrill, that freedom comes inextricably coupled with fear.

Thrill-seekers voluntarily choose to play with speed and gravity: water-skiing, bike racing, sky-diving, skidding a car in a parking lot. Freedom-seekers want to return to activities they did *before*—riding a horse one has already ridden for five years, ice-skating after a major surgery—activities chosen not in a search for thrill but to use as a shield to repel the fear pressing upon them. They need to feel comfortable again living on this earth. In between the extremes lies the majority of us, sometimes leaning toward one side, sometimes toward the other. But whether we seek thrill, freedom, or a mixture of both, the moment we must pass through can feel the same.

CHAPTER 2

Skiing: A Metaphor

The strongest, surest way to the soul is through the flesh.
— Mabel Dodge

Many of us covet the unconscious, fearless freedom we had before—before we were injured or traumatized or aged. We want to return to that innocent state. We don't want to get stuck before we jump. We don't like our feet to tap and our hands to shake before we speak. We want that moment, and all the fear inherent within it, banished. But it can't be. That moment of passage before we willingly surrender is an essential part of any leap forward, any creative act. It is not a moment for *us* to control or manage. We need to become *its* students, its devotees.

Through skiing, I began to study the nature of this moment. Since the age of three, I felt skiing's fundamental tussle—shall I surrender my body *down* the hill or hold my own *across* the hill? As I grew older and began to race, this question became more tangible and more subtle. But it was not until I began to teach fearful students that I was able to characterize this moment of surrender, and in the thirty years since, I observed a wide array of responses.

To ski is to flirt with gravity. We go up only to come down. We pay to travel in a chairlift or a tram up the side of a mountain in order to feel gravity's pull, to feel ourselves in a delicious, selective fall like a moment in love. Like love, skiing has within it, inherent in its very nature, *the act of letting go.* And it is this letting go, this feeling of a controlled fall down a mountain that brings the thrill, the freedom, the feeling of being swept along in the fever of a new crush. But to willingly let go, to fall, we must move through that small passage of time which contains not only exhilaration but fear.

Lodged within the very idea of falling is the risk of getting hurt. Even if the evidence were there that no risk is involved in a particular fall, the mind still binds the two together in a long and tight association. In skiing, the actual risk we take might be negligible but we can nevertheless experience that *feeling* of a fall and therefore the feeling of standing on the edge, a push-off point, the moment.

Skiing is not an ordinary risk sport; it offers a huge range of risk-taking. My father can play it safe at eighty. My son can scare himself silly at eighteen. It's a democratic sport that accommodates every level of skill, every degree of athleticism, and almost every age and body-type. You don't have to be particularly natural or experienced or skillful or daring.

This broad gradation of risk makes skiing a compelling, almost magical medium in which to work with fear. The degree of risk can be finely regulated. We can stay quite cozy if we want, we can even get bored, or we can dare to let go a little farther than we did yesterday, stay a little longer with that feeling of falling. Then we can ease up, ski slowly and comfortably for a while until the appetite for thrill or the need for freedom rises again.

For some people, the desire or need to dare does not arise on its own. The presence of risk causes conflict. A part of them wants to push off from the edge and feel the body surrender. But another part cannot let go of the safe and familiar. Like Cece and me, they often start to start but then back off as the conflicting voices get louder and louder. This is not a conversation. This is a fight.

Many feel the fight is not worth it. They stick to the safe and familiar, their comfort zone. As one student said, "I've almost skied myself to sleep." But some feel they're losing something, a joyfulness or freedom they once experienced. "I felt my spirit fading," another said. "Each year I got worse. I became so...*tame.*" They want to learn how to take that one step over the edge again, even if it's a small step with little risk.

It does not matter if taking that step means feeling safe driving to the store again or if it means leaping off a cornice. What is important is learning to guide ourselves through what we recognize and acknowledge as the pivotal moment, to give the voice that says, *Yes, I can do that* a chance.

Trusting The Body To Play

A survey done in 1996 by Ski Industries of America asked a group of women who no longer skied why they quit. One of the main reasons was that they did not feel athletic enough. Many of the women I teach go to the gym, jog, take tennis or riding lessons, and yet they do not feel athletic either. "I'm basically a klutz." "I'm gonna be your worst student." "I've never been good at *anything* even slightly athletic."

Some of these women are actually very coordinated. When I described one as a "natural," she said after her initial surprise, "I guess I've always had a big chip on my shoulder and any mistake I made I chalked up to being unathletic. When actually, I just needed to keep practicing."

Is athleticism only a permanently fixed, primal condition? Isn't it also a quality capable of being developed?

At any beach you can see even young girls strut like they're on a fashion runway, wily and self-conscious, already caught in the tight grip of convention while packs of uninhibited boys twice their age still play wildly in the waves. (This is not just a modern dilemma. The ancient Greeks felt that if young girls fell too soon under the influence of Aphrodite, the girls-turned-women would become too civilized and tame. During those susceptible adolescent years, Grecian girls participated in the bear cults of Artemis to sustain for a little longer—and even cultivate—their solitary, uncivilized wildness.)

Spontaneous play—rough-housing, snowball fights, Frisbee on a beach—gives the body a store of knowledge that it can translate into disciplined, precise movements. The body begins to know, during each millisecond, precisely where it is in space and also where the *other* is—a person, a Frisbee, a ball—and exactly how far and in which direction to move to meet or avoid that other. As this body-knowledge grows, so does our trust. It is simple: the more we see that the body does know, the more we allow it to do what it knows. We stop micromanaging. We "let go." Practiced movements that might have been robotic and mechanical become naturally playful, a fusion of discipline and freedom that we associate with being athletic.

Many women have not felt this trust in the body for thirty or forty years, even though they jog daily and take a battery of tennis lessons. They abandoned athletic *play*—jumping, running, diving for a ball or flinging themselves into a snow bank—as early as eight or ten. The slow, methodical work of practicing a movement—a slice backhand, a chip shot—in a standard lesson format is easy for them. What feels scary if not impossible is to translate that work into what is unmanaged, creative and free of prescription, in short, play. However, even at a low level of skill development, "play" is possible if we have the trust to let go of the learned micromanagement of the body.

One of skiing's curious gifts can help revive the spirit of play. This gift will never be marketed: the unexpected joy of a fall, a real fall, losing control and landing on the ground. Whenever a person falls and slides on the snow without getting hurt, they almost always laugh out loud or hoot and holler, surprised out of their prescribed patterns of movement, their bodies taken beyond their habitual limits. An unintended "letting go." Even if they feel a little shaky at first, they are still energized.

My six year-old kid kicks out and runs excitedly back and forth with his Sheltie in our too-small house. He hits the slippery rug, slides happily even on the wooden floor. "You're outa-control," I yell from my desk, smiling. "I'm outa-control outa-control outa-control…" he sings back, sounding partly like a motor, partly like a drum. It has not occurred to him that being out of control might be scary. The freedom of his movements makes even the word *"control"* seem irrelevant. No wonder he's only using it as a beat he can bop his head to. How can we say he has moved *out* of control when he never attempted to stay *in* control? He didn't intend to fall, but I doubt his body registered even a momentary request to stay upright. As soon as falling became inevitable, it became desirable, part of the play.

At the other extreme is my eighty-two year-old friend setting her foot carefully down on her stone step. The next foot starts to peek out. She keeps her arms close to her body as she holds to the railing. Just the thought of falling will cause her to tighten her grip.

I see I'm halfway between. I go rollerblading for the first time. I feel the fight. I want to move freely but I also want to stay safe. I become keenly aware of my limitations, the perimeter of movement I have grown accustomed to. Any movement beyond that boundary feels frightening, as if my body were suddenly out of reach, outa-control. My mouth tightens. I pull my arms closer to my trunk; my legs stiffen. I start to circle, but I can no longer let my feet go out from beneath my hips. I stay very upright, like a kid turning slowly on a bike. This self-imposed control isn't much fun. Just like my ski students, I want to break free, but I don't, I want to, I don't… Faster, then slower, my body reflects every nuance of ambivalence. But then, I fall… and I can't help it, I laugh, each time, before I start to hurt. Every year our bodies move in a smaller space as more and more, we hold our limbs in—in control, inside the shrinking perimeter of our comfort zone. Falling breaks that, shakes our arms and our legs free, surprises the body into an unexpected direction.

But I don't want to fall. Again. Falling on pavement hurts. And my old friend assures me that you do get smarter as you get older. *You can learn to pick your falls.* A good fall down a ski slope where you can slide gently to a stop... or better yet, falling into three feet of new snow. It doesn't hurt! No wonder it's impossible to keep from laughing. It breaks the mold and revives the memory of spontaneous play. Even if you do get smarter as you get older, that same friend added afterward with a mischievous grin, "But you keep making all the same mistakes."

Skiing is a silly, useless thing, nothing but play, and I've often begrudged that, after practicing for days to perfect a minor movement. But I have found that very uselessness makes skiing useful as a metaphor. Because we are not running a business our families depend on, or raising a teenager, we have the luxury to *practice* surrender, giving ourselves over to gravity. We can learn how to be guided through that moment, either to release our edges down the fall-line or to allow our legs to swing farther out to the side than they did before. Because it is play, we will not lose our jobs or hurt our children. We can allow ourselves to fail.

One woman said to me a year after she took a fear workshop, "Skiing helped me get bold!" Then she added proudly, "I'm separated!" Whether we need such boldness or just a little comfort, the beauty of metaphor is that it works "down under," beneath our conscious control, crossing boundaries, out of the body and into our work, our families, our relationships to each other and to the world.

Perhaps skiing's inherent silliness—going up to come down—is its greatest gift to us. It protects us from our goal-driven, good intentions. Even if we practice *hard* to achieve a list of clearly drawn objectives, once we push off down the mountain, we cannot help but fall into our senses—sliding, almost floating down, the feeling of acceleration in the belly, the lightness of the body, the frictionlessness of the ground, the wind, cold teeth, the constant adjustment of feet, ankles, knees, hips, arms, the feel of the

skis arcing over the snow, the snow changing, the hill changing...
Our senses give us an immeasurable gift: a time of total absorp-
tion. We forget our daily expectations. We forget even to castigate
ourselves for our most recent mistakes. We drop down from our
self-absorbed mode, drop into our bodies and out to the mountain beneath us. "Let the beauty we love be what we do," Rumi the
twelfth century Persian mystic says. "There are hundreds of ways
to kneel and kiss the ground." (Translated by Coleman Barks.)

Total Immersion: Body-Mind-Heart

BUT! skiing does not always feel free and easy. As we move across
the hill, our skis on edge to track cleanly in the snow, we are in
control over gravity's pull. The moment is about to come when
we must *willingly suspend that control*. We must release our edges
and as they flatten, give over to gravity. We surrender to a larger
force, the pull down the hill into the fall-line. This is where we
sometimes get stuck. We can stand frozen at the top of a steep
pitch—heart pounding, thighs shaking, shoulders locked, our
breathing shallow and quick—wanting only to be airlifted out of
the moment and transported into a feather bed with hot tea and
homemade cookies. Or we can be torn apart by a state of profound ambivalence—the voices of the body, mind, and heart in
an all-out fight: to go or not to go. Sometimes the body speaks the
loudest, sometimes the mind and heart do. It can be difficult to
tell them apart. They each reveal the other. The body signals any
unconscious trepidation. The mind reads, moment by moment,
the body's orientation and discomfort. If the heart retreats, the
body sags and withdraws, too. Where does one begin and the
other end? This complicity of the body, mind and heart makes
that active surrender more profound and therefore more difficult. As one of my students yelled out once, "I wish skiing weren't
such an emotional sport!" Then she quickly corrected herself,
"No I don't!" It is not just the play with gravity but the totality of
the surrender that we are attracted to.

To stay in balance over our skis, all parts of our bodies must surrender together. We need to "leap." But often, one part of the body mutinies—holds back and retreats from the fall-line where we feel gravity's pull the most. (I discovered two very different kinds of people, those who retreat with their genitals and those who retreat with their heads. If this tendency to protect suggests what we value most, the majority of us—maybe 70 percent—prefer our genitals.)

When this mutiny happens, we lose our balance and rely on the backs of our boots to hold us up, a situation the body knows is unstable. It sends us warning signals. We become uncomfortable, and we should be. We have compounded our initial ambivalence with a precariousness, which although self-created, is real. We need to prepare for this "leap," so that we are able to "throw the *whole* self in," body-mind-heart, actively releasing ourselves to gravity.

The import of this surrender obviously transcends those moments in skiing where we face the fall-line. The other day I visited a friend who was in mourning. When I saw her face, and the way she held herself, continually tapping her elbow, my mind went blank. For just a second, I stalled before that same all-or-nothing passage: should I stay back and silent? or jump?

What the moment asks of us is our full participation. A lawyer friend of mine explained the total immersion she felt was necessary to succeed in a trial. If we are distracted by the thought: "How do I look, Ma?" part of us is still hanging back, clinging to the rock ledge, viewing from a safe distance. It is impossible, though many of us try, to take a leap...*partially*.

Newness: Our Resources Reconfigured

Greg Louganis, the great gold-medal diver, only visualized his dives in practice, never in competition. He wanted to allow his body to do more than he could "see." His will surrendered control of the dive, allowing his body to be the artist that shaped his existing skills into never-before-imagined movements.

Like Louganis, when we pass through the moment, what we are about to do is *new*, beyond what we can know up to that point, beyond any previously conceived limits. Our limits will be re-configured into a new creation, born of a synergy between our individual resources and the universe at hand. This takes undivided engagement with what is imminent—a newness we cannot be fully committed to if we try, with our paltry and limited perception of the possible, to stay in control.

This is a time of great risk and therefore great vulnerability. When we were children we were not fully aware of our vulnerability so we breezed through risky situations unconsciously. Now we are adults and the Nike ad: "*Just do it*" does not cut it. Just do it, stay unconscious and face the consequences later. It is the flip side of the "Just say no" slogan, mirroring the same simplistic tendency to polarize the world into opposing absolutes. A mindless activity or a mindless inactivity. This is a *mindful* moment that demands our entire attention. Not bumper sticker slogans but an original response true to each person's complexity. An observant four-year old told me the color of snow through her goggles was "a dark dark dark dark white." We live in a world where opposites coexist, even meld. When we take the risk the moment offers, to surrender safely—mind, body, heart—we need to prepare. We need to plan for our abandon.

CHAPTER 3

Imagining

*My self-imposed rule is to retain the courage of one's
doubts as well as one's convictions, in this world of
dangerously passionate certainties.*

— Eric Sevareid

Stalled in front of a drafting board or a new project, we can
recognize the pivotal moment, but it is hard to imagine it as
an entity in itself. But if we do, this slight turn of the imagination can separate the moment from our own response. "I'm just
a fearful person," people usually say with shame. But the fear this
moment carries is not a curse to be cured. It is not an affliction, a
complex, a syndrome, or a symptom. It belongs to no gender, no
particular group.

It is important to wrest the unique nature of the moment
from the personal sphere, to free it from our reflexive thinking.
Once we see fear as an essential element of the moment rather
than the result of a personal pathology, we have taken an important step. We are once removed from our individual reactions. I
know a writer who laughs about how clean her house gets before
any new project. For her, the moment visits like an old, cranky
friend. This separation from our personal narrative liberates the
imagination. Not only can the writer see "it" as being part of the
creative process with its own integrity, but she can see herself

from a distance as well, as a character, and laugh as she bustles about straightening not only the drawer full of hand towels but the silverware, too.

The imagination is essential to this process. Like a gust of wind, it can loosen what has been stuck: the same boring mono-logue, the same self-deprecating tape played over and over. The imagination is the ocean of images. Images do not judge or criti-cize, so the ego isn't on guard against them. They never explain themselves so our theories and rationalizations miss entirely. What an image can do is move. It can change. It can transform. And because images are the language of the soul, they can carry us along.

We are loaded with phrases that carry no personality and no image. Negative self-talk, destructive internal dialogue, fear of failure, fear of success, bad self-image, low self-esteem.... How can we learn to live with such words? How can we negotiate with them? Barter? Or bribe them? How can we give such concepts a kick in the pants, or brace ourselves for the kickback?

The Nag

When we begin to imagine this moment, the moment we push off from a reliable, familiar ease into an uncertain future, we see it is a narrow passage that is not easy to move through. What is there that wants to stop us?

When I ask my students, "Why did you back away?" (or, in one case, "Why are you avoiding that trail you love to hate?") the phrases that most often surface are: "afraid to make a fool of myself," "want always to do my best," "hate not being perfect," "get so frustrated," "take so long to learn," "embarrassed in front of others," "want to do it right." This is their nag talking. And only the very old or the very young seem to be free of this creature's sting.

The nag is that little man or woman, about four inches high, who sits on our shoulders, always ready to whisper in our ears.

She is the calculating critic that accumulates and files correct, relevant data just to use for her one great purpose: to tell us very specifically and accurately how we will fail, and that it might be better not to try at all. She can make us hesitate and falter when we need to do something well, when a lot is at stake. Then she'll smirk and taunt, "I told you so."

To my nag, raised Catholic, everything is a moral issue and intrinsic evil is the cause of failure. If I make a mistake skiing in the moguls, or I forget to take my lunch sitting on the table—no matter what the infraction, how small or large—my nag boils it down to one simple thing: I am a *bad* person. But that's not the real curse of the nag. It's her perfect timing.

The nag rears up and spits at the pivotal moment, just when we need a little encouragement to willfully take a leap. Why does this particular moment spark the nag's attention? A surrender of control, an initiative toward an uncertain future *necessarily* allows for the possibility of failure. Accepting this possibility is anathema to the brittle ego, the nag's loyal, long-term companion. The nag hovers protectively nearby, ready to pounce.

I've heard, out of the mouths of my students, Baptist nags, Jewish nags, Lutheran nags, Existentialist nags, and WASP nags. I met a Sicilian nag who spoke very colorfully, a German nag who liked to work hard, even a New Age nag. Some nags are jock-like, some intellectual, some butch, some fem. One woman I taught had two, a Catholic nag on one shoulder and a Jewish nag on the other. A confirmed rebel said hers was not personified at all. It was a dragon, thank you very much. Another called hers the Cheshire cat.

Each nag has a different style, uses different pet phrases, attains different decibel levels, but they all have one thing in common: they are very smart and they can win any argument. It's like trying to argue with your teenage kid—hopeless. Our nags have watched us a long time and they not only know all our weaknesses, they can identify, in each situation, the one weakness that will completely deflate us. No wonder we want to turn back and not even try.

The nag affects how we stand, how we carry ourselves, how we move. Do we let go? Do we hold back? Can we dance alone with ourselves? Are we able to express what we love?

In order to allow our bodies to move freely and purposefully, we must learn to converse with the nag. Not fight, not cower. To converse means to listen. Listen with *imagination*. This kind of listening both discovers what already exists and creates it at the same time. Although it does not make sense, all artists live with this paradox. An artist knows on the one hand: *I am merely discovering these shapes, these colors.* The work lies dormant but intact. But an artist also feels at the very same time, the opposite: *I create it as I go along. I make it up. I am imagining.*

With this kind of conversation, full of attention and imagination, we can get real information from the nag, information about our imperfect bodies and our convoluted minds that can help us when the stakes are high.

Culturing of the Guide

We need to imagine another figure, the guide, both wise and canny, sitting on the other shoulder. Instead of confronting the nag ourselves, which often leads to a back-and-forth that ends in argument, we can say simply, *Talk to my guide.* Setting up this triangulation makes negotiation possible.

The guide may not be as colorful as the nag, but she can be very powerful if given the chance. Her practical intelligence can lead us through the sticky passage of the moment. Once our imagination brings her to life, she gains authority by absorbing and applying ideas she can use to help us. I call this process the *culturing* of the guide because that word has two important connotations. The first conjures up the image of some strange coming-to-life in a petri dish, and the second is associated with the broader reaches of education. Both connotations are appropriate here. A particular magic happens that gives each internal guide a life of her own, a distinct personality born from a synergy between education and imagination. As one of my students said, "With each new idea, the guide has more to say. So it's more *there*." I have witnessed some guides coming to life for the first time. Others that have "been there all long" revealed themselves more plainly. They went unnoticed because of a monotonous steadiness or a penchant for specific details that made them seem boring, too boring to listen to. But as a guide gets educated, she becomes "louder," more confident of her knowledge. We feel compelled to listen.

"Oh, I got it!" one student said the last day of a fear workshop, "It's that very quiet voice in the back, the smart one, sort of..." she paused, "...*aged*. It's been there all along. But I never heard what it was saying."

Some people find that bringing to mind a companion or teacher animates the rudimentary form of their guide. At first, they need the influence of a real person. But for the guide to grow into her unique shape and voice, that person's presence must retreat, leaving a necessary void, a receptive impression for the imagination to fill.

Once cultured, the guide can loom up larger than life and take us places we didn't know existed. And when her job is finished, what do we owe her? Nothing. She loves her work: encouraging the body to move with an accuracy that comes from freedom rather than control. She wants us to dance. And as a Yup'ik Eskimo song says, "If you do not dance, you will become moldy. So the secret in life is to keep on dancing no matter what." (Translation by Chuna Mc Intyre.)

Preparing

CHAPTER 4

The Guide's First Question

Out beyond ideas of wrongdoing and rightdoing,
there is a field. I'll meet you there.

— Rumi (tr. by Coleman Barks)

In our culture, the word *product* has reproduced itself in the most inappropriate places, ski education for example, where a major trend is an "outcome-driven, bottom-line approach aimed at producing results." At major ski resorts, lessons are now called "product," one more inert item to be consumed, even though for most teachers, a class is more easily imagined as a complex organism with a life of its own—more like a puppy than a spatula or a couch. This inert language, diseased and deadening in itself, arises quite naturally from the corporate mindset that has infiltrated, or rather infected, even humanistic vocations.

This cultural obsession with *product* (and its progeny *productivity*) influences our attitude even when we go on vacation or play a sport. I said *play* but as Witold Rybczynski points out, we don't play tennis anymore, we *work* on our backhand. We drive all morning to get to the beach. Driving, we feel we are not any *where*, no place in particular so no place at all. Suspended in a not-here-not-there-yet anxiety, we worry about time. Once we're at the beach, we can finally sit down and relax. Or can we? We're so wired from habitually moving to achieve some goal, we can't sit still. We shift the lounge chair five times blaming it on the sun, the shade, the bugs, the wind, the kids. We've reached the point where we need a workshop to learn how to vacation.

The same thing can happen when we arrive for a weekend at the ski slope. We worked 9–5 Monday through Friday. We perform. We produce results! Saturday morning, we wake up to the alarm and rush out to "get a good day in." We check our watch three times riding the chair. We begin to ski.

Freely? Is it possible? More likely, we are miles away from letting go with our bodies, our hearts, to feel the surrender skiing offers. Even the *word* surrender sounds scary. This is where we need the guide to step in and ask her first, but loaded question: *Do you approach skiing as performance or experience?*

Our usual answer is performance. Performance in sport sets up a polarity: *success* as opposed to *failure, right* as opposed to *wrong.* Say "*win!*" to an athlete who is neurotic (or, as I prefer to say "psychologically complicated,") he invariably thinks *lose.* Say *good* and the first association is often *bad.* (Unless you've been raised Catholic like me, then it's *evil.*) Words like *winning* and *success* enjoy the limelight in our culture but they do not live there alone. They carry their shadows with them: the possibility of losing, of failure.

In contrast, experience suggests a one-of-a-kind event, a singularity. Associated words like *play, exploration, adventure, discovery, innovation, emotion* do not trigger a string of polarities in the mind. Like colors, they can live as unique entities.

When we ski, we usually *want* an experience, some type of adventure. But we often end up locked in performance mode, with its competitive, polarized mindset. Hasn't the sermon of success been preached into us since the first grade? Don't we receive performance evaluations on every detail of our jobs from communication skills to timeliness to professionalism? And no matter what I think about the validity of the "eval," I have never been able to ignore a check in the wrong box. Of course, many times, the drive for success and perfection is valuable, even imperative. But once in its grip, we cannot easily switch off that polarizing mindset.

The most common question asked of a ski teacher? "What am I doing wrong?" It doesn't help to say to ourselves riding up the chair, "OK, this is downtime now. This is recreation, nothing but play." No, those of us that are performance-driven would then try to be really good at playing. We would try to succeed at downtime.

When we treat an activity as performance, we feel judged by an external standard of measurement. This creates the feeling that someone is watching, the "Hey, look Ma!" syndrome. That external eye offers a reward outside and separate from the actual experience. (In fact, the word *reward* comes from the Old French "regarder" which contains both denotations: to "hold in high regard" and also to "observe.") Praise is a reward the ego lustily drinks up, but praise lives in polarity with its opposite, blame, so the ego must swallow them both.

My husband, Eric, was shooting a few baskets alone at a friend's house. We yelled out that dinner was ready and he called back, "I'll come in as soon as I miss." But as if he were caught in a spell, he could not miss. After the first ten baskets, he was amused, but he was hungry and wanted to come in. He backed farther away and threw what were for him crazy, wild shots, even hook shots from twenty feet. And they went in! Finally, he just threw the ball backwards over his head.

Eric arrived at the door, amazed. The entire time, his focus never turned in on his own performance. Nor did he care whether he sank a shot or missed. With any suggestion of "Hey! look at me," or even the desire to make the shot, the spell would have been broken. His hunger tricked him momentarily into a taste of what Gandhi meant when he said, "We're entitled to our work but not to the results of our work." And because of that, Eric carried away no inflated sense of his own skill but rather the memory of a heightened rapport between ball, basket and the free, unhindered movements of his body.

Immersed in any activity, *experience* evokes this same rapport, a relatedness or engagement with the "other," whether it be the event itself, or the world. Our orientation shifts from the *me*-to-be-praised toward the *other*-to-be-experienced. While our focus remains outward with no "look at me" distractions, our engagement stays complete and the only "prize" we gain is awareness intrinsic to the event. The ego remains lean.

Skiing offers a wonderful medium in which to foster a rapport with the world. "Skiing has no win or lose," my son said when he was six. There is no basket, no net, no game, no score, no performance or competition unless you go out of your way to create one in a race or bump competition. But still, you are never alone. The mountain stands beneath you, waiting.

In this regard, skiing differs from many sports. It is more akin to sex, which obviously doesn't have to be a performance. It can be savored as experience. (When I made this analogy in a lecture, a woman piped up, "Either way, I'll take it.")

Experience	Performance
Singularity	Polarity
Discovery	Win/Lose
Adventure	Success/Failure
Sensation	Good/Bad
Newness	Right/Wrong
Emotion	Pass/Fail
Relatedness	Competition
Other-orientation	Me-orientation
Internal Gift	External Reward

Performance in sport, associated with competition, triggers a polarity in the mind. Experience suggests a one-of-a-kind event, a singularity.

The Performance Mode in Ski Schools

Ski schools fall headlong into the performance mode. Their systems habitually draw comparisons between individuals which throws us smack into the "Hey! Look at me!" mindset, a mindset so collectively supported, it can trample any fragile hope to feel some rapport with the mountain or movement. Even the most enlightened schools unwittingly emphasize *hierarchy*, the "I'm OK, You're Not" brand of teaching. It starts with the jacket the instructor wears which clearly depicts the hierarchical structure that now you, the student, are a part of: he is the expert, you are the little shit. He dutifully demonstrates the "proper" technique. And his aim, of course, is to do it as perfectly as he can, the way he has been trained. And then you try. And he, in good faith, tells you accurately and specifically how you are not quite as perfect as he is. You want to be, especially in front of the other students, because the whole atmosphere is geared toward perfection and success. You try again. But now you are more careful and conservative with your movements. You don't want to make a mistake. You don't want to fail.

The ski teaching profession is, of course, trying to evolve. "There are no wrong turns." "Teach only to a student's strengths." "All feedback should be positive." The instructor is no longer called an instructor. He is "a pro." A student is now a "guest." Schools are no longer schools but "development centers" and "fun parks" and "adventure camps" that are "guest-service-driven" and "outcome-based." But no matter the stiff, corporate language and attempts at euphemism, the profession still remains trapped by an obsession with success. Whether they are called instructors, teachers, or pros, these men and women are trained to set up all "learning situations" with success as the goal. "Guaranteed learn to ski" marketing schemes feed the public the illusory pablum of risk-free learning. But this one-pointed focus toward success actually *heightens* a student's fear of failure. Even the word *failure* or any near equivalent has become taboo: the f-word. "Ineffective" is the sanitized word of choice. I've actually heard very illustrious teachers say to their groups: "*Some of you are...*" betraying the fact that they think an ineffective movement—an arm flying up or an errant knee—is such a heinous crime, they can't even mention your name, they wouldn't want to embarrass you and destroy your self-esteem. It's like misguided, misapplied PC.

The results from this "positive" approach are no different from those attained in the "I'm OK, you're not" style of teaching. As long as the idea of *success* hangs in the air like a blimp, students will move carefully and conservatively, fearfully trying to avoid the embarrassment of a mistake, no matter what it is named. This is a long way from skiing as a metaphor for sex. Or skiing as an adventure. And unfortunately, it is a long way from learning as well.

Learning a new movement is a radical act. We have to travel with our bodies, quite literally, into the unknown. To do so, we necessarily face the moment when we risk the possibility of failure. But there is a paradox inherent in that moment of risk-taking. To be willing to risk, a person must first be comfortable with (or at least tolerant of) feeling vulnerable. In a performance-oriented environment, with its goal of perfection, no one wants to feel vulnerable; no one wants to make a mistake. The willingness to risk is suppressed, the desire to learn thwarted.

If we temporarily jump off the performance ladder with its opposing dualities, the word *failure* loses its meaning. It becomes obsolete, and so does the corresponding fear of failure. Even the word *risk* loses its charge because what we are risking is no longer considered failure. The environment becomes safe for learning. The body can now explore the limits of its movement, perhaps even break through the pivotal moment into what is new and unknown.

But *how* do we "jump off?" It is not enough to say that the consequences are negligible for most of what we call failure in skiing. We cannot pretend our fear of failure has mysteriously evaporated. Instead, we must consciously re-see (or "re-vision") what we perceive as failure now that it is shaped by a different context, the context of experience.

Intentional Failure

Ian was the first teenage boy to come to the fear workshop. He was seventeen, sensitive, intelligent. But under his meek exterior, he was extremely competitive. His father told me how he burst into loud sobs at the breakfast table when he was about four. Both worried and curious, he and his wife spent a long time calming him down until he was able to say what had so suddenly upset him. His father had finished his cereal first, he had "beaten him."

Ian was so frightened of failure, he was almost paralyzed in a group. Even on terrain that was easy for him, his movements were stiff and contracted. He had an intense desire to succeed. I decided to make "failure" the actual goal so that he would try to succeed at failure, and consequently begin the process of "re-vision."

I began by asking Ian to ski on one ski but I didn't want him to flail about hitching and twisting, trying to keep his other ski high off the ground. I told him he could keep both skis on the snow, but gradually (as gradually as he needed) transfer most or all of his weight onto his right ski. (That was his strong leg.) Then I stated the goal: falling sideways onto the snow, an easy and fun fall for a teenager. At first, he was extremely conservative for his skill level. He did not want to get his skis even slightly out from under his body. He was like a small kid trying to turn his bike without wanting to lean.

Ian would start comfortably down the fall-line and in each turn, he would try to lean progressively more to the inside, his skis taking a wider and wider path. Then he'd stop. But eventually, after about an hour, he let his skis go out, farther, farther, bam! He was on the snow! He threw his hands up. "Yeah!" He had allowed himself to go beyond the limits of his body's balance. He had surrendered control and passed through that elusive moment.

For those, like Ian, paralyzed by fear of failure, this is no small epiphany. But more accomplished skiers can benefit from this same approach. Ski racers often, either consciously or not, turn failure into the goal. A racer, although usually associated with competition, trains most effectively with the experience mindset. Instead of aiming for perfection, she stretches her skills by testing the envelope, pushing continually into the realm of the unknown. If she wants to go faster, she will start at a comfortable pace and attempt to speed up until the point of failure, where her skis start to slip sideways, or they run too straight, or her body gets too far back or too far forward... She won't want to hang out at the point of failure long if she can help it. She'll recover, back off a bit, then gently start to push the boundaries again. This is what it means to ski on the edge, at the limits of one's skill. In this way, racers learn not only to risk failure, but to be on familiar terms with it. They have de-sensitized themselves to its sting, learning with their bodies the words of Blake, "The road of excess leads to the palace of wisdom."

Each time Ian froze up in the group, we would decide what would be an appropriate and meaningful point of failure for him to try to reach. In this way, his guide learned how to erase the unspoken goal he always felt: to be perfect, to succeed, to be the best. Ian eventually stopped comparing himself with others in the group. "I actually forgot," he said. He was focusing so hard on moving toward the point of failure, recognizing it, learning to recover, learning how to back off, being more gentle with himself. He was fully absorbed in learning.

Ian was learning the limits of his body's balance by going beyond them and falling, and that is a learning to be valued. His balancing movements on the "edge" began to sharpen with familiarity and his current limits started to stretch.

But most important for Ian was that his concept of failure was slowly being transformed. What he had previously named failure was no longer to be avoided and feared. It was his teacher, able to stretch him with its call.

> *…Whoever was beaten by this Angel*
> *(who often simply declined the fight)*
> *went away proud and strengthened*
> *and great from that harsh hand,*
> *that kneaded him as if to change his shape.*
> *Winning does not tempt that man.*
> *This is how he grows; by being defeated, decisively,*
> *by constantly greater beings.*

> — Rainer Maria Rilke (tr. by Robert Bly)

CHAPTER 5

The Gentle Art of Listening

*It's a rare person who wants to hear
what he doesn't want to hear.*

— Dick Cavett

Marley, a highly paid interior designer from New York City, had introduced herself as the quintessential perfection addict. I watched her first attempt down a steep, black diamond pitch interspersed with icy moguls, a difficult trail for her level of skill. Still, she managed to keep her rhythm and control her speed. She even looked comfortable. As she finished her last turns, her entire, astonished group started cheering and clapping. But Marley skied up to them and broke into tears. She said she skied awfully and felt embarrassed, even "disgusted." What was going on here, a harsh nag working overtime or something else?

Marley was astute kinesthetically. She was keenly aware of her movements, even the sensations of her skis on the snow. She was able to feel her right arm on maybe two out of twenty turns shoot up over her head as her outside ski slipped. But that awareness flooded her with frustration that colored the other eighteen turns in which her arm stayed quiet and her ski steady. She was so overwhelmed by her negative judgement of the sensations that she could only read the data as signs of failure. She could not use it as information.

To learn new movements in any sport, we have to develop an awareness of how the body is currently moving, where it is *now* in space. But this listening phase can be painful for those of us like Marley who judge every movement against a strict, narrow ideal we call perfection. This continual judgement distracts us from the more pertinent issue of what our bodies need to do next. How do we learn to listen to the body and use the information it gives? Can we stop obsessing on whether it is positive or negative? This is where the guide comes in.

Whether we feel we are just playing or are involved in serious learning or work, the guide perceives every mistake of ours as minor, as mere data to be evaluated and used in future attempts. This is one of the guide's most generous gifts: no-bullshit honesty mixed with kindness. This alone can often lift us out of the self-importance we have burrowed into and bless us with the space we need to calm down and listen.

Marley was stuck in the polarized duality of the performance mode. She compared each turn to what she considered the perfect, *carved* turn, that she had felt on groomed, intermediate terrain. Skiing was, in her mind, a monotheistic religion devoted to the one god of carving. Any turn that wasn't carving was bad. (Her nag was a Lutheran.) She couldn't imagine that skiing this slope demanded another kind of turn, one that could give rise to a whole pantheon of different sensations, each a unique experience.

Marley's internal guide started to get educated. Carving had its place, a large and venerable place in the world of skiing, but there were other gods, too. There was not one perfect turn against which every other should be judged. In fact, carving through icy, irregular bumps might be, at best, inappropriately fast, but carving down a steep couloir could mean grave danger.

After a few days, Marley felt her skiing world had "just cracked open." There were so many possibilities other than carving, so many available sensations. Her imagined guide would say in her head while she was skiing, "Be open now. Here's a new sensation. Feel it. Feel it." *Wow!* Marley would think, *But is it OK?* "It might be," her guide would assure her, "We'll find out later. You're still standing up. Keep on going." This was her first step in learning how to listen.

Now Marley's guide could begin, gently, to discern *what to value*. There were movements that were more effective and others that were less, sensations that were enjoyable, others that were "instructional," even "character-building." Without reverting to a harsh, critical mindset, Marley's guide needed to translate the perceived data into pertinent feedback. This data is not to be personalized or "owned" or used as a judgement on one's self-worth. A guide, by virtue of his or her distance, treats our bodies with this objectivity so we can fully engage with the task at hand and the world underfoot. If Marley's arm flew up and her skis started to slip sideways, her guide immediately responded, "Hand down. Outside ski!" The guide told Marley what to attend to without making any judgmental statements.

Marley's kinesthetic sensitivity became a boon to her skiing. She had felt handicapped by it at first, but sensitivity wasn't the problem. It was the "monotheistical" and ego-focused performance mode. Kinesthetic acuity should be cultivated in any sport, and especially in skiing. Skiing is never static or habitual. It calls for a constant feel, a "touch" born of a continuous fine-tuning between the skis, the snow, and the mountain. To cultivate this touch, a highly-focused connection with "otherness," we need an approach that frees us from our tendencies toward self-obsession.

Many of us, like Marley, are merciless toward ourselves. And we are often vain as well, expecting to learn much more in a short time than even the greatest athlete could. An educated guide makes it possible for us to be kind to ourselves, with a voice that is neither vain nor insecure about what to expect. He or she gives only the information that we need. "When I saw you tell other people what to do, it seemed so matter-of-fact," Marley said. "So my guide took that and applied it to me." In fact, the guide's gentle matter-of-factness is so absorbed by the task at hand, it trivializes the impact of "making a mistake." The ego and the nag get sidelined. "Whether the feedback is good or bad becomes totally irrelevant," Marley said. "It just *is*."

After about a year, Marley began, in her own words, "to really ski." Her body was learning to respond to the variable terrain beneath her. "Not bad," she said, "for a 48-year-old perfection addict. I almost feel," and she lowered her voice, "athletic." Then she added with a quirky laugh, "It's my guide now that's working overtime."

Marley also began to approach her work as an interior designer differently. At times when she needed to start an especially difficult job, she had been frozen by fear. Her mind could not consider new ideas because The Critic, another version of the nag, would shoot them down before she had a chance to develop them. Marley started to cultivate the same habit in her studio that she adopted on the mountain. She "pushed off," throwing a few lines onto the paper that might be good, bad, ugly—it didn't matter. She had begun! Now, she could respond *matter-of-factly* to the internal voices guiding, modifying, or refining the design until she reached the level of excellence she wanted. She hung Winston Churchill's words on the studio wall: *Success is the ability to move from failure to failure without loss of enthusiasm.*

Kinesthetic Anesthesia

For those who have not grown up training for a sport or a performance art like theatre or dance, hearing the body can be difficult. The body speaks a different language with an alphabet made of movement and feeling, and it can seem both painfully direct and awash in a sea of nuance and vague suggestion.

Carol's relationship to her body was the antithesis of Marley's. (She came to a fear workshop mainly to spend time with her daughter.) She was quite comfortable skiing, she confessed to us in a rather hushed tone, and never considered trying anything new or difficult. "That's probably why," she said, "I haven't improved in years." Once she started down a mountain, Carol had no clue about anything that went on below her neck, even whether her skis tracked forward or slipped sideways. She was kinesthetically unconscious. She would watch where she was going, feeling only the wind fly by.

I had Carol try something totally new for her: skiing backwards. She watched me slide in a backwards wedge down the hill and then she stepped her skis around and did it herself. But she could not feel the inside of her edges rubbing against the snow. Or the change in her body's attitude, tilted forward up the hill as her shins pressed against the front of her boots.

Carol spent almost a year trying to hear the "loud" sensations as she skied backwards, lifted one ski, or jumped off the snow. I suggested what she might feel so her guide would have a hint of the possibilities to focus on—her knees and hips straightening when she jumped, softening when she landed, pressure on the arch of her downhill foot at the end of a turn. She began to feel what I mentioned but still, no other sensations came spontaneously to her attention.

We made a lot of jokes that Carol should run from any teacher who tried to meddle with such blissful ignorance. But no one really wanted to trade places with her. As one man said, "Even though a lot of it isn't that hot, I still like *most* of what I feel." "I don't get it," a woman said, "It's like she's missing out on, on... skiing itself." She was missing the incomparable feeling of the skis floating over the snow.

People expressed surprise at the extent of Carol's kinesthetic numbness, but it is not uncommon. Even though I grew up training to sense a range of movement in skiing, I felt a similar numbness horseback riding. Undifferentiated sensation blurred together like white noise. Now I have learned to isolate some feelings—the horse's rhythm, the softness of his mouth, elasticity of his back, my right elbow stiffening, a flash of resistance, renewed suppleness, my thigh bracing, dust in my nostrils. But at first, these sensations jumbled together. So when my teacher asked, "Did you feel how your left ankle locked up?" I could only answer, "Whose left ankle?"

In much of our daily lives, we seem to *prefer* numbness, sensation dulled by a culturally encouraged anesthesia. If we sense any pain in our knee or back, we reach for the ibuprofen. Walk into your bank to cash a check and it is seventy-two degrees twelve months a year. Or drive up to the window, and you can stay in your car, set to the degree you find most comfy. A cold draft blowing through the kitchen from a north wind is considered an abnormality. In my hometown, the old slate sidewalk may be removed because slates, are, of course, irregular. The norm is uniformity: undifferentiated sameness. If you have eaten one McDonald's hamburger, you truly have eaten them all. Contrast that with a glass of wine from an unirrigated vineyard in Italy, its taste dictated in part by the amount of rainfall that year. One year is special, another is not. But both are connected to a collective memory kept sharp—a severe drought, the 100-year flood. Distinguished means different. When we distinguish flavors—fruity, bitter, musty—does it encourage us to envision a particular hillside? Can we sense also the worry of the farmer, the touch of his hands on the vines, the hope for the cloudburst to come? What else do we shun when we shun sensation? Memory? Emotion? Ties that hold us to this particular home, this year's weather, the contours of this mountain?

The following winter, Carol skied down a challenging pitch and said innocently at the bottom, "Damn, I felt my right hand keep crossing my body." The rest of us looked at each other in a "Did you hear what I just heard?" moment. It was the first time Carol had noticed any movement that was not called to her attention beforehand. When she realized that she actually said the words, *I felt*, she dropped to the ground, laughing. It was time to celebrate! That awareness was hard earned and a thousand times more valuable than a "perfect" run.

After Carol began to hear her body, she could move in new ways, replacing old movements with more effective ones that would not "screw her up." She began to improve. But most important, she was experiencing more—not only of what skiing could be, but of what her body was doing. "It's not just a thing that carries my head around," she said. "I was the true talking head."

We need to develop an awareness of what the body or skis are currently doing before we can learn new movements. Developing this awareness can be the most difficult stage of learning.

As Carol's "hearing" became more keen, she experienced less static, less noise. In that quieter, focused atmosphere, her awareness could detect increasingly subtler details. Her senses felt, she said, "like they had come alive." And then she added, "Now they're being stretched."

Carol had never imagined skiing as an experience full of sensations. Before she came to the workshop, she simply wanted to do what was right and stop doing what was wrong. Now she realized that learning involved listening to increasingly refined sensations on a continuum from the gross to the subtle.

With this almost silent but heightened awareness, a great skier can hear the most subtle nuance of movement and feeling. Senses extend, like antennae, beyond the body to the ski and the snow. It is difficult to detect where the language of the body ends and the language of the mountain begins.

Skiing with this touch is an art. It invokes the hard-core love that impels passionate skiers to drive six hours through a snow-storm or spend years working the odd job to live in the mountains. Skiers of all persuasions and levels of machismo joke constantly about this love, comparing it either to their spouses or their lovers, to the best of sex or the worst of addictions, but certainly beyond compare to whatever money can buy. You can feel this love in the ski culture, thick as honey and permeable as air, as spiritual as the devotion of a bhakti, but disguised in raw talk, in years of discipline, or in the simple gift of a beer—gratitude for a taste of that touch.

CHAPTER 6

Expanding the Comfort Zone

*Courage, when you don't understand what it is you
have to face, is no better than ignorance.*

— Penelope Fitzgerald

L istening to the body means, in part, knowing when it is comfortable and when it is not. Although this seems obvious, it is not always easy because our comfort zone, our safe haven, can shrink or change shape. It can contract slowly with age or abruptly after an injury, a trauma, or any emotionally powerful event. Sometimes it can surprise us and take any course. We often want to ignore these new limitations and override the body's discomfort with simplistic or vain expectations: "Well, I did it before…" or "I *should* be able to…." or "If he can do it, I can…." But if we do, we risk violating our bodies. We need to keep our antennae sensitive and accurate.

Avoiding the body's discomfort by simply avoiding challenge can also hurt us. If we stop attempting what was once familiar, we can lose confidence that we can do it at all…soon we never want to try it again, then we begin to do even less…our comfort zone progressively shrinks when we do not regularly stretch it.

To work with these limits as if we each have a new body takes patience, kindness, and a delicate sense of timing. Our guide needs a feel for pacing and also for rhythm, that elemental quality that is as essential as it is elusive to define.

Emmy started skiing when she was twelve. Her family traveled from Ipswich, outside of Boston, to Sugarbush, Vermont every winter weekend. By the time Emmy was eighteen, she skied comfortably all over the mountain. During her college years, she skied on most of her winter breaks. Although she didn't ski the double black diamonds well, she felt no fear getting down any of them "her way."

After college, Emmy stayed in Boston where she found a great job photographing historical architecture. She also found Michael. They fell in love and she took him up to Sugarbush for Thanksgiving to introduce him to her family and skiing.

By noon on his first day, Michael was soaked from both sweat and melted snow which had managed, he said, to get quite intimate with him. He was, nonetheless, hooked. But what was even more fortunate was that everyone got along. Michael not only didn't mind listening to Emmy's dad; he actually enjoyed his diatribes. And he loved her mother's obsessive feeding instincts. Michael and Emmy eventually moved into an apartment together and got engaged.

A month before the wedding date, Michael was killed in a car accident. Emmy became clinically depressed. She quit her job and moved back to her parent's home in Ipswich. Emmy's dad thought skiing would help. Even her therapist thought so. On weekends, Emmy and her family drove to Sugarbush.

Emmy told me that in her depression, she felt contracted and apathetic. She didn't have the energy to ski terrain she once enjoyed and stuck to the easy slopes. Soon she felt she no longer *could* ski anything more difficult. Her comfort zone started to shrink and for the first time in her life, she became afraid. She skied less and less demanding slopes until after a year, she was skiing only beginner terrain. Even the thought of skiing anything more difficult would make her start to hyperventilate. Her comfort zone continued to contract until one day she went up the easiest "bunny" lift, got off the chairlift and froze. She could not move. Two hours later, she walked down.

Although the contraction of Emmy's comfort zone was extreme, many people feel the same tendency to a lesser degree. And they don't like it. They want to revive their spirit, the feelings of freedom or liveliness they remember from before. The actual physical accomplishment is not what is important, whether they ski this or that black diamond run—they want the juice to flow again, stirred up by the energy of the moment.

The Rhythm of the Wave

The first thing Emmy's guide needed to know was the concept of rhythm. If her movement in and out of the comfort zone (or synonymously, in and out of the Yikes! zone) followed a rhythmical wave, her comfort zone would gradually expand.

When our movement in and out of the Yikes! zone follows a rhythmical wave, our comfort zone will gradually expand.

It looks like a simple sine wave on paper. And the concept is definitely simple enough: we need to build momentum gradually toward our leap (through the moment) into the Yikes! zone. This is important for the guide to know now, as we prepare. I have watched many people force themselves into the Yikes! zone before they were ready—at worst risking injury, at best adding to their nag's lists of I told you so's. I've also watched many stay in the Yikes! zone too long, thinking it will do them good. Either mistake will actually shrink the comfort zone. It needs to be stretched, but gently. This can be a tricky concept to apply. After a taste of Yikes! we should return to the comfort zone to replenish our resources and allow our appetite for another "moment" to build. To do this, the guide needs to understand our rhythms— the rhythm of the hour, of the day, the overall rhythm of our lives.

Building Momentum

The first day I skied with Emmy, we stayed on the beginner trail. Perhaps because she was with a "fear teacher," she skied well within her comfort zone and showed no signs of freezing up. In fact, she resented being "held back." Even though she hated the Yikes! zone, she wanted to waste no time "dealing with her fear." Couldn't she just blast through the moment now? What her guide needed to experience was how the concept of momentum worked.

The sensation of being held back builds potential psychological energy. Emmy looked around, got a feel for the snow, for the mountain. She looked at ease, sure of herself, even cocky. The energy built. She wanted more. I skied faster, I made shorter, tighter turns; she stayed right on my tails. On the next run, when I headed for the same beginner slope, both relief and disappointment flickered across her face. But I didn't want to risk squandering her psychological momentum by trying a trail that was too difficult too soon. I continued to raise the challenge slightly, almost imperceptibly, so that at each stage, she felt "no problem." I skied near the woods where the groomer made a few waves in the terrain, then headed straight to build speed before a blind knoll, listening to her skis behind me, following close. An appetizer, a tease, but never a full course. The energy intensified. Her trajectory was now taking her close to the Yikes! zone. It became just one more simple step, a very small leap—how and when did it happen?—she slipped through the moment. On the next run, without any warning, I took a turn onto an intermediate run she hadn't skied in over a year. She followed close behind. I could tell by the sound of her skis, that she was still travelling happily forward through the turns, not trying to brake by pushing her skis sideways in harsh, panicky moves. We took only one run on that trail, however. Emmy looked uneasy riding the chair lift back up, as if primed for another challenge. So before she started skiing defensively (and she could easily hyperventilate or freeze up) I took her back to her refuge—the beginner trail—to restore her energy. But this time, I followed *her*. The limits of her comfort zone had been massaged enough for now. Its borders were softer, with more stretch and give.

That was an easy day so the process may seem straightforward. But when we ski, we deal with more than one variable: a steep pitch, an icy patch, a person cutting in front, a sudden whiteout. These are the stubborn givens of matter and laws of this earth that we need to respect. The simple sine wave you see on paper is actually condensed from a complex of variables.

The Variables

Most skiers first notice pitch or steepness. You can hear them talk about it in the bar afterward: the jovial boasting of those who skied this or that double black diamond. But actually, the difficulty that a steep pitch provides can only be considered in relation to other variables, especially snow conditions. The same run never skis the same way if the snow has changed. Frozen granular, a marketing euphemism for ice, demands an entirely different mix of skills than a foot of soft powder. The slope's length, its narrowness, the presence of rocks, trees or lift towers, even the vista can all add to its difficulty.

And then there's the weather. It continues to assert itself despite the efforts of the corporate-minded resorts to cater to every customer convenience. Impeccable grooming, tissues at the bottom of the lifts, billboards announcing the waiting times of lines can fool us into believing that this is a creation of Disney, a simulation. Even the daunting number of signs instructing us how to keep safe can replace our natural reliance on our own physical awareness. The weather, blatantly beyond our control, reminds us of the truth: this is a mountain. It can change without notice. The fog comes in, a cold wind starts up, the sun-baked snow develops a crust.

What the mountain offers, its intractable givens, meets of course our slippery subjective response. Some people are frightened away when the radio reports a foot of new snow. Others cringe when they hear the sound of skis scraping against ice. So the guide learns to take into account not only the actual conditions the mountain offers but also the person's history, her acquired skills, what she has previously been exposed to, her biases, irrationalities, the peculiarities of her body. The guide considers these personal aspects *impersonally.* A subjective response gets treated with the same objectivity as the trail's pitch or an ill-fitting boot.

"So you're squeamish about crowds," the guide says, "one more variable to consider as we plot our course toward the Yikes! zone." No big deal, no personalizing, just another given, as simple a fact as the fog. Or your body is out of shape and is fatigued; you are suffering from PMS, cramps, a menopausal flash, or a hangover—these become the givens the guide works with rather than serving as food for the nag. The morally inclined nags tend to gorge themselves on any personal morsel they can, "Well, *he's* not afraid of trees, you shouldn't be, either. You hit one, but that was years ago. Get over it already." Moral nags love the word *should.*

To learn the many variables of skiing is a form of respect for the world. It takes attentiveness and time, but it provides essential knowledge. At first, it might seem like you are merely accumulating a mental check list. But to *understand* how each variable affects us, to weigh its impact, to measure it in relation to our own momentum takes a cultivated wisdom. "It's a feel you start to develop," one woman said, "rather than a list that you click through." It's an *intelligent* feel that the guide develops. He becomes like a dance partner who by listening to the energy and rhythm of the music knows just how to advance, just when to give.

But often we find it hard to listen to the music that is actually playing. We pretend it is another song entirely. "I wanted to think I was still 30," one woman said, "Slowly—very slowly—my fear is being replaced by respect... *honest* respect. Not only for what's out there, but also toward myself."

It can be difficult to cultivate this objective honesty when emotional variables are in play. We often castigate ourselves when a fight with a partner or trouble with a boss affects us on the hill. Many of us want to shut our emotions out entirely as if skiing could be locked inside the sport category, sealed off from any connection to the rest of our lives. We consider compartmentalization as essential as Prozac for a productive life. It's in bad taste to bring our home into our work. The heart should be kept tight in its box, all colors within black lines. On the flip side of this control lies our obsessive personalization of feelings. We drag in our mothers, our gender, self-esteem, or sibling order. The bulk of our culture lurches between these two poles: boxing emotions, and being boxed by them. "It's all in your head." "Get it together." "Get over it." While continually denying the validity of emotions, we still try to analyze them for meaning, control them, own them, stuff or drug them. We find it very hard to simply feel them, as real entities that visit, hang around, or leave, remaining, like the weather, beyond our control.

The guide, once removed yet involved like a close, savvy friend, neither compartmentalizes nor obsesses. Feelings come and go like the fog. Having an equally powerful affect on one's abilities, they are acknowledged as givens, phenomena in flux. This tricky mix of acceptance and de-personalization frees us to engage with the mountain.

Limiting the Variables

To monitor the wave well, we should only go into the Yikes! zone in one, or at the most two, variables.

PITCH (STEEPNESS)
VISIBILITY
LEVEL OF FATIGUE
CROWDS
EQUIPMENT
CONDITIONS
WIDTH, OBSTACLES
COLD
NEWNESS OF PLACE
PERSONAL FEELINGS
GROUP ENERGY

Y I K E S !

Now that it has become icy, better not try to go to a steeper pitch. I'll ski the same pitch I've been feeling steady on. But I'll try the narrower section I've been avoiding. I feel ready for that now.

Pitting our skills against more than two variables at a time can cause a backlash in our confidence and learning. The nag will thrive. We emerge from the lodge in a post-lunch-coma wanting to revive the late morning fervor so we decide to ski the same steep trail we skied then. But now our muscles are not only tired but cold after sitting and digesting, the conditions have deteriorated, the light is flat, the crowds are peaking. Pretty soon, we feel the nag start up: "I'm regressing... I haven't learned a thing." Sometimes, too many variables can converge to create not a Yikes! experience but a reaction akin to terror. After we "make it down," we land in what I call the Scotch zone, whether we drink or not.

Another course that can land us in the Scotch zone is sustained exposure to the Yikes! zone. Sometimes we can't avoid this. You take a wrong turn or the run is much longer than you expect. You try an easy run but it's full of moguls. After any of these mistakes, you should relax your mind and heart as well as your muscles. Take a bath, a walk, ask your spouse to cook you dinner.

Many people, however, prolong their stay in the Yikes! zone intentionally, out of a misguided Puritan work ethic. They fight a steep run again and again without returning to their comfort zone. A "comfort run" can re-fuel us both physically and psychologically, either capping off the day so we are hungry for the next or building toward another peak for the afternoon.

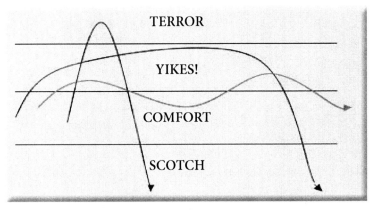

Pitting too many variables against us can either send us into a state of terror or prolong our stay in the Yikes! zone. Rather than expanding our comfort zone through following a rhythmic wave (in gray), these two courses can cause a backlash and send us to the Scotch zone, a self-explanatory state.

The Effect of a Group, a Powerful Variable

Skiing has a private aspect; when you go down the mountain, you are essentially alone. But it can also be very social. People rarely ski by themselves. And it is hard not to use superlatives when pondering a group's effect. Some groups provide exceptional support and take us places we would never travel alone. But many don't.

I have found it especially easy to land in the Scotch zone when skiing with others. A lot of groups (especially of instructors) start skiing faster and harder when abilities start to weaken. This is a peculiarly American reflex—the anti-siesta. As soon as any data starts coming in that suggests or even directly states, "Hey, slow down! Things are falling apart," we often heroically attempt to drown out the message with a compensatory machismo. And consequently, our skiing gets worse and worse, a flailing with harsh, tired, crude movements. Gone the subtlety, the finely-tuned gradations of giving with some muscles while resisting with others, the buildup of psychological momentum, the careful monitoring of the guide. We slash and burn to the end of the day. And usually no one person is to blame, because no one person ever runs a group. The group is run, rather, by current prejudices and hierarchies that have not been examined or articulated.

Sharon, a ski teacher, was extremely patient with her students but had a difficult time accepting one simple variable that affected her own skiing. She was a gifted skier and every morning she took some runs with the "hot guys" before lessons started. But her body warmed up slowly on the hill (no matter how much stretching or exercising she did beforehand). If she began at a gentle pace, she had that "fluid feeling the whole day." Her body would relax and respond to the undulations of the slope with a gifted ease, in love with the flight *down* the hill. But if she gave in to the group pressure to "rip the first run," she stayed sloppy and ragged for a long time, her movements defensive and crude.

This was the seemingly minor bit of information her guide needed: "First run, turn the skis across the hill till they point all the way to the woods. Start slowly, build up gradually." No extraneous baggage, just a simple given. "Yeah," she laughed, "simple for someone else." For Sharon, skiing at a slow pace fought against expectations and goals she set for herself as an athlete. The morning ski was her time to prove herself. Her simple given became tangled with the gender issue and with pop notions of self-esteem. *The guys can rip, I can't, gotta keep up with the guys, gotta toughen up, gotta hold up my entire gender, I'm petite, not strong enough, just don't have the balls, such a bad self-image,* her

nag went on. (The irony is that it can take more skill to turn farther across the slope—strength coupled with grace.)

While we were standing in the lift-line, Sharon turned to a
stranger next to her and stated with a flourish, "Hi, My name is
Sharon and I warm up slowly. *There*, I said it!" She enjoyed bringing to light the silliness of taking her givens too seriously, but she
knew the next morning, it would still be difficult to challenge the
group energy and respect this one, necessary fact. It was the fantasy of the guide that helped her treat herself with patience and
knowledge as if she were one of her own students.

The next morning, she started at a gentle pace, shaping her
turns with a skilled mix of care and ease. She let the speed build
gradually, but without losing the snaky shapeliness you see in a
series of gorgeous turns. The guys looked up from the lift line
at the bottom and saw her ski the last pitch so well, they nicknamed her "the veritable vision." Encouragement she desperately
needed. They started emulating *her*. They didn't want to go rip
a bunch of sloppy, ragged turns either. But they were driven by
their own nags: *Gotta rip, gotta keep up with the guys, gotta stay
ahead of the girl...*

The Dubious Role of Expectations

Like Sharon, we can all be so severely driven by our expectations
that we cloud our grasp of the circumstances at hand. For this
reason, I get nervous when a student talks about goal-setting and
all its various by-products, the short and long term, lists upon lists
of objectives. The very notion of goal-setting is a thinly disguised,
culturally condoned certification program for adhering to our
insatiable expectations. For years, I have been longing to create a
bumper sticker that said: DARE TO LIVE WITHOUT A GOAL. How
did the rampant assumption that goal-setting was necessary for
a productive life take hold? Think of all the great achievements
that came to be before the endless numbers of vision and mission
statements got constructed (always by committee) full of bloated

abstractions and tired, sexless words. I have never read one that didn't elicit in me that true-but-useless sigh.

A couple of years ago, I was asked to state my goals at the beginning of the ski season. I refused. I hadn't even skied yet that year. Goal-setting has become a cultural control freak run amok: every act intentional! But who creates the intention? Our self-centered, limited conception of the possible. Do we need to be so governed? How arrogant to think that my small, single mind could know what was in store when I started to ski, or what *should* be in store. The act of goal-setting states that the ego knows best. Instead, I wanted to welcome the unexpected. I wanted something to happen *between* skiing and me. A synergy that I could not intend, a conversation with the givens— and gifts—the mountain offered. After I refused to set goals, I received quite a long lecture that was probably true, but useless.

Think of sex. Doesn't a lot happen between partners without a mission statement? (Just think of the list of short-term goals that could be couched in that corporate language which robs the soul from even the most ecstatic of moments. "Bi-lateral thigh-strokage" would have to be quite early on the list, working up to "maintenance of a breast-driven orientation" that would impact a multiple-outcome-based bottom line"...) As with sex, can't we let our relationship with skiing or any other passion develop naturally, in an organic, let's-take-it-as-it-comes way? (Pun not intended but noticed.) To live with that approach means we cannot delude ourselves with the false security a mission statement provides. We are not protected by a list of sure-sounding objectives, or tricked by the authoritative language of an invisible corporation. Rather, we must pay attention, learn to feel, to listen and respond. Just like in sex.

CHAPTER 7

The Malleable Variable

At the boundary, life blossoms.

— James Gleick

"You won't believe how stupid I was," a friend of mine said on the phone from a hospital near Mammoth Lakes, California. "I can hear you using me now as an example in your next lecture." Corporations hire Judy to develop team building through bike and wilderness tours all over the United States. She's familiar with her body's limits, with the wilderness, with the rigors of travel. "So how did you end up with acute altitude sickness?" I asked. "Never take a vacation," she answered, and then the list began. She worked 15-18 hour days the entire week to "finish up" so she could go. She didn't eat well, some days barely at all, and she drank lots of coffee. Her digestion acted funny.... but she made it! She wrapped up the last project...then at four in the morning, drove to Boston...("Did you sleep?" "Well, not really.")... and caught a plane to L.A. to spend time with her new romance: rich food, wine, coffee, *very* few hours' sleep. They drove the next day to Mammoth. Ah... the Sierra Nevadas where she had spent much of her childhood.

Spurred on by love, she began to hike, fast; she was back in her element. But the variables clicked away like a metronome: no sleep, irregular food, digestion troubles, altitude change, jet lag, wine, lots of caffeine, sudden aerobic activity. "The worst was," she said, "because it was *me* and not one of my clients, I didn't believe the signs when they started to come. I began to shake and thought, *Oh, I need a little water.* Even after I started to faint I didn't guess what was happening." Her familiarity with altitude sickness tricked her into an illusion of immunity. "I guess I'll be paying attention now," Judy said at the end of her call.

Judy's comment reminded me of another. "I came here to deal with my own fear," a student said, "but I ended up learning to pay attention." Then she threw her arm toward the mountain, "To that out there. And to myself, too, but only as part of everything else."

To track a course in and out the Yikes! zone, we must stay attentive to the world, as well as our bodies and emotions. If Emmy had grown tired, if it had started to rain, or if a wave of grief had blown through, we would have had too many variables against us to try that intermediate trail. So monitoring our simple sine wave grows tricky when it is understood as a complex of variables in flux. When applied on the mountain, our wave often looks like this:

There is one variable, however, that is not a given. It is malleable and can be the guide's best ally: the *task* we set for ourselves. By modifying the difficulty of the task, the guide can finetune the wave. If we are halfway down a steep pitch, we can't say, "Airlift me out of here. I'm ready to go back to the comfort zone." Or when a boot buckle breaks. Or when a cloud descends just as we reach the top of a no-way-out cornice we decided to attempt while it was still sunny. All these variables keep the guide alert. Raising and lowering the difficulty of the task is the guide's artful response.

Raising the Difficulty of the Task

Let's say we can't decide whether to try a steeper trail. We don't know how much we have left in us, or what the conditions will be, whether it was groomed recently or was full of moguls. Maybe one of our knees feels tender. Still, we aren't ready to ski the afternoon away in our comfort zone. We want a little Yikes! but we want the ability to fine-tune the wave. That's exactly when we should *raise the task*.

For one person, raising the task might mean to ski short turns in a self-imposed corridor, then repeat the same thing but without gaining speed. For another, it might be learning to carry speed across the hill by gradually lengthening the turns. One woman who felt stuck in what she called a "chronic snowplow" spent about three runs a day learning to pick up speed. She'd begin straightening her turns out, more and more in cahoots with gravity, until she reached her own version of terminal velocity and then she'd begin to count out loud. The first day she made it to five before she turned sharply across the hill to slow down again. The next day, she reached eight. On the third day, something clicked and she was up to twenty-four before she began to slow down again, her wedge or snowplow long gone. When she finally decided to stop, she was breathless. She was a very articulate woman but all she could muster was "Wow!"

About two or three times, she'd open her mouth to speak but still nothing came out but "Wow!" Finally, she added, "So *that's* what skiing is." Afterward, she reverted to her "chronically controlled plow" only occasionally.

When raising the task, the other variables should be kept relatively constant. Remember Ian, the competitive boy whose goal was to fall? He learned to ski on one ski on easy terrain with groomed conditions. And he learned by turning only slightly out of the fall-line at first, staying in a gentle rhythm, gradually gaining momentum. That momentum and rhythm helped him keep raising the task till he tricked himself into falling onto the snow.

The Power of Repetition

Sometimes, however, we cannot learn a new movement in progressive stages. A flip on a trampoline for example. You certainly want to fully execute the flip the first time, making it all the way over, even if your execution is crude and rough. It takes repetition to refine and naturalize the movement so it becomes part of the body's repertoire. The amount of repetition needed to master a move comes as a shock to many nonathletes.

One day I took a group of fearful students to observe a cluster of teenage snowboarders practicing the latest move, a hybrid between a flip and a twist. I had heard pejorative comments about "the young people today," how they were lazy, not interested in learning the way *we* were when we were kids, almost the same sentiment Aristophanes recorded in *The Clouds* back around 400 BC. At those moments, I often launch into a reactionary lecture on the self-discipline I see manifest in the younger generation, but this time I found I could show it off firsthand, and with a particularly motley bunch with particularly colorful language. I made the participants count the number of times these kids practiced their new move *without complaint or self-castigation.* (They'd also spent over an hour building the ramp.) Each jump, they raised the task slightly by increasing either the difficulty or the level of refinement.

As we watched, some women in our group said they had never gone to a sports camp or even played on a team. Those opportunities didn't exist for many girls twenty or thirty years ago. They didn't know how *slowly* the body learns, how stubborn matter is compared with the fluidity of an idea or feeling. They were naïve about the work involved (the sheer number of repetitions it takes) not only to learn a move but also to naturalize and refine it. We often believe: *I know it in my mind, my body should know it, too.* But the body's intelligence works at a different pace. This ragtag crowd showed all of us what it means to be patient, diligent, and kind to the body. And what the kids showed to their own bodies, they also showed to their friends. Each of them knew when he "hit it" and when he didn't. No words were minced, but there was no trace of any condescension. And when someone took a chance, flying higher or farther than before, it was soundly acknowledged even if he didn't quite hit it. They knew they learned plenty from a move that wasn't executed perfectly. They didn't need a sports specialist to do a study and finally "discover" the role of exploration in learning.

Few adults I know would practice all day long enduring so many apparent failures to learn only one thing. The one-pointed focus and persistence of the kids won my students over. "Certainly no sign of attention deficit disorder here," a man said, breaking the silence after we witnessed a spectacular fall. "I guess I didn't realize how long it takes to learn," a woman said. "I thought it was just me. I mean these are young, agile kids."

Well, some were agile, some were not. Most were average. But the differences in natural abilities and age had no negative effect on the atmosphere; no self-esteem issues seemed to erupt. There wasn't a leader or teacher, but there was a hierarchy based on ability and experience. Another woman noticed how carefully the younger kids watched the bigger boys, observing and imitating in obsessively thorough detail. "This is really the perfect classroom, isn't it?" a man said who at first had been put-off by the very imperfect language.

What I noticed that I hadn't before was the kids' humility. They didn't expect perfection on the first or even the twenty-second try. In fact, they didn't seem anxious about perfection at all. Their discipline was animated and guided by desire. They wanted to try a cool move, and they started in, at whatever level they happened to be, some just trying to go off the jump without exploding, some doing pretty spectacular refinements on a twist and/or flip. No matter the result, they grabbed their board and walked back up the hill, took their turn and tried it again, and again, and again, and again... They politely waited for their bodies to master the trick. That takes humility. "I guess here's a model for my guide," someone said. "Shit yeah!" another (caught by the spirit) answered.

Preparation for Difficult Terrain

I raise the task for myself and my students when preparing to ski difficult terrain. This begins to move the wave gradually toward the Yikes! zone before we attempt the new slope. It is a physical warm-up that works psychologically. One group in particular taught me how important this preparation can be. Five middle-aged women—beautiful without exception, and elegantly outfitted with great hats and fantastic lipstick—were about to attempt a more difficult slope than they had ever tried before. It was steep, icy, and full of irregular moguls. I needed to raise not only their skill level, but also their physical and psychological intensity; hone a hard-edged attitude that would be reflected in their movements. Their seductive bodies had been themselves seduced by a chronically blasé ennui—*Well, maybe I'll turn here, oops it's too hard, I guess I won't. Or maybe here. Oh well, missed it*—a squishy, lackluster mediocrity. One woman was vice president of a major HMO; I knew she wasn't soft and vague in her business life.

We faced a demanding trail. Each woman needed to be able to yell out, "Now! Now! Now!" and have her body keen and eager to respond. Refinement would not be as important as intensity, the drive to keep going no matter the minor mistakes.

I felt myself start to shapeshift, incarnating as General Patton. I lined them up, shouted the orders. "There will be no stopping, no whining, no adjusting of suits or belts, no wiping of lipstick or sweat, and absolutely no *I can'ts*. Talk to your nag later if you have to." I raised my ski pole in the air ("Readyyy, go!") then slammed it on the snow in a rhythm, making them turn, turn, step, step, hop, hop, turn, turn... I slammed, I screamed, I demanded and commanded and I got it. I asked for more, "Harder! Higher! Faster!" and I got it. And then I realized what I was seeing. They were fantastic! And I had taught nothing but seriousness and intensity. I never imagined they could ski this well. I had never asked them to. I unwittingly supported their mediocrity by not demanding this intensity from them. I had been blinded by the very prejudice I tend to rail against. Such is the power of the beautiful, fem persona.

After I taught that group, I began to observe body intensity more clearly. I saw that most recreational skiers (even men) don't raise their intensity level until they start down steep terrain that intimidates them. At that point their bodies are unprepared. There are suddenly too many variables for the body to absorb. It is not able to increase its intensity level constructively and on command because it must also react to the increased pitch. The body responds psychologically.

I was talking about this intensity training with my friend, Abby Tassel. "That's what *I* do," she said. Abby works in an agency for women subjected to domestic violence and sexual assault. One of her jobs is teaching women self-defense. "When protecting yourself against assault," she told me, "it is the intensity of your initial reaction that is most crucial." She focused as much on marshaling that intensity in her students as honing punches and kicks. Even though it has been shown that an intense, aggressive reaction often shocks the assailant into backing off or running, some women accept the popular misconception that submission is safer, that an aggressive reaction will excite the assailant into more violence. Abby constantly needed to counteract in both herself and her students this culturally condoned tendency to submit, to fall silent and limp. Responding aggressively in class to a simulated assault at first seemed strange and scary, even without a real offender. "For aggression to work, you must be completely comfortable giving it your all." And then she added, "Both you *and* your body. And you can't fool the body." What she was teaching women was a body attitude that had an expanded *range* of intensity; it could whisper, and it could also yell.

Lowering the Task

William Stafford, a wonderful American poet, wrote a poem every single day. Asked about those days when he didn't write well, he said, "I lower my standards." My guide grabbed that little bit of wisdom and it has proved to be a great friend: truthful, humbling, and loving at the same time.

I had grown accustomed to the typical American warm-up which is to cruise fast on an easy, well-groomed trail, "a cruiser." Then, in 1987, I arrived for my first visit in St. Anton, Austria. I found myself at seven-thirty in the morning, looking off the back of the Valluga, a peak that was open to skiers only if you were accompanied by a certified guide. We were to spend the entire day off-piste, skiing to Lech, a few towns over, where we would eat lunch around two in the afternoon. Along with a few Austrian sight-seers who were allowed on because they had no skis, our guide took us up in a small cable car that ran to the top of the Valluga. The deck at the top had a secure railing that went 360 degrees around the building. I couldn't figure out where we were going to ski off, because the ground all around us fell sharply away, you could not see any part of the mountain below. I started to feel weak.

Why not ski a bowl, I thought? No matter how steep a bowl may be, it *feels* more supportive than a peak. Even a cornice or coulour seemed cozy compared to this. This was like being on the top of a pin above the rest of the world. I had heard the guides say last night that yes, you can fall *off* a mountain. "Just wait!" they said to me, a naïf who could only imagine falling *down* a mountain. I was an American *girl* and not even from the Rockies or California but from the old and folded Catskills in New York. What was I doing here?

I took off my gloves to buckle my boots but my hands shook so violently I put my gloves back on. I didn't want the guide to see; he was not about to offer support. Already wary about both my gender and my nationality, he stated in a smug I'm-OK-you're-not tone, "Don't go outside my tracks. You end up in Bavaria, dead."

"Oh, thanks very much," I said. On the inside I screamed, *Excuse me, sir, but I want a cruiser. A warm up. Do they have those here? Can I buy one?* I talked to my mom: *Thank you. I love you. I'm sorry for everything. I'm sorry I'm in Bavaria.*

Then William Stafford's calm, assuring voice spoke to me from the flat plains of the Midwest: *I think it is a good time to lower your standards.* Yes. Because in fact, I wasn't as afraid of getting hurt as it might seem. I knew I had the skill to get down safely. But I didn't want to *just* get down, I wanted to ski well, and it was *that* combined with the sheer drama of the landscape with little leeway for mistake that shook me. *Time to lower your standards.*

I took off gently, stemmed my skis for the first turn, got a feel for the pitch, for the snow, stayed conservative through the second turn (but hey, it's not so bad), now letting it out a bit for the third and fourth (I'm in it now), got a rhythm, fifth, sixth, the gravity pulls ooh... with such seduction, my belly feels the roller-coaster fall of each release down toward what I can still only sense but not see, I stretch my legs, reach for the snow that catches and holds me till gravity pulls again, and then again, forget to close my mouth, swallow too much snow, my teeth so cold, thanks Mr. Stafford, you're a wise man.

If, as in my past, I had charged off, pushed on by adrenaline bathing every cell, I would have ended up sitting back and jamming my skis back and forth defensively the entire trip down. Or worse, saying good-byes all the way to Bavaria. To get started, the variable I modified was the task. I lowered the task I set for myself, and left behind those grand and stubbornly vain expectations. In return, I was given more than I could have previously imagined.

Remember Marley? The interior designer who worshipped only one interpretation of perfection to the exclusion of all others? At first, she wouldn't try more difficult terrain, not because she didn't have the ability, but because she wouldn't adjust her standards. She wanted to ski new slopes with the same finesse with which she skied easier terrain. The *first* time. There was only one way she wanted to feel on skis. (You can't get away from those monotheistic notions without a struggle.) Eventually Marley's guide started lowering the task and with it, her expectations of what was realistic on more difficult terrain.

Her first time down a new run, she set the task very low: exposing herself to the new pitch. Perhaps an energetic side-slip at the top to get the juice flowing in her ankles and knees, a small wedge on the first turn and then bam she was in, skiing her fluid, shaped turns the rest of the way. She built up a momentum starting from as low a task as she needed to get started.

I had a dream recently that I was skiing a narrow trail through the woods, the kind I had skied as a child. It turned into a sheer cliff that fell away abruptly onto a flat. I approached, looked over and then backed away. But I couldn't see any other way down. I looked over the lip again and it was no longer sheer. There was a small ledge about half way down that I could jump onto and from there land safely at the bottom, which I did, aware, but not surprised that I was now naked, wearing only boots and skis.

At times the moment arrives as a sheer wall between you and the Yikes! zone. But at second glance, it can open and what you see may be more like stairs, a series of small, humble leaps, as small as you need them to be, in order to begin. Each small leap offers a landing spot, where energy can gather itself and serve as impetus for the next move forward.

Encouraging Energy to Flow Out

Anne was a sixty-year-old ski teacher I taught in an instructor training clinic at Snowbird, Utah. She was technically the best skier of the group, with almost uncanny grace and a refined sense of pressure control, easing and pressing against the skis with such subtle skill, she was a joy to watch flow down the hill. She had warned me that she sometimes "froze solid for no apparent reason." But after seeing her ski, I discounted her concern. The dynamic of the group was fantastic: sensitive, encouraging, fun, even bawdy. Nothing was censored. There was room for feeling, for vulnerability; everyone was skiing beyond what they thought were their limits.

We warmed up on the easier slopes by raising the task and intensity level, gradually working our way toward the Cirque, a steep bowl scooped out of the top of the mountain. We passed the narrow, rocky chutes that lined the beginning of the bowl and headed along the ridge for the mid-section that was freer of rocky outcroppings and obstructions. It was still a risk; there were ten people. With no trees for shade, the sun had turned the snow into heavy, wet glop. But their skiing had been primed, the group dynamic was right, and I had an assistant who could offer individual support. I took the chance.

There is a near-vertical lip at the top of the Cirque that can make it daunting for some to get in. Once in, if you look back up, what you see of the next skier is only the bottoms of two skis jutting into the air. Those who didn't want to ski straight down off the lip could lower the task by slipping in at an angle to ski across to a stop if they needed, or into their first turn if they had the psychological momentum. I didn't worry about Anne. She'd had such a spectacular morning. My assistant and I were busy coaching first one and then another and everyone seemed to be making their way down until Anne froze just after she slid in, about twenty feet above me. Stuck. Crying. Her words echoed in my head: "for no apparent reason."

I stepped up through the glop as fast as I could. Her energy had not only stopped moving outward, it was beginning to retreat. She was trying to back up which would move her into a section of dangerous, rotten snow. When I got there, her chest was caved in. Her breathing was fast and shallow. She was shaking like a leaf. My presence offered a safe ledge, a flat place for her to gather energy. She needed to breathe by completely filling her lungs, lowering her diaphragm and extending her belly instead of taking fast, shallow breaths that lifted and stiffened her shoulders. I put my hand on her stomach and had her breathe in deeply and slowly until her belly pushed my hand out with each breath. The energy in her body began to calm and gather itself. Still, she was holding in her tears, trying not to cry. I started to make sounds, loud, breathy sounds, as she breathed out. She joined in, her voice at first full of crying. The energy now had a direction; it was moving outward again. Her sounds became louder and more forceful. Then we started to bounce, just small bounces timed with her breaths and voice, as if we were standing on the edge of a dance floor getting ready to jump into the fray. Now her skis were bouncing, too, and we moved a little forward, not turning, just bouncing more and more till we moved maybe a foot ahead, a foot down, her skis still across the hill. I stayed beneath her. She made louder, stronger sounds. But it was still too early to attempt a turn. She needed more energy.

The timing was crucial. If we had tried to rush or force a turn, we would have squandered the reservoir of energy that we had so carefully collected. And if Anne saw how quickly she could lose that energy, she would distrust the process itself.

We were quite a scene. On the outside, you saw two women bouncing and yelping sideways down the steep off-piste. On the inside, I was fully absorbed in measuring and monitoring Anne's energy level for the exact moment she could bounce into the fall-line and turn. What seemed before to be a huge leap was getting smaller and closer, until it seemed like just another step, Anne released her edges and turned with the loudest yell yet. Yes! She did it but now she needed to recoup. We waited, then started again, bouncing, yelling, bouncing and yelling until her next turn and the next and the next. Five turns exhausted her energy. Gather again. Begin again. The group came into focus: a party of nine sending up cheers, and love, looking cozy as a campfire after a long trip. As Anne approached the group, I saw from her face that she, like others I've witnessed after their leap through the moment, suddenly became aware that she was stark naked.

For a person to willingly leap, their energy needs to flow out. If the energy faces too great a barrier in that crucial moment before the leap, it will start to back up and swirl like water before a dam. The energy will vortex inward and manifest in crying, cramped breathing, shaky muscles, and the desire to retreat. As Anne's guide learned, she first needed a safe gathering place (in this case provided by another's presence) to stop the inward swirl and collect a reservoir of energy that can move *out*. Then the task needs to be lowered so the barrier of that crucial moment drops to whatever level is necessary for the energy to begin flowing. A mere sound, a loud breath. That is how the sheer cliff dissolves into a series of stairs, one leap leading to the next. As soon as energy begins to move, more seems to break through, and it is time to steadily raise the task again, building momentum in small increments toward the pivotal moment.

This is no different from the rest of life. Let's take writing this book for example. I sit down at nine in the morning to write. *Something.* But there are days when there is a profound blankness to the page, not an emptiness, or an openness, not an availability or a possibility, just blankness: nothing. The muse is miles away in another country speaking in a foreign tongue. At such times, having to write a grocery list can be overwhelming.

When asked about writer's block, Tobias Wolfe echoed Stafford when he said, "I don't believe in it. You just have to be willing to write badly for a while." To work this idea into my daily schedule, I continually lower the task I set for myself (and with it, my pride) until I start to write, even if that means only getting the fingers moving, the mere physical act: *Nothing much happening. Nothing at all. Oh my dear computer, you bored with me? Well, here I am, stuck with you, a sitting duck, stuck... and lunch a long*

ways away and nothing happening. Nothing. You think I like this?
You think I'm not bored, too? Gonna pick a fight today? Throw a
tantrum? After a while, maybe two words rub together and spark.
A flicker of light, or maybe an image or an idea comes, just a
small glimpse is enough. I wait in the dark like a beggar, ready
for more.

> *One word*
>   *—one stone*
>   *in a cold river.*
>   *One more stone—*
>   *I'll need many stones*
>   *If I'm going to get over.*
>
>   — Olav Hauge (tr. by Robert Bly)

CHAPTER 8

Rushing or Retreating

I've tried relaxing but—I don't know—
I feel more comfortable tense.

— Hamilton cartoon caption

A tough motorcycle mama once confessed to me that she was scared to get on her bike because she knew that once she pulled onto the road, she'd be oblivious to any fear and ride too fast and too hard. I looked at her and smiled. I understood. There are many ways to react to the fear locked within the pivotal moment. Some constantly retreat in the face of that leap and avoid that willing surrender. But others, including myself, sense the moment's fear, close their eyes and ears and hurl themselves as quickly as they can over the edge. It's as if we believe this all-or-nothing attitude can conquer all. But we sense it doesn't, because we are frightened, too, either before or after the fact. What do we need to begin to slow down and move through the moment with our eyes and ears open?

While working with the concept of modifying the task, I discovered that the ability to lower body intensity is as important as the ability to raise it. We should be able to modulate that intensity level along a well-differentiated meter, the more gradations the better. I learned, in short, the importance of subtlety, especially for athletes who ski in terrain where, for their own safety or for the group's, they cannot make an irreversible mistake. They need to know exactly what 87 percent is, 93.5, 99.1. Many coaches are ignorant of this aspect of athletic awareness. They suffer from a heroic attitude clichéd into absolutes: "Just go for it!" "Give it everything you've got!" "110percent!" always with an exclamation mark and a smack on the back. My own coaches instilled that mentality in me when I was young and it almost killed me. Like this motorcycle mama, I had an on switch and an off, and it *was* dangerous, especially as I aged. To negotiate the variables I found skiing on difficult off-piste terrain, I needed to learn how to back off without turning off entirely. And this motorcycle mama and I were not alone.

Robert and Jane

Women, men… definitely one way the world is divided up. And it remains such an either/or issue despite the efforts of transvestites, cross-dressers, the butch and the queen, all those on the fringe of each gender who fuzz, smear, or rip at the great divide. They try to open the sticky gate locking us inside claustrophobic male-female stalls. With just a slight opening, we could wander beyond strict gender polarity and express with new latitude who we are or who we want to be, or who we imagine we could be at this particular moment…. Sounds good, but not always easy or even possible in this petrified world. As a six-year-old, my son said to his little friend Michael, "I love you," and the kids screamed, "Hansen's gay! Hansen's gay!" With a shrug of his shoulders, he said, "Maybe."

But the next year, he came to me with his serious, got-a-question face. "Mom, when the kids call you gay, it is *not* a good thing." When we talked about it more, he said, "It should be hating someone that gets you in trouble, not loving someone." By eighth grade he reported, "The homophobia, Mom, goes very deep." The sexual stereotyping found in public schools is, of course, almost everywhere—the blatant expression of the entrenched values of our culture. We have crossed into the second millennium and we still find ourselves cemented by fear into literalized stereotypes and one-dimensional roles.

The ski world is no exception. And dealing with fear calls up the feminine stereotype as if it were made to measure. Timid women talking about being *scared* trying a *sport*, a *physical* activity *outside* (in the *cold*) on a *big* mountain. But a man, no, he would never be scared... well, maybe one of those sensitive new age guys, but not a man's man.... I've heard it over and over. And I had to acknowledge that it *was* mainly women who came to me expressing some fear. But I was reluctant to look at this hackneyed issue again. Introducing gender into yet another conversation was like flavoring one more dish with the same old spice. Too many discussions ended up tasting the same.

But then one fortunate weekend, I was asked to teach a couple who appeared to be spitting images of the gender stereotypes. Robert and Jane lived with their two kids in Rowayton, Connecticut. Robert commuted to his work in the city. Jane stayed home, but wanted to get more active since both kids were in school. Every Friday night, from Thanksgiving to Easter, the family traveled the three hours north to Windham. Their house is right on the mountain, and Robert and the kids skied out the door at 7:59 Saturday morning to make the first chair up. "They love it," Jane said, so, of course, she loved it, too. But did she really? For herself? Well, actually, no. "But I *want* to want to ski," she said.

Robert "lived to ski." He worked almost sixty hours a week running a business and skiing "took his mind off everything." It both relaxed him and absorbed his total attention when he "worked at it hard." He started as an adult so he was not a great skier but he could get down even the toughest trails if they weren't too icy, especially with his new shaped skis. And his kids were active and happy, off with their own friends in season-long programs. After spending Monday through Friday dutifully being the good provider, the good husband, the good father, skiing was, at the end of the week, finally, *Robert's* time. He wouldn't trade it for anything.

Jane had skied intermediate slopes for the last ten years. She started with Robert twelve years ago thinking it would be the perfect family sport. Now, even her seven-year-old whizzes by yelling his perfunctory hello as he speeds on toward the expert slopes with his friends. Robert would like to ski with her, but... that's the best case. The worst case is that he *does* ski with her, practicing many forms of well-intentioned ski harassment: he takes her to terrain that's "good" for her; he gets behind her and yells, "Turn! Turn! Turn!"; or, he skis on "her" terrain but gets frustrated, speeds ahead, waits, she pulls up, he takes off. (My husband reminds me at this point that I often do this to him.) Jane would really rather ski by herself and mostly she does, but then she gets bored skiing the same slopes, and she is too afraid to try anything new, so she goes in early. And while the rest of her family stays out till four, she ends up in the house cleaning the breakfast dishes, starting dinner. She sort of, almost, maybe had a good time.

Fear in the Mind, Fear in the Body

As I looked more closely, I saw the one part of this story that is usually omitted. An essential part: what Robert's and Jane's bodies were saying on the slope. Skiing makes visible a dialogue not only between the mind and body but also between the body and the changing pitch, the snow, ice, bumps, compressions, bowls and valleys. Jane's body was upright, slightly flexed at the joints, relaxed. She was relatively centered fore and aft, and made easy, round, skidded turns. She didn't rush to get her skis across the hill, which meant she basically enjoyed her gentle ride down the hill. In short, her body showed no fear.

Robert's body, on the other hand, turned *on* then *off* then *on* with no subtlety or finesse. He moved abruptly and defensively, his weight far back of center, actually leaning on the backs of his boots. With his stiff downhill leg, he habitually braced hard against gravity. He did all the work himself, determined that under his reign, gravity wouldn't have to help him at all. He pushed his skis around the corner as fast as he could almost as if he didn't want to go *down* the hill. His mind seemed free of fear as he conquered slope after slope, but his body looked scared to death.

So there is fear in both Robert and Jane. Jane's mind says no to anything new or scary. She retreats from whatever she thinks could be a frightening situation. Because she remains on easier terrain where she is comfortable, fear never becomes manifest in her body. Robert either does not feel the fear or in a culturally induced coup of denial, he rushes through it. Consequently, with no place to occupy in his mind, the fear manifests itself in his body. As he dutifully tries to manage terrain above his skill level, his body responds with stiff bracing of the legs, and harsh, defensive movements.

Even though Jane is technically fine for her skill level, she has been on the same plateau for many years, constricted by her own self-imposed comfort zone. That, in itself, has deflated her confidence in her body's ability to learn, to do something new. Jane assumes she is not athletic, although there is no evidence for that assumption—she works out three days a week at the gym. But she has retreated from any opportunity to try new terrain; along with that cushy ease comes a lack of thrill, a lack of that feverish delight coursing through the blood. Jane feels bored, a little dull, trapped. Did she ever have any of that feverish delight? She thinks she did, once. And she sees it in the eyes of her ten-year-old daughter, red-faced from the cold and happy, as she sets her poles in the snow to push off down the hill.

Robert can ski more terrain than Jane can, but his body has reached a plateau, too. It is so busy defending and rebalancing itself, he cannot use his new skis to accomplish what they were designed for, a rich and subtle smorgasbord of feeling that one has to be quiet and receptive in order to detect. And he cannot take messages from gravity or the terrain. In short, he has cut off his receptors and stoppered his feel for the intricate data coming to him as he makes his way down, in a whatever-works-for-the-short-term mode. Another slash-and-burn fight to the end.

I got stuck in a snowstorm while driving home on the highway, and I could feel both Robert's and Jane's reactions at work in me. Jane wanted to stop and wait till it was all over, even stay in a hotel. Robert reminded me I had to get back to work. So what did I do? Like Robert, I pushed ahead, feeling pressure to maintain my speed. Trucks flew by tailgated by black SUVs with dark windows and bumper stickers that said "Beware of Dog" or "Forget the Dog! Beware of Owner." I grew accustomed to the conditions after a while and didn't actually *feel* frightened, but suddenly I realized my fingers had turned numb from gripping the wheel so tightly. How could I have any feel for the road when I could no longer feel the wheel or even my hands?

De-literalizing Robert and Jane

The original Robert and Jane showed me two potential reactions to the pivotal moment: a retreat from or a rush through. I found this similar pattern recurring so many times in others that I called it the Robert/ Jane Syndrome. But now, with our motorcycle mama's help, let's sever this concept from gender. There are actually quite a few of us Roberts in the female gender. I also see a lot of Janes among men, although as a (male) colleague of mine said, "You wouldn't get me to admit that." But more and more men are not frightened to admit feeling fear. We must also be careful as we try to lift the Robert and Jane response from gender, not to drop into another trap: physical appearance and manner. Butch women are not necessarily Roberts. Effeminate men are not necessarily Janes.

Even though some workshop participants are consistently either a Robert or a Jane on the hill, others vary their responses.

One woman is notorious for being a Robert before lunch and a Jane after. Sometimes a season, a phase of the moon, a period of intense creativity, or a deep, transforming experience can shape-shift a Jane as she decides to jump off a cornice. Or an inveterate Robert might turn his energies within, attempting to honor another dimension of being alive.

Expanding Our Use of the Intensity Meter

Both Roberts and Janes need to expand their use of the intensity meter to help them modify the task. A Jane should push the needle farther up the meter, adding more force to her outward energy. Like the beautiful women who inspired Patton to rise from the grave, her body's show of intensity has, up to this point, barely registered. She only whispers now. To move out of her comfort zone, she needs to talk, shout, scream, jump, and play. A Robert, on the other hand, should use more gradations on the meter, not just on or off. He needs to approach the moment as one approaches a sacred spot, showing a respectful receptivity, a readiness to respond with whatever is called for, sometimes 30 percent or 70 percent or 91.6, not just with a blind 110 percent dash.

What the moment seems to demand is a complimentary blend of these two different energies: strong outward force monitored by a subtle, differentiating receptivity.

The person who taught me the most about developing this receptive awareness was the workshop's most challenging Robert: my mother. On the slope, Josephine acted fearless. Other participants were surprised to find her attending the workshop at all. "Fear? What fear?" they said, "You don't have fear, you just go." But Josephine insisted, "I'm frightened to death, so I take off really quickly." As I watched her, I recognized the instinct to charge as soon as fear appears. She would go straight into the fall-line, and like the original Robert, she retreated to the back of her boots and her movements became stiff and erratic. Because she rushed through the moment, her body was forced to express the fear.

My mind was full of questions. Were Roberts more frightened of the fear than the slope? Is that why we rushed? If Josephine stopped for a second and listened to the fear, if she respected the wisdom locked inside, was she afraid she would then have to back away and go home? Could it be age that she was running from, the changes in her physical abilities and in her body? But Josephine was not one to worry about getting old. What was it that frightened her the most?

We were at the top of the Wall, a short but steep pitch at Windham Mountain. "If I don't do it now, I'll never do it again."

"Then you can never stop skiing this slope?"

"Never!" she said, part jokester and part rebel. I understood the complexity: her tone carried the same rebellious vehemence she skied with, but her grin showed a full understanding of the absurdity of the answer.

Josephine was seventy-six, with osteoporosis and almost total blindness in her left eye. Over the last decade, she had broken more than fifteen bones. Still, she wanted to ski the entire mountain as she had for much of her life. But what exactly was worth the risk? Her bones were fragile, easily injured, and her age made it hard to recover. Also, she was the only caretaker of my dad, now brain-injured. Lots of people would say, "Hey! Go home. Read a book." And it certainly would have been easier for me to say that. But her spirit was too earnest, courageous, and hungry to learn. Skiing was not a trivial pastime for her. It had woven itself into her soul and had become one of her teachers. If she had not been able to ski, she would have transferred her irrepressible zest to some other area. But as long as she *could* ski, she wanted to accept its challenge. It still had something to teach her. She wanted to quarrel with it and she was not about to give up, go home and skip the debate. And it was true, she did have the skills to ski this run, the Wall, safely. It was well within her ability. Her age and condition posed a greater risk than the rest of us were facing, but it was not a crazy risk. However, if Josephine was going to stay intact and mobile, she had to stop charging ahead in that hurried, rattled manner. Charging might have worked in years past, but now it was time to break what had become a habitual response. Was this what skiing had to teach her? Were her age and physical limitations demanding from her a more complex and subtle response to the moment? This would not be an easy lesson since this woman was as impetuous as she was vulnerable.

Learning the Language of the Body

When Josephine's body retreats to the back of her boots, she places her knees in danger. Her knees know that, and they don't like it. Her body gets more frightened. Then her head retreats, too, and now, out of balance, she cannot keep the ski turning, and as she goes straighter, she picks up more speed. A vicious circle she got away with for many years. Now Josephine needs to let her *body* say what she can or cannot do. *She needs to lower the task until her body is fully accommodated.*

Lowering the task creates a small retreat, a necessary retreat when too many variables are stacked up, a retreat that will help the body stay in a safe, relaxed readiness, still wanting to move down the hill. We must learn to pay attention to the body's desire. When we feel the body begin to retreat, we can change the task and lower the intensity, sometimes ever-so-slightly, to keep all its parts moving forward *with* the skis, so the body stays in balance, instead of being left behind. So Josephine's first lesson was learning to read what the body wanted.

The body speaks a language that is, for most of us, foreign, even inscrutable. Yet it is familiar for its presence. So familiar in fact, we easily ignore it, a background noise we have learned to tune out. This is true for most skiers, not just my mother. Even many trained athletes (and their coaches) don't understand what the body is saying. We are trained to adopt a Newtonian perspective, treating the body as a skill-development machine. If the body retreats as we turn into the fall-line, we don't ask what it wants or needs. We don't approach it with the curiosity and regard we would a lover. No, we simply yell, "Stop doing that." And if our bodies keep repeating themselves, we call them nasty names.

The first step for Josephine was to recognize the moment her knees stiffened and retreated, placing them in a vulnerable position. Then, she could learn to modify the task to lower the challenge. She could stay in the turn longer, keep the skis turning farther across the hill until they were 90 degrees to the fall-line so she could reduce her speed. If she were skiing in bumps that dictated where she had to turn, she could step one ski out into a stem. This would minimize the time the skis were moving *down* the hill in the fall-line, where they would pick up speed and frighten her body. Or, if she were on the top of a steep slope, the Wall let's say, she could begin in a small wedge for a turn or two, until she gained her rhythm.

We can employ different tricks for different slopes, but each one has the same purpose: *to accommodate the body's fear.* That accommodation would help her technically as well, by keeping her body safe, centered fore and aft, and relaxed at the joints while she was moving—in short, happy. Then, as her body felt looser, gaining rhythm and confidence, she could begin to raise the task. She could perhaps pick up (a little) speed, maintain more constant momentum or flow, try a few short turns, or aim for a series of small moguls. She was covering, with each run, more gradations of her intensity meter. She had choices now. Instead of being torn between "Never again!" and "Charge!" She could regulate the challenge she offered herself. She could start low at 50 percent of her capability, move to 60, back off again to 50, gradually move to 70 or 80 percent, responding to the variables that her body and the mountain presented.

Josephine started to ski much better in her late seventies than she had for the last twenty years, with more skill, balance, and control. Lowering the task does not mean lowering the level of skill required; it means only lowering the level of challenge that you feel. For example, turning more across the hill actually takes more skill, skill that Josephine *did* possess, but could not use because the vicious circle had already taken hold: after her initial rush, her body retreated, and once left-behind, it was out of balance and unable to keep turning the ski which then gained speed, adding to her fright, her body retreated more… So by simply turning more to slow down, Josephine frightened herself less but utilized more skill. She was replacing what appeared to be raw grit with subtlety and finesse appropriate to her age. "Someday you might actually mature, Mom," I said after a particularly beautiful run. "Don't count on it," she answered with a defiant grin. (At eighty-one, she skied one of the best runs of her life down Windham's Wedel, a steep run she hadn't skied since she broke her collarbone there years before.)

Lowering the challenge while still raising the *skill* level can be an important tool for Roberts. After injuring his shoulder, a horseback riding friend of mine does flat work when he is not up to jumping. The skill he shows in his circles, canter departs and downward transitions is actually higher than the skill he needs to jump but it is still, he says, "easier psychologically."

This seems like common sense. But a Robert who has not yet tuned in to his body has no idea that it habitually exhibits a defensive attitude. To re-train a Robert's body from defensiveness into a relaxed, elastic readiness, he needs to be on what he considers easy terrain where his body is thoroughly comfortable. To keep him off the steeps for a while might require some coercion, but if he yields, he will begin to ski with more skill, grace *and* athleticism.

When we lower the level of bodyfear, we hear less static, allowing our Robert to tune in to the body's various subtleties, as did the kinesthetically numb Carol who also learned to listen. Distinctions become audible, then turn into discreet messages, making it possible to detect the difference between the slightly bent and ready joints of a relaxed stance and a braced downhill leg leaning on the back of the boot. A Robert begins to feel when his thighs are free to continuously roll his edges or when they are stuck holding him upright because his head flew back as he turned down the hill. This is the language the body uses with utter precision and brutal honesty. As Abby said in her self-defense class, "You can *never* fool the body."

When we start decoding this language, we can respond by modifying the task. Our beginning responses are, however, often in broad strokes and after-the fact. *The hips retreated, oops...* But the more deftly a skier follows or even anticipates her body's desire, the more fluid her skiing becomes. The body stays in love all the way down the mountain. This is the touch that remains unteachable and yet we can point to it, we can say, "Here is the idea, now listen, now dance."

Differentiating the Generic Mindset

The more I worked with the various Roberts and Janes, the more I discovered, to my surprise, that they were not opposites. Although fear manifests differently in each, in the body of one, the mind of the other, neither of them negotiates their way through the moment wisely. They both, upon sensing the moment's intensity, respond with an all-or-nothing mindset, the main difference being that a Robert charges and a Jane retreats.

By working with the all-or-nothing mindset of Roberts, I began to understand the similar mindset of Janes. A Jane needs to tease apart the elements that contribute to her amorphous experience of fear. Then she can see options other than a fast and complete retreat.

Becky was a typical Jane. When I asked her what she was *particularly* frightened of, she said, "Oh, everything." When other students mentioned the variables that frightened them the most—ice, powder, steeps, fog—Becky kept nodding. Finally, someone said, "Crowds," and Becky yelled "Yeah!" before she could censor herself. That was the first sign that her fear had begun to differentiate.

As Becky and I skied off the lift, I saw that the top of the slope was mobbed. I felt like I was entering Yankee Stadium, and had the sudden urge to scream out, "Peanuts! Popcorn!" I looked back at Becky and she was holed up in a corner almost underneath the lift ramp. "Can I ride the lift down?" she asked.

Becky's mind was overrun by one thought: *I'm freaking*. Her hands were cold and shaky from the adrenaline that flooded her. She had never transferred this physical reaction into movement because she always retreated before asking her body to act. She would rather ride the lift down. An all-or-nothing response.

"I'm a real mental case," she said as I came near her. To Becky, her own fearfulness had become the only problem present. She was so absorbed in her own freaking that she discounted the existence of the external situation, the actual crowd. This happens to many of us. When my college friend, Andrew, told me he was about to ask his boss to transfer him, he listed understandable reasons: the lack of mentoring, the inappropriate fit of his qualifications, long, unrewarding hours... but somewhere along the line his tone changed and soon he was grossly under-qualified, didn't have the right temperament, was too unstable, he should quit. Soon all the problems that did exist in his job dissolved, and it was "just me, I'm a mess." Both Becky and Andrew spoke as if their responses took place in a vacuum, a world devoid of troublesome characteristics. And the variables themselves—the crowd, the company, the conditions, the hours—were mere projections of their own minds.

"This is not skiable here," I said to Becky. "There are too many people." The statement shocked her. I was acknowledging the impersonal reality of the situation and separating it from her response. This particular given belonged to the world. We should work with and respond to it, but it was not ours to own, it was not to be personalized as "a problem with me."

"We can slide down this right side till we get to the knoll where we can wait till the crowd clears," I said, taking the role of the guide.

"Is that *legal*?" Becky asked. "I thought I would just have to go."

"Even here? Through this crowd?" I asked.

"Yeah, all the time. I thought that in this workshop, I'd just have to force myself to ski it."

"All the time, no matter what?"

"Yeah." Given this either-or alternative, of course Becky would choose to run.

"Let's return to the roots of skiing. Ready?" I said with a grin. "This is not only legal, this is laudable! This is ancient history. Skiing began as transportation and we will *transport* ourselves down this side to a more friendly, unpeopled spot. When was the last time you side-slipped?" Becky's face cracked into a friendly frown. Her undifferentiated response began breaking into parts simply by modifying her retreat. "Side-slipping is a very worthy skill to practice right now."

"But is it laudable?" she smiled. "I *only* do laudable."

"Oh, very. Through side-slipping entire civilizations have been saved." We side-slipped and slid and stepped down the side (which is very safe but not particularly easy) discovering as we went the travails of a historical reconstruction.

"Remind me never to follow you when you are wearing that grin," Becky said.

It was still quite crowded below but once Becky was free of the claustrophobic pressure of her all-or-nothing mindset, she felt the desire to ski. As desire began to outweigh the work of stepping down, she took off skiing even before we reached the knoll.

Modifying the Retreat

Just as my mother's guide had to learn to read all the various nuances of her body, Becky's guide needed to read the discrete elements of the fear that her mind had previously experienced as an undifferentiated mass. Becky was not "just a mental case." Her guide started to pick out the different variables that *the world* offered, and then found tactics to modify the task.

Rather than learning to modify the charge through the moment, Becky's guide learned to modify the retreat, 10 percent, 5 percent, 1 percent. "Baby retreats," Becky called them. Sometimes, we noticed that the retreats became almost infinitesimal, and then even nonexistent. Her guide would read the world accurately and time precisely the moment when Becky could break through. "I actually *liked* scooting down the middle between those people," she said once, "It was like dashing into the subway and grabbing the last seat."

CHAPTER 9

The Necessity of Desire

Ideas we don't know we have, have us.

— James Hillman

So here we are preparing to negotiate our move through the moment. We build momentum gradually in order to develop the energy necessary to break out of our comfort zone. In monitoring the rhythm of the wave, we consider the givens of the situation. We fine-tune our course by modifying the task as well as our expectations. We tailor our approach differently if we tend to be a Robert or a Jane, identifying particular messages from the body or disassembling the fear that inhabits the mind. Our guide becomes well versed in tempering either a retreat from or a charge through the moment. In short, we have probed and poked at the fine art of differentiation.

Knowing all that, having taught it over and over and applied it in hundreds, maybe thousands of situations for both myself and my students, I arrived in Utah to compete for a spot on the National Demonstration Team for the Professional Ski Instructors of America (PSIA). Every four years, Snowbird hosts a six-day competition to select thirteen ski teachers from across the country. My husband and son came with me for the final week of preparation. I felt ready, confident; I was skiing well, and working out the final details of the equipment I would use. I kept waffling between two different lengths of ski. The short pair seemed too light for the expansive terrain (as if I were skiing on pencils) and the longer pair seemed too heavy and cumbersome for tight chutes and narrow, deep bumps. But I decided to take my chances with the big pair. So the day before the tryouts, I skied a bump run to see how the skis reacted, and I took a spectacular fall. I was uninjured but I landed hard—both sore and shaken.

As I rode back up the lift with my son, I began to cry and blurt out in short gasps: "I was so confident... up until now... and I've lost it all... that fall got me... I can't ski those narrow bumps... with these... damn skis... I gotta go right back there... and try..." This is how the fear guru was carrying on until her fourteen-year-old son interrupted with, "Hey Mom, Mom! Stop! Settle down. It was just one fall. But it was a hard one. Of course you're shaken. Instead of doing those bumps again just to prove to yourself you can ski them, why don't you back off, ski some easy cruisers with us, relax and have fun. Let your confidence come back naturally. It always does. You just have to wait for it." I stared at him. My crying and carrying on simply stopped. "Damn you!" I said, and kissed him.

On that chair ride, I was—what is commonly called—losing it. I lost any ability to listen to my guide. No penetrating, discerning perspective bailed me out. What was my guide missing? Why couldn't she get through to me?

Before my son filled in for the guide, I had defaulted into the prevailing paradigm of our culture, bouncing from one cliché to the next. You should get back on that horse! Just do it! You're not a quitter! You gotta stay confident! You gotta stay up! You gotta prove it! The Puritan work ethic specially loves to possess me, expedited by my German grandmother. But there was more than the work ethic in my diatribe. The tone bespoke an utter intolerance of my body's limitations. I might have yelled "These goddamn skis!" but that was a minor, speakable blame compared with the unspeakable rage I reserved for my body and its incorrigible penchant for making the same mistakes!

I never did get back to those bumps. But I did, like my smart-ass son predicted, recover all my previous confidence. And there was something else I gained, something I only sensed at first, and could not explain. I skied easy, and each run, more of my feel for the terrain returned. I felt again the exquisite sensuality of the razor-thin edge arcing, as if each ski were floating one-sixteenth of an inch above the snow. That palpable beauty proved the whetstone upon which my senses sharpened, my desire grew keen. I was charmed by each sensation as it seduced from my body its gifts and skills—more speed here, a tighter line there, a sudden change-up... I started to move down the hill like I was in love. And who in love would castigate the body? It becomes not only the means to express but the expression itself. By the end of the day my body felt delighted, sharp, hungry, my senses stretched. Two days later, when we got to the bumps in the actual tryouts: *What fall?*

So what had happened? It was not the Puritan work ethic, not body-punishment or a series of thinly disguising affirmations that brought me back. It was not even confidence that I needed to recover, it was my *connection with desire.* I had lost more than a discerning perspective in that fall, I had lost what *moves* me, and what in turn, moves my body to ski. Up until that day, my guide had not fully understood the necessity of this desire.

The word *desire* gets a lot of bad press. Unlike the words *justice* and *honor* which stick to the high road with a civilized, noble bearing, or *hard-working* which carries a sanctified weight no matter where it goes, *desire* feels low, personal, indulgent, and lascivious. We strip desire of its sacred nature when we focus only on the final fix, self-gratification, desire as a personal whim to satisfy. We need to restore desire to its true status. Like a sacred form of magnetism, it is the fundamental force that draws us out of ourselves and toward the other. It pulls us into relationship with the world. Our desire reaches toward what attracts us, toward what we find beautiful. Beauty moves desire; it gives desire direction, an outward direction toward itself in the world. As we extend our attention outward, the border that hems in our individuality blurs and becomes permeable. In touch with the world, we can no longer pinpoint where we stop and it begins.

Without desire moving us toward beauty in the world, we contract (as I did on the chair lift) into individual, imploding me-ness. Oriented inward, my mind swirled into a self-assaulting whine. The rage and castigation toward my body was just another form of my inward implosion. I fortified my border and set up camp, both isolated and isolating. Receding from the world, I looked on it as if it were cold and remote.

> *...It is hard to live inside the flawed*
> *and gritty chambers we*
> *believe ourselves to be,*
> *but we have strapped our bodies in,*
> *we watch our lives through airplane windows,*
> *small and dim and scarred...*
> — Ruth L. Schwartz

Fear severs us from desire, and consequently redirects our energy and attention inward. This inward–turning isolation comes in all forms and in all degrees—the greater the fear and anxiety, the greater and more lasting our rupture from the world. The fear Anne experienced on the Cirque forced all her outward energy to retreat and trapped it within her own body as her hands shook and her heart pounded. She was not merely alone on the Cirque, she was imprisoned within her skin. Fear had drawn strict lines and the world *out there*—the skis, the snow, the mountain—had become the enemy.

What had seemed so simple, merely backing off and skiing easy on that tryout preparation day, turned into a major lesson. I needed only the time and place where I could feel again that exquisite and profound desire. It was what freed me from the self-obsessed black hole I found myself in. Then I could allow the taste of beauty to be what moved me—both physically and emotionally—first, out of my inward swirl and then toward the mountain beneath my feet.

We cannot control desire and demand that it perform. We can only listen for its voice. We must wait, with utmost attention, for desire to emerge. We can protect and nurture it during its first and sometimes fragile waking moments. We can attempt to prevent what will overwhelm it, flatten it into silence. But still, desire will remain inherently unpredictable because it is not only about *us*, it moves in response to the world. We might be in control of the goals we set, imposing them upon our schedules, but we will always remain at the mercy of desire.

The guide can now name its master, I thought, reflecting later that day. Each of the guide's decisions on the approach to the pivotal moment—whether lowering the task, or gauging the body's level of relaxation, or differentiating fears to modify a retreat—all these methods could now be governed by the underlying force of desire, its fundamental and sacred pull.

The Body as a Machine

A major impediment to restoring desire as a value in sport as well as in the culture is our mechanical concept of the body. We have come to view the body as a machine. The machine gets in shape and is monitored by other machines. In fact, some coaches direct their athletes to work out *only* while hooked up to displays and monitors that can accurately specify the exact percentages and rates and totals of the machine's exertion. We keep the machine going, and in return it carries around our brain, which we have scientifically reduced to an exchange of chemicals. All the while, the soul is in exile, permanently relegated to some netherworld where it is allowed to concern itself with "spiritual" matters.

This mechanistic perspective of the body is not benign. The now soulless, chemically based machine gets stimulated and repressed by other chemical substances.

In the athletic world, this translates to the ubiquitous use of drugs. The International Olympic Committee reacts with absolutist measures like stripping the all-around gold from Romania's sixteen-year-old gymnast, Andreea Raducan, at the 2000 summer games for taking over-the-counter cold medication. The officials' knee-jerk reaction against the rampant use of artificial stimulants makes them miss their enemy entirely. The fault of such use lies, not in the steroid or in the doctor or in the athlete, but in the entrenched materialist view that reduces the body to the exchange of chemicals. With that perspective, what is the significance of one more chemical substance? Where is the line between what is "artificial" and what is "natural"? Viewing the body mechanistically equalizes every opportunity and every advantage: the latest machine, the latest training tactic, the latest chemical.

Our materialism toward the body becomes most evident when we train after an injury. We believe that as soon as the valve or tendon or bone is healed, the body is back to normal. It is the same old knee, the same old heart. We get on with it. We charge ahead.

How do we begin to restore to the body a psychology of its own, with its own memory, its own perceptions, and especially its own desire?

Liberating Desire

Rick, a twenty-two-year old man, came up to me after a lecture I gave at Snowbird, Utah. I noticed him because he was in front of the line of people who wanted to speak to me, but he let person after person go ahead. He waited till he was last. There was no one else in the room. I could see his eyes start to water. I listened to his story: two torn ACLs (anterior cruciate ligaments), one torn MCL (medial collateral ligament), three knee reconstructions, and now another injury. The reconstructed ACL on his "good" knee hurt so much that they checked it out and found it had torn again. He was losing his drive, he told me, and then he said, down to the floor in a barely audible tone, "I don't think I have it in me." He couldn't say anymore. He looked ashamed. I understood. When I was sixteen, my coach called me into his office and told me that I had the talent, "but I just don't know if you have the drive, if you have what it takes." He looked at me piercingly. "You know what I mean?" And then he added for good measure, "Like Susan does. She has what it takes." Susan, the new cherub, the rising star. It was a sentence thrown (and received) with a guilt that weighed me down for months. Somehow I never completely swallowed Sister Mary Patrick's sentence of hell for children who "held their privates instead of going to the lavatory." (Although I still can't see a little kid squirming and holding without thinking of that nun's sober face announcing such doom.) But even so, I couldn't ward off the incriminating judgement from my race coach. I lay in bed trying to defend myself: "I *do* have what it takes! I do! I do! I'll prove it to you!" I felt misunderstood, misjudged. I couldn't untangle the truth from the cliché. My drive, my desire *had* shifted. Something in me knew that and instead of exploring it and welcoming it as the next movement of my soul, I felt shamed. I had fallen out of love. And for my coaches, that meant I was no longer a person of substance: I didn't have it in me, the big, mysterious IT.

I saw in Rick the same torment. Was the IT changing? Were all his dreams, hopes, expectations, and goals (those big inflated words) losing air? "Maybe I don't..." but then he swallowed hard. That was all he could get out. He didn't want to cry in front of me. He was a trained athlete. I could see the hours dedicated to weightlifting through his shirt.

"When is your next operation?" I asked.

"After the ski season."

I asked him to come ski with me.

The next day, riding up the tram, Rick was composed. We talked about his previous racing, and his current coaching career, slowly approaching his ambition to make the PSIA National Demo Team. His first injury had felt almost like a badge of honor: everyone gets hurt and everyone comes back. He skied a few summers in Chile. "I was really on 'em." All the signs seemed to promise a place on the Team until his second injury came, and then the third, and then the fourth with no fall. The ligament just gave.

"What did you do to get your trust back in your knee after the rehab?" I asked.

"Oh, it just came," he said. "After a while, I just trusted it."

"After it was OK physically?"

"Yeah, after all the PT, once it was all healed."

"Till it betrayed you again?"

"Yeah," he smiled. "I guess." I asked him if he still liked to ski.

"That's what I do," he said, surprised. "I ski. That's what I am, a skier."

"But do you like it?"

"Sure. I can't imagine being in an office all day."

"What do you want to ski right now? You like moguls? The Rasta chutes? The Cirque? You want to cruise on a groomer?"

"Anything," he said. "I ski it all."

I started to poke, "But what do you *want* to do?"

Silence. "You ask a lot of questions, don't you?" he finally said.

We got off the tram. I didn't have a clue. I was looking for a place to start, a place where his desire seemed to coalesce, but all I could get from Rick were vague, even-tempered generalities. Even so, I could sense the subterranean, militaristically controlled feeling. It had been beaten down into its place. Just like his body. Pushed down for the DREAM that was looming over us like a hollow piñata …. I wanted to smash open the paper maché and let him see for himself if there was anything inside.

Rick was a technically great skier, but a graph of the intensity he expressed would be a flat line. His skiing was like someone on the dance floor moving with a constant amount of energy through the entire song as if the music's tempo never changed, never built to a climax or slowed again. He was a perfectly controlled and perfectly dull vision. A technically sound, tight-assed white boy.

He needed to ski at the borders of his ability but without hurting his knee. As I did with Ian, I wanted him to reach the *point of failure*. I asked him to do a series of turns on one ski (using his strong leg), continually slowing the pace by shaping each turn progressively more across the hill while still keeping the ski tipped on edge. No pivoting sideways on a flat ski was allowed. As you go slower, the degree of tipping must steadily decrease until the subtlety demanded is reduced to a hair's breadth. It eventually becomes impossible. That was the point. I wanted him to move toward the inevitable failure to see how he reacted. I wanted him to notice *where* he broke down. What did he trust? What didn't he? What gave? Where exactly were the boundaries?

Then we took that same idea into his free skiing. *Raise the difficulty* by continually tightening the radius of the turn until the ski starts to slip sideways and "wash out." And then *immediately*, upon reaching the point of failure, back off, get the rhythm going and then tighten the turn again and again. What your guide will be doing, I told him, is creating a course in your mind that is made to order for your particular skiing. He will be stretching your skills, sometimes just past the breaking point (101 percent), sometimes just up to it (99.5 percent), then easing off, coming on again, never staying at a constant level of difficulty or intensity.

Rick's imaginary guide not only set the course for him, he also provided the necessary distance for Rick to view his body. Rick could imagine it as a separate entity. This allowed him to accurately monitor his body's reactions and movements because they no longer were a measure of his self-worth. No energy was wasted repressing judgements. No big questions lurked for him to assiduously avoid answering.

Rick was afraid of what his knee was going to say to him.

What if it pointed to the core question: did he still have *it* in him? While his head was haunted by the unlimited dream, he couldn't afford to listen to the very real limitations of that knee. When he shut out his knee's voice, his whole body began to contract. It was as if his body said, "OK, since you won't protect your knee, I will, I'll shut down. I won't risk a thing." Rick became strangely unpresent, skiing with a superior technical proficiency, but without thrill or love. No wonder the dream felt hollow, it had lost the body that fed it.

Rick had never intentionally changed the intensity level in his free skiing. "Except I guess when I was a kid. I would go faster and faster till I self-destructed." He was so technically accurate that even when he flew off a bump he was in perfect balance, never going too high or too far. Even in a race course, he admitted, he went out of the start with a generic go-get-em mindset he maintained till after the finish line.

"What about when you blow out or miss a gate? Do you push and push till you lose control?"

"No, it's just an unintentional mistake," he said.

He was learning just how much he had stopped testing his limits. After each injury, he relied on greater skill and precision, continually refining old moves but never trying new ones, which necessarily are rough-hewn and crude. He became a techno-machine. And what his body had to say about it got drowned out of the conversation. But by creating 99 percent and 101 percent intensity levels, he was forced to converse with and explore his body's boundaries.

And he found out a lot. "I guess I don't trust even my good knee," he said and cocked his head to look at me.

"Thank God 'cause it's not trustworthy," I smiled. "And it's been trying to tell you that."

As Rick's body became more vocal, it began expressing that missing energy, liberating his desire. The next day, Rick's skiing expressed a much greater range: fast, Cadillac turns on the groomed and then short, quick, pops down the chutes like he was handling a sports car. His skiing no longer looked boring or measured: it looked fun here, silky there, sometimes strong and indestructible, sometimes light and delicate.

He said, "I can feel the terrain again. I didn't even realize I had stopped feeling it." His guide started getting more imaginative. He used the contours of the slope to set his course, the fall-a-ways, and the knolls. "I'm think I'm starting to get it. I really *did* shut down."

"Well," I said, "you were so worried that you didn't want IT…"

"Yeah," he interrupted, "that I stopped knowing *what* I wanted, I stopped wanting anything. I was like…"

"A machine." It was my turn to interrupt.

He laughed, "A damn good one though."

By the end of three days, Rick knew exactly where his knee stood, but like Houdini, he kept eluding its limitations by utilizing other skills. His skiing showed an insatiable thirst for gravity, especially in the unexpected drop-off, as well as the satiated love of the feathery landing. He took a run down Great Scott that sent chills up my spine. He slipped through the rocks at the top like they were rapid gates and then, on its unrelenting steep face, cut some perfect GS turns, hit one bump, jumped over the next and landed perfectly on the back side of the third, his skis flying from one turn into the next, carrying momentum like water curving seamlessly down the pitch. He roped it in and pulled to a stop. "I liked that!" he said, smiling. "I liked that very much."

"You certainly did," I said, "you were dancin'."

He looked over at me. "Not bad for a tight-assed white boy, huh?"

Viewing the body as a machine, without voice, dampens its desire. A catch-22 takes hold. When shame leaks from the words, "I don't know if I have what it takes," diminished desire has become confused with feelings of self-worth. Then an athlete fears even more what the body will say; he represses its voice at all costs. Soon body-as-machine, with no expression or purpose of its own, becomes co-opted entirely by ego.

When Rick's guide allowed him to disconnect his body from self-worth, it could speak again without having to defend his manhood. Rick's previous training gave him a deep familiarity with his body; when he began to test its limits, he immediately tuned into an animated dialogue. Rather than hearing his body through one generic spokesperson, he heard the various voices expressing negativity, but also love.

The Puritan Work Ethic

I mentioned my German grandmother. Although a staunch Catholic, she upheld, above all other values except cleanliness, the Puritan work ethic. She was no fun and not very loving, but she did manage to get a lot done in a day, holding together (back in the thirties, forties, and fifties) a family of seven kids and a full time career with the U.S. Treasury. One of her proudest accomplishments, however, was transmitting, in a pure and unadulterated form, this work ethic to her children and her children's children. Despite our collective disdain for her sharp-edged temper as she plowed through her must-do lists, we became, sometimes for better but mostly for worse, the beneficiaries of her gift.

The Puritan work ethic, now affectionately called workaholism, slowly and thoroughly kills our connection with desire. "What do I *want* to do? I don't know. What's next on the list?" We are so overrun by *shoulds*, we can't even remember when we did something for the hell of it. We even relax occasionally because we should. We are probably happiest when we have time to get caught up. Perhaps that is why we stay permanently behind. The odd desire might sneak up in an off moment and leak out unsuspectingly. But when we are in control of the day, when we have taken possession, we march on like a no-nonsense army conquering our not-yet-finished work. Sometimes while the world watches the brightly lit march, the odd desires gang up in the dark and silently gather force. Then we call them obsessions or addictions. Sport, like art, can open a middle course where discipline remains under the command of desire. This middle way is not easy or obvious. Some of our personal militaries are bloated from years of overfunding. Gabby, a nationally ranked kayaker from Seattle, would arrive at race day, ready to trot out her well-schooled armies. She was a dutiful, conscientious, God-fearing athlete, a workaholic if I ever saw one. (I felt my grandmother beam from her clean, heavenly abode!) Gabby was constantly evaluating and re-evaluating her training program. She recognized she was often slow to read and respond to quick changes in the water, but she improved with repetition. Armed with that self-knowledge, Gabby arrived at each new race site a few days early and train and train over the difficult transitions, the waterfalls, the change-ups... Sounds like a good tactic, right? No. By the time race day arrived, Gabby was exhausted, and frustrated and her confidence was shot. Her nag, of course, had made use of every opportunity in practice: "See? I told you that you sucked at those new transitions."

We worked out a different program for her guide to follow. Gabby needed to feel that she was doing the *right* thing for her training. The concept of the guide provided for her a figure she could invest with the necessary authority to deliver this new, pre-race schedule.

First, the armies took a short vacation, just till the race was over. (She sent them to sun on some beach in the Caribbean and learn the Samba.) Gabby would wake up when she wanted and saunter down to the water. Then, she studied the difficult transitions, imagining herself kayaking through them as many times as she wanted, kinesthetically living through the details she had so carefully observed. In her imagination, she focused on the sensations she most *loved*. She no longer practiced mechanically, but evoked the proper technique by moving (in her mind) toward the desired sensation. "I can feel myself," she said, "reaching, stretching to create those feelings. I can feel my body being fluid. I don't get stiff and robotic." Then she would get in the water (if she felt like it) and kayak through easy parts of the stream to produce the real sensations that teased her, and made her want to move. She could do the transitions if she wanted *but only in pieces* so her desire remained piqued. When others worked and trained late into the afternoons, her authorized and certified guide made her leave early, relax, and enjoy whatever the equivalent of a glass of wine was called in her training schedule.

At first, Gabby found it difficult to adopt such an easy program. She talked about kayaking the way some people talk about their spouses: "I knew I loved it. I mean I've spent my life…But I had stopped *feeling* the love." The new program worked. When Gabby entered the race still full of desire, any newness she experienced became a welcome play of the water. She had saved herself for the moment, waiting until race day to be satiated.

Restoring Beauty and Desire as Cultural Values

Both Rick and Gabby, by losing their connection with desire, also lost their *touch*—their senses callused, their sensitivity to the mountain and water dulled. Rick stopped expressing any love or risk in his skiing. Gabby's movements became so habitual, she lost her responsiveness to change. Both became mechanical—hardworking and technically proficient—but severed from the part of the world that their sports explore.

This severed state is not isolated to the occasional self-castigating diatribe or to the dulling of an athlete or the quick withdrawal of someone stricken by fear. Think of the ubiquitous presence of the words *isolation* and *alienation* in our society, a society in which desire is often condemned as immoral and beauty dismissed as merely decorative and superficial. Aesthetics get stuck at the bottom of the list after more important values like safety, convenience and speed have been righteously funded.

The imaginative thinker James Hillman points to the connection between the reduced status of beauty as a cultural value and the corresponding, destructive obsession with the personal, the human, and the self, a contained entity turned within and away from kinship with the world. He is an ardent proponent of beauty and the aesthetic response as primary, collective values necessary to resuscitate a vital relationship between us and the world.

Today, our definition of "myself" continues to contract into an isolated physical entity, the appearance and performance of the body. With the body receiving such inflated, but malnourished status, no wonder we spend more money on weight loss than on either education or the damaged environment. Looking at a popular women's magazine at the dentist's office, I found the words *fitness* and *self-esteem* sharing space in thirty-four sentences. What have we come to? Do we measure our self-worth by whether we have cellulite or not? Are we working out merely to enhance our appearance, a word now almost synonymous with pride and dignity? Has the apparent fitness of the body become the core value of our culture replacing what we do for our family, our country, our land? Is our community fit? Are we fit as a society to live on this earth? Is there a fit meaning to our lives?

With such evidence on magazine shelves, I find it encouraging that within sport, where self-indulgence and self-obsession so easily run rampant, and even within skiing, whose elitist tendencies make it doubly suspect, ordinary expressions still hold a contrary understanding of the self extending into the world. "I'm *into* it." "I was *in* it." "Touch for the snow." "Got a feel for the mountain." Where does the awareness of our senses end and the ski-snow-mountain begin? With the ski as the initial contact point, the skier's sensibility keeps probing farther into the world.

I once taught a talented ski teacher who skied with a prosthesis on his right leg amputated below the knee. At the end of the day, he skied a run through the bumps so smoothly that the slope appeared flat as he absorbed, with sensitive precision, the undulating terrain. When he pulled up to the group, he said, "Hey! I felt my ankle!" Everyone nodded like "of course you did." He said, "No! I mean I felt *this* ankle! The one I don't have. I felt it." We understood. We knew how the senses could extend beyond the physical realm. Every lifelong skier I know winces or yells *ouch!* after skiing over a rock and damaging a ski. It hurts. If we could only breathe that same life into the rest of our world.

CHAPTER 10

Injury

...Why should I mourn
The vanished power of the usual reign?

— T.S. Eliot

Injuries are like annoying guests. They arrive precisely at the worst time. Usually fluky, and filled with fate, they never make sense. They tug at our minds: *why, what if, if only...* An injury can upset in an instant what seemed to be a solid, settled relationship with our lives; it stops our forward march. We're stuck on the couch and have been there four days, the novelty wore off after the first nine minutes. We wonder, *Where did my old life go?*

Every time I lecture on fear, I am asked about injury. And if I talked about one injury, I'm asked about another: "But *my* injury..." Injury feels personal. Although the stories and specifics vary, the unarticulated questions behind the struggle are often the same: *How do I live with this new fear? With this now imperfect body?*

Our response to injury is often reactive. We feel our comfort zone suddenly shrink and we want to push against it, especially if we are used to expressing ourselves physically. We don't want to live with fear pressing upon us. We feel we might suffocate, like grapes that once dangled freely from the vine, but are now pressed tight against plastic shrink wrap.

My close friend, Johnnie, a smart, complicated lawyer broke three ribs and punctured a lung and liver in a horseback riding accident. She so hated the feeling of a shrunken comfort zone that only one day out of the hospital, she wanted to get right back on Rain, her horse. It was not due, however, to a Puritan don't-be-a-quitter mentality. It was something else.

"I am *so* scared," Johnnie said, walking very carefully (an egg rolling around on her head wouldn't have fallen), "I want to get right back on as quickly as I can. Now! Yesterday!"

"You mean to catch this fear right away?" I asked.

"Yeah, otherwise it will keep growing, get bigger every day and I'll end up in this kitchen just sitting here afraid to move." Her husband smirked. We both knew that was not likely.

"Let me get this perfectly straight," I said. "So now, when it hurts to laugh or sneeze..."

"...or cough..."

"...or cough..."

"... or move in her sleep," her husband added.

"...and you're sitting and walking bolt upright as if your torso were strapped to a board, you want to get back on Rain when you know, you've *learned* how much your rib cage rolls and gives with a horse's movement."

"I'm frightened of time," Johnnie said, "or what the fear will do with time."

"Or frightened of how far your comfort zone will shrink," I said. "But it *will stop* shrinking. And when you *are* physically able, you'll have to do what everybody else has to do when they get injured: slowly expand it again."

"Ugh!" Johnnie groaned, "I worked so hard to get this comfortable on Rain."

"I know. And now you'll have to begin again. But it'll go a lot quicker. Your guide is smarter now."

"But dealing with this old, injured body."

"Just as it is."

"Shit!"

"And what else is there for your guide to do?"

"We could pretend!" Johnnie cracked a smile but winced because she almost laughed.

"That you're twenty-five? And get hurt again 'cause you're so dumb?"

"But I'm not taking care of you *next* time," her husband piped in as he cleared the painkillers from the table and put plates down for lunch.

"Because the sin is stupidity?" Johnnie asked.

"Because the sin is *knowledgeable*—no, worse—it's *intentional* stupidity," he answered.

"This could be fun," I said, "to watch you learn a little patience with your self."

"You're a sadist."

"But you, my dear, are a masochist."

"Only when I'm scared," she said.

A Robert's Reaction to Injury's Inward Pull

Do we recognize Johnnie's tendency here? Is this the charging if-I-don't-do-it-now-I'll-never-do-it-again mentality of a Robert? The injury had sparked a Robert reaction in Johnnie because *she was so scared of turning into a Jane,* of receding and retreating into her nest and never walking out the front door to move freely again.

Johnnie was haunted by fear that her comfort zone would continue to shrink forever. But determination and will were not the solution. As every massage therapist knows, the body remembers injury and stores shadow images of the pain and fear on a cellular level. The dimensions of that memory shape the boundaries of the comfort zone. Johnnie's attempt to disregard the memory could not stop her comfort zone's contraction. It only intensified her frustration. What is repressed rumbles below the surface and threatens to burst. Johnnie could easily have made an irreversible mistake because she wanted to "get her fear over with," to bolt or at least frenetically scramble through the moment. Her guide had to enforce great patience during this antsy state and keep her near *but off* her horse.

After an injury, we often feel both very close to and very distant from our lives—closer to their pulse since we know viscerally how lucky we are to be alive (even though unlucky to be hurt) but distant because we are blessed with a perspective that comes from a sudden change of angle. We have a new and very different job: healing. Peeing becomes a major expedition, pouring ourselves a glass of wine from the fridge inconceivable. When we fantasize, it is for a painless shift of position. We are stuck with the rare, discomfiting, and inconvenient gifts of injury: a new vantage point, slowness, inwardness, depth, and naked time, time we cannot run from, busy up, or cover over.

These gifts run counter to values our culture holds dear: speed, convenience, productivity, progress, independence, self-sufficiency and mobility. Intentionally or not, we all pay homage to the collective mandate to march forever onward toward our goals, and to never, by God, look back. And our bodies pay the price. They get sick, they get injured and single-handedly hold us back from our constant advance—our next meeting, next job, next home improvement. They demand we stop and look. Injury is a time for reflection (from the Latin flectere: to bend, divert, turn away or aside). Turning away from the march forward, we bend, we fold, we curl inward "and cast the eye or mind upon" our lives. We take stock.

The inward reflection that injury demands is not the same as the inward implosion of self-obsession. We do not sever ourselves from what the world has offered. In reflection, we do the opposite. We slowly sift and sort through the experience we are given.

This inward time balances the outward thrust of our lives. We pull the bow back before we shoot. In kyudo, the Japanese art of archery, the focus for the archer is on drawing the bow, not the target. He pulls the bow back for what seems like an interminable time, fifteen minutes or more, before he releases the arrow. He no longer sees the target. Its darkened image flashed before him for only a moment! What a metaphor for the glimpses we are allowed in our moments of reflection.

To yield to injury's inwardness, so contrary to our culture's push and productivity, is difficult. Our lives have slowed to three walks to the bathroom a day, another at night. We are tired of reading, and although we keep punching the remote, TV wears on us like too many store-bought cookies. We feel guilty for being a burden, for not carrying our own weight, for not being fun. We feel weighed down by loss. Injury is a time most of all for feeling, especially the feelings we most shun: failure, depression, frustration, anger, rejection. Injury drags us to a halt and into the depths.

Injury not only gives us the time to look back and reflect, it also gives us a fast forward, a preview of old age; we see the inevitable need to *cultivate different resources.* Weighty, subterranean resources that we will carry into the rest of our lives. In time, we will recover and we will charge ahead as before, making each appointment and planning the next project and juggling the kids' schedules. We will sign this contract and pay that bill, and fix the broken window, but we will be different. We will carry with us a weight, an anchor that connects us to the slow-moving depths.

Johnnie could not, at first, welcome injury's inward, reflective pull. It provoked in her a manic resistance. Since our culture itself is manic, it's not easy for the Johnnies of the world to find composure sitting, or solace in "learning patience." But the body becomes our teacher. Its knowledge, secured in the form of memory, can, as Eliot says, "teach us to care and not to care/ Teach us to sit still." The physicality of the body's memory grounds us in the value of slowness. Its weight teaches us to wait. We wait to begin again, to feel the body's desire pull us up from our chair and move us out the door at the appropriate time.

A Jane's Response

While some react to injuries like Johnnie, others never get back on the horse. And no desire pulls them to do so. This is a perfectly sane and appropriate response for some. They offer their energy to the world in other ways that can prove even more rewarding and valuable. But others feel diminished. "I shut down a big part of me when I stopped skiing," one student said. "I no longer *lived* through my body."

"I'm becoming transparent," another woman said, sensing her physical vitality recede.

Often, this feeling of something missing begins to take form. It can be a stirring from within or it can come from the world—a new sweetheart, a move to the country or a new city, a new job— some green shoot springs up after a long drought. Or a wife, a friend, a sister signs you up for the fear workshop as your fortieth birthday present. That's what happened to Lorraine.

"I guess I got sick of re-watching the re-runs," Lorraine said, "and I called up my sister. But I *never* said I was interested. I just asked if she were going."

"That's right," her sister added, "but when I asked her if she wanted to go, she *paused* before she said no."

Lorraine worked nine to five at a job she enjoyed, as an administrative assistant in an environmental foundation. She was not psychologically depressed, but she said, "my *body* feels depressed." Her response to a knee injury six years before had limited her body's expressiveness; it "never played anymore." Where once she had felt vigor, she now felt an habitual lethargy— her body's spontaneous, outgoing nature dulled into sleep.

But Lorraine did call her sister, and whether she sensed it was time to re-balance her life or not, that call was the first move out from under injury's pull and the chronic inwardness it imposed. The desire was there, in fantasy form, and fantasy is our first outward act. But just as it makes no difference who first says "hello" in a budding relationship, it does not matter if the original stirring is from within or from the world. What is important, in either case, is that we watch for these hints—some inexplicable excitation, an invitation from a friend—and that we are ready to accept them, no matter how faint they seem, so they can grow under our attention.

The more we sit with this new stirring, the more curious we become, the closer we look, the more it comes to life. Under Lorraine's thought and attention, her faint desire gained both force and definition. "It really started last Christmas," she said. "I had just come back from visiting my mother..." Her language revealed that what began as an indistinct ruffling now had a life of its own, ready to rouse her from her six-year hiatus. A week before the workshop, Lorraine's sister got cold feet. It was Lorraine who brought them both.

A Flesh and Blood Model for the Guide

When Lorraine skied, she felt a generalized weakness in her knees but she was not hampered by any *specific* memory of her injury. She had no lingering trepidation about the particular slope where she was hurt. Her knee had torn in a slow fall when her pole got stuck between her legs, but now she had no apparent fear of using her poles.

The particular challenge she faced was her complete lack of familiarity with the pivotal moment. "I haven't felt adrenaline in six years," she said. "Since it happened."

What Lorraine needed was a model for her guide. A knowledgeable, supportive *real-life* companion. Without that flesh and blood form, her imaginary guide, no matter how educated, would remain an anemic shade.

Lorraine expressed the shame others often feel when they

"can't do it alone." Her nag haunted her with the insinuation that she didn't have the "integrity to face physical fear." Like Rick, the ambitious athlete, she was frightened of not having what it takes. This guilt is certainly fed by the up close and personal stories surrounding the Olympics. We hear the slogans of independence, self-sufficiency and an undying faith in oneself, as if athletes were self-made, in isolation and against all odds. But no athlete (not Phil Mahre, not Bill Johnson) has risen into glory without tremendous support and interdependence, but these qualities do not slide so easily into our American ideology.

Guilt accompanies our neediness in part because it expresses an inherent contradiction: we need a companion or coach to help us learn how to face the moment which we must, finally, move through alone. Unexamined guilt can wrap us with self-concern and inhibit our involvement with the world. But in the presence of guilt are the seeds of humility. Just the attempt to consciously face the moment begins to press this guilt into what can sustain and enliven our relationship with the world—the humility of our basic, mammalian nature: our herd instinct, the slow and simple weight of our physicality, the smallness of our individual gestures, our embedded dependence on others. This humility prepares us for the willingness to surrender, to offer our gifts, no matter how small or insubstantial.

In an ancient Vedic story, a small bird lived in a forest that was being ravaged by fire. He flew to the ocean to carry back to the burning forest all the water his tiny beak could hold. Back and forth, back and forth he flew. As the gods looked down and saw the few drops of water falling onto the raging fire, they were so touched by the bird's effort, they commanded a huge storm to put out the fire.

What a sublime mix of humility and audacity! We can carry this image with us as we prepare to meet the moment.

Moving Toward Independence

Whenever the pitch frightened Lorraine, I would spin around and ski backwards to offer her my eyes and voice, establishing a connection. But I would not have helped her flesh out her internal guide if I kept her level of dependency constant. So when the hill flattened and she grew more relaxed, I would face forward again and drift a little farther away. I would stretch the distance between us as far as our connection would allow, then fall back toward her so she could take a breather and ski easy for a while. Using both the terrain and my physical presence (both its proximity and position), I retreated and advanced, back and forth, rhythmically moving her toward independence, the replacement of my presence with Lorraine's imaginary, lifelong guide.

Just as touch, after its removal, leaves a residual sensation or after-image, so our imagination continues the influence of the physical guide after he leaves. Both the positive suggestion of the guide and the negative space left by his absence are necessary to feed the imagination.

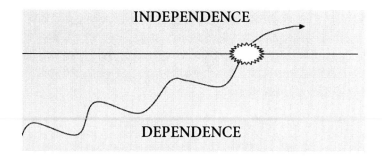

*Our move toward independence follows the same wave
we have become familiar with, as we gradually replace
the physical with the imaginary guide.*

Using this process of connection and replacement, we can attempt more challenging moments than we might alone. Even after the workshop, Lorraine would not ski a new trail on her own. She did not want to freeze at the top, her thighs shaking, so she didn't even try, she just said no. But then she learned she could temporarily use her friends as real-life guides. "I'd ask them to ski my pace for just five or six turns—they never minded—and I'd shadow them. After a few turns, I could actually breathe and ski at the same time. Then it was OK if they flew ahead. Sometimes I'd ski the run alone the next time, but sometimes not till the third, fourth, maybe even the fifth time down."

The following year, Lorraine and her sister traveled to Stowe, Vermont for Christmas week, her "first fun, physical vacation" since her injury. "I hung out near the top, waiting for strangers who skied my speed. They didn't even know I was hitching a ride," she said. "We nicknamed her *the stalker*," her sister added.

When I first met Lorraine in the workshop, she said, "I'm leaning on your faith in me."

I answered, "Well, that's smart because I know what I'm doing."

Her guide was looking for any available faith in Lorraine's skills that it could find. It knew what it needed for sustenance and it knew where to look. As our guides mature, they start to find that necessary faith in many places—a well-earned compliment, the success of a peer, the relaxed image of a five-year old sailing by. The guide's eye to the world sharpens. In the same way that our bodies are nurtured by what we eat, the guide is sustained by the substance of the world.

Welcoming the Body as New

Our identification with the-body-we-once-had can so dominate our attitude that we often try to whip it right back into its past shape so it can do everything it has always done. NOW. "This is *my* goddamn body and I can do what I want with it and I can do what I want to it." And if the body doesn't perform as it once did, we counter with a manic training schedule, working harder and harder…succeeding less and less.

But if we imagine the body, as it ages or after an injury, as new, with new memories, new knowledge, and new desires, we can more easily welcome what it is about to say, and where its voice will lead us. We are ready and waiting for a surprise. Again, the guide comes in handy. The fantasy of the guide offers both distance and imagination, two necessary ingredients of a welcoming mind.

When Josephine's brittle bones called attention to themselves, their injuries and age demanded that she not only listen but carefully gauge the levels of eagerness and fear that her body felt. To do this, her guide needed to disregard what Josephine wanted or expected her body to say as well as what it had said for so many years. In short, the guide created a semblance of silence so she could hear. If, in rigid adherence to her past, Josephine had dismissed, in any way, the stubborn reality of her bones, she would have shut out her body's voice and never learned to read its new, actual desires. Instead, her body, annoyingly vocal, led her to a more subtle and engaged response to the moment. Josephine kept the conversation with her body alive, and in doing so, animated her particular conversation with the world.

This silence is a cultivated state of disregard. We actively ignore all our pre-injury intentions, goals, and expectations in order to find out what is going on right here right now. Those old expectations come from the blaring voice of a single ego, a controlling monopolist whose vested interest narrows its foresight and restricts its rule to a top-down management style, listening to no opinions from below. By turning the volume down and muting the ego's din, we redirect our attention toward other voices— we engage the body. We place our ear to our individual ground, ready to mine for the substance and boundaries of desire: how our life wants to extend itself into the world again. This does not mean that we are glued to a course of constant self-gratification whining away till we get what we want. It means rather that we welcome the unintended and unforeseen, even injury, which like the teeming, marshy ground of an oasis, leaves nothing sure underfoot, but gives us the rare chance both to reflect and to imagine newness.

> *The easy part is following the trajectory with dedication. We often feel what we must do... The hard job is making sense of accidents, those trivial gusts that take you off course and seem to be delaying your projected arrival... Are the hindering gusts distractions? Or has each one its particular purpose? Do they together combine to advance the boat—maybe to a different port? You will not be able to find any point in an untoward incident if your compass is pointed too fixedly on the far horizon and your teleological vision knows where you should be going, what you should be doing to get there, and where you are right now.*
>
> *...What matters is not so much whether an interference has or does not have a purpose; rather, it is important to look with a purposive eye, seeking value in the unexpected.*
>
> — James Hillman

When I first met Tom Passero, my son was only three, and there was no one more fascinating to him than this man who could take off his leg and put it back on. While my son was busy trying to take off his own leg and put on Tom's bigger and better one, I asked about his story. As a pedestrian, he was hit by a truck driven by a drunk driver and squeezed against another car. He was twenty-four, back from Vietnam, an Italian stallion, a jock, a basketball junkie, and eager to sail with his beautiful fiancée into what he imagined to be the rest of his life. But life had other ideas. His leg was amputated, below the knee.

Years later, when I met Tom, he said, "I would never give back what losing my leg has taught me and where it has taken my life." He went on to explain that when he had asked for a better prosthesis that would enable him to run, the prosthetist answered: "We don't want to spoil you." Tom decided to become a prosthetist himself, one who would attempt to understand the depth and complexity of recovery for his patients. The loss of his leg as well as the indifference of his prosthetist were catalysts for Tom's re-engagement with the world. Through events obviously not intended, he discovered why he was here on this earth.

The extreme nature of Tom's injury radically altered his perspective and rewrote the course of his life. But it is often the small, niggling injuries that while less brutal are more confusing. They seem only an annoyance. We cannot continue "life as normal" but neither do we feel any closer to the deep issues of life and death where we most keenly feel the sacred. It is hard to stay open and welcoming when we are, in short, pissed.

While writing this chapter, I injured my own Achilles tendon. It was just before a riding event my friends and I had enjoyed for three years running, a hunter pace (a long trail ride through woods and across rolling, mowed fields with cross-country jumps, scheduled at the peak of the fall foliage season). I was determined to go even though I couldn't walk down stairs or even down a slight hill without hitching sideways. But dammit! It was all planned! I just didn't want to let it go. My close friends taunted me, "And you've been writing all week about injury! About listening to what the injury is saying. But will *you* listen? No!" "Better warn your readers: *Do what I write, certainly not what I do.*"

My mother (remember Josephine, the incorrigible Robert?) added without a hint of sentimentality: "Maybe this tendon is stopping you from killing yourself."

I waffled between overblown feelings of failure, and a to-hell-with-my-body callousness, between a spoiled-girl-whine and Puritan strictness that begs a hair shirt. In the end, I made the call and cancelled, and the big deal I created from a minor change of plans was embarrassing. But it was also a small and fleeting revelation. Injury tells us over and over again:

> *"We are all struggling; none of us has gone far.*
> *Let your arrogance go and look around inside."*
> —Kabir (tr. by Robert Bly)

CHAPTER 11

Voices

...I hear bells ringing that no one has shaken...
— Kabir (tr. by Robert Bly)

A few words came to me as a gift, carried by the voice of a four-year-old girl. Her father was teaching her to ski with the help of a harness (a tether wrapped around her belly which he could use to hold her back). She had skied this way before but this time, four inches of wet snow lay on the ground and she kept falling. The father finally realized that the snow was too heavy. He took off the harness and was about to carry his daughter down when she looked up at him and said very purposefully, "I can do this."

But she had never skied freely before, never mind in heavy snow, and her father, being a rational, responsible parent, asked, "What makes you think you can ski this?"

She shrugged, "I just know."

He still didn't believe her, but let her take the dare. And she took right off and skied, in a perfect little wedge, turning this way and that, gliding through the new snow to the bottom.

This was a few months before the PSIA National Demonstration Team Tryouts. It was my second (and last) chance. Four years before, I was prepared, I arrived, and I choked. This time, I needed armor. I needed to protect myself from myself. I heard those words "I can do this" carried in that sure but small voice and they sank down inside my body. They felt true there. They were for me. For that particular week.

I did know (in my stronger moments) that any task they threw at me, I could handle, but I needed the smallness of the little girl's voice to carry that knowledge. Others had been giving me the hefty pat on the back, their votes of confidence. I had heard over and over "You can do it!" often in deep, jovial voices that sounded in the know and in control. "You can do it." The word *it* was partly the problem. I guessed that *it* meant that I could make the team, and *that* was a very big thing to do, too big a thing for a two-letter word, and certainly too big a thing to say casually that I could do. The competition was steep. That "you can do it" phrase was so ubiquitous, it almost slipped by me unnoticed, except by someone small and frightened inside who would answer, "But, but... you don't know *me*, the vulnerable one, the one with shaky hands and wet palms, the one who loses her voice or blurts out the wrong thing whenever she's nervous."

This same vulnerable and very internal one smiled, however, when she heard the little girl's words come toward her like a string of small pearls, *I can do this*. *This*, this particular thing before me, nothing else. She grinned, and answered, "Yeah."

I carried another voice, but not such a sweet or comforting one. Scott Lenzi, the U.S. representative for Shorei-kan Okinawan Goju-ryu karate, told me that students always wear white to a karate examination because that is the color of the death shroud and the offering is: "This is as good a day as any to die."

The words shine in the mind as naked as an unsheathed sword, at once presumptuous and humble. The totality they imply at first sounds like the generic "give it all you got!" but they carry a corresponding, liberating hopelessness that protects us from our all-too-human hubris.

Our attempts are merely an offering. To believe otherwise is to be swept away by a great irrational inflation, the feeling of control over one's life. As prepared as I can try to be for those particular days, I still stand before a power that looms large, or a combination of powers that add up to the great uncertainty: ANYTHING CAN HAPPEN. My knees could give out, a bone could break, a binding, a car, a plane... This is the realm of fate, of what is invisible, and all we can do is wait humbly before it, as hundreds of variables line up and maybe, maybe, like geese in formation, take flight in our direction.

"I can do this."

"This is as good a day as any to die."

The two voices balanced each other. They spoke over each shoulder, one voice a small, feisty girl's, one a submissive warrior's. And together they were complete: "I can do this." Here is my small individual gesture, my prayer. "This is as good a day as any to die." I stand ready and open for the response.

Moving Through

CHAPTER 12

The Focus

*The seat of the soul is where
the inner world and the outer world meet.*

—Novalis

Eleven-fifteen in the morning. The air is crisp. Trees covered with frost glint in the sun, hot pin pricks against a deep, inhuman cold. Arcs of birch bent by snow come and go against the white slope as we ride up the side of the mountain, our faces a happy cold, our muscles warm. At the top, we skate through a small opening in the trees, under the lacy filigree of branch spread against a hard blue sky. We head toward a steep chute. We've been out since nine and are ready. We practiced and perfected, tuned to the appropriate level of intensity. The visibility is clear, the snow perfect, the variables have been narrowed down to one—pitch. We look out over the precipice. The body begins to speak: hands sweat, mouth goes dry, stomach tightens, it knows we have never been here before. But the preparation is over, the timing is right, the moment is at hand. We are here. How do we push off into the air? Where does our planning meet abandon?

We know that once we pass through the moment, we cannot turn back. We have entered the metaphor of the leap, and we cannot foresee how we will respond to the freedom of the fall. Because we can never be certain of a safe landing, we need to replace that uncertainty with trust. In order to jump, we need to trust that we will somehow muster the necessary resources to land—unharmed.

The *focus* is the bridge that carries us into that trust even though we are full of fear. A focus acts like a rope, tempting us away from the material security of the ledge and pulling us into the emptiness as we swing in the tension between the words *control* and *release, will* and *surrender.*

Narrowing Down the Nag

I was riding up the Gad 2 chair at Snowbird two days before the National Demo Team tryouts when the nag whispered in my mind, "STH (Steeper Than Hell) is gonna be nasty. Just like *before.*" My heart sank. At the last tryout, I had choked on that very trail. Right in front of the selectors, I gained too much speed, got in the back seat, started jamming my skis around, one poor excuse for a turn after another, blew my line—what line?—bounced all over the place. The nag took that memory and ran with it. What a set-up! All my confidence drained, no, flushed out of me. The fact that in the last four years, I'd had some gorgeous runs on that trail, that I had spent hours teaching there, that I had helped probably fifty others have their own great runs, the fact that I knew every nuance of that trail and had come up with focus after focus to pierce each demon there... all those facts were overrun by that insidious comment of the nag, which inflated into an amorphous mass of anticipated failure as undifferentiated as the mindset that had besieged the Roberts and Janes before me.

As the fear of blowing STH ballooned through my mind, I knew I needed a focus, the specific *this* of the little girl's words. The value of a focus lies not only in what it is but in what it is *not.* Whenever we locate our attention on a particular, we ignore everything else. Just like in painting, where the challenge of choosing the right color lies not only in finding the one that is suitable, but in knowing the many to exclude. It was time to find buried *within the nag's generalized ranting*, the precise, hardened information I needed to pass safely through the moment. I called on my guide to help.

My guide quickly turned into The Interviewer, impersonating NPR's venerable Terry Gross. "What exactly are you scared of?" was her first question.

"That I'll do what I did before."

"Which is?"

"I won't keep shaping the turn enough, I'll get going too fast, sit back, lose my line, get out of control, and blow up."

"What was that *first* thing there?"

"That I'll stop shaping the turn."

"Why would you do that?"

"Well, it's a whole pattern but it starts on the left side, I tend to rotate..." an admission that carried some shame.

The undaunted Terry Gross turned clever: "If one of your students did that, how would you tell them to prevent it?"

"Well, I guess I'd tell them to keep the left pole swinging continuously, and move it forward, down the hill, instead of letting it cross their body."

"That keeps you from rotating?"

"Yeah."

"And that prevents that 'whole pattern' you mentioned so you can shape your turn?"

"Yeah."

"And then you won't pick up too much speed?"

"Yeah."

"And if you don't pick up too much speed, you'll be able to keep your line?"

"Yeah."

"And if you keep your line?"

"I'll be home free."

The nag had been cornered into giving out valuable information! (The little girl smiled: "I can do this: continuously swinging my pole forward and down the hill.") This simple command would serve as the catalyst, the personal trigger to keep the rest of my body moving accurately. The fear that inflated so quickly through my mind had popped and what was left was a specific, do-able focus, well-defined and solid as a small stone in the palm.

Letting Go of the Focus

But my work was not over. If I had kept my awareness narrowed to my pole swing for the *entire* run, I would have skied in a contracted bubble, a glass house. How could I have reached out to the snow below and felt the terrain falling away beneath me? How could my legs have expressed just the right amount of elasticity to keep my touch, which includes *both* the feeling of floating *and* the lovely contact with the ground? How would I reveal the love that I know skiing can be? Just as you do not want to separate for a second from your lover, you do not want to miss a moment of the snow below. But if bound by the constricted awareness of the focus, I would have reduced the art and passion of skiing to a narrow spectrum of experience, a robotic series of movements.

So first, we must learn how to choose an appropriate focus, a specific cue so that when we jump, *all the resources we need will be drawn into action.* The focus ensures that our move through the moment will not be reckless. By invoking a localized attention— "I can do *this*"—we liberate both body and mind from the nag's generalized threats. But if we stay constricted by the tight grip of the focus, we micromanage our body and never transcend the limits of our previous technique. Once the focus serves its purpose, we must let go of it. Only then can our awakened resources create what is fresh and unforeseen.

The focus weaves for us an illusion of security, feeling like a lifeline until we broaden our attention and extend our antennae into the world again. And it is at this juncture, where we meet the world, that we express our love. There is no specific now to limit our commitment, no support to hold on to. We hear the complimentary words of the warrior—*This is as good a day as any to die.* We know that in this leap is the entirety of what we are, and what we have, but it is puny in the presence of the true powers of the world; we feel their proximity.

Until one is committed, there is hesitancy, the chance to draw back, always ineffectiveness. Concerning all acts of initiative (and creation) there is one elementary truth, the ignorance of which kills countless ideas and splendid plans; that the moment one definitely commits oneself, then Providence moves too… A whole stream of events issues from the decision, raising in one's favor all manner of unforeseen incidents and meetings and material assistance, which no man could have dreamed would have come his way.

> *Until one is committed, there is hesitancy*
> *Whatever you can do,*
> *or dream you can, begin it.*
> *Boldness has genius,*
> *power and magic in it.*
> — attributed to Goethe

CHAPTER 13

Choosing and Using a Focus

*It does not do you good to leave a dragon out
of your calculations, if you live near him.*

— J.R.R. Tolkien

Sally, a freckled, funny, forty-two- year-old landscape architect
was an accomplished skier, having skied most of her life and
even raced some while in high school. But for the last five years
or so, fear had begun to visit her, turning her mind into a blank
slate. "I become Ms. Tabula Rasa," she said.

When we skied together at Killington, Sally wanted to ski
Outer Limits, a famous bump run she had never tried. We took
the chair that rises alongside it so we could check the conditions.
The moguls were large but well-shaped. There were icy patches
but most of the surface fit under the marketing term "packed
powder," a euphemism for a severely compressed, machine-made
mass that is dense, durable, and so unresponsive it could be diagnosed as dead. It is white, however, and relatively slippery so it
does resemble snow. Sally easily had the skills to ski the trail. In
fact, 90 percent of the skiers we saw there did not ski nearly as
well as she. She had already warmed up by skiing lots of bumps
on easier terrain, using a focus that seemed to work "like magic."
In fact, an easier run would have bored her. Still, being careful,
I asked again at the top (in a casual tone), "You want to ski it?"

She nodded, giving me a mischievous smile. "Time for Ms. Magic to meet Ms. Rasa."

I followed her down the top section of Outer Limits which felt like an intermediate trail that had been souped up with bumps. Sally skied down in a happy rhythm negotiating each mogul with a lightness and agility I had come to expect from her. She was mouthing her focus to herself and smiling. But then, as she reached the place where the trail opened up, she lurched to a stop. Before her, the great swath of bumps fell a thousand feet to the bottom. Her eyes glazed over like she was witnessing the Mississippi on acid. Her focus, her rope, her lifeline was nowhere to be found.

In order to understand what Sally needed to do at that point, we should return to the choice of her initial focus.

Focuses of Different Sizes

A focus can target a part of the body—the downhill thigh, or the left knee, or the arch of the foot. Or it can be centered on a composite, a larger whole, rolling the ski tips on edge, for example, a focus which calls into action many different body parts. Those integrated parts are no longer micromanaged but trusted to fulfill the demands of the larger focus, the action of the skis. In the same way that individuals make up families, and families make up towns… there are composites of different sizes, each, in turn, part of a larger whole. But no matter what the size, each whole is a new entity equal to more than the sum of its parts. In a sense, the parts organize and become subservient to the newly identified whole.

When choosing a focus, it's best to find the largest whole that works, one that will liberate the greatest number of resources appropriate to the task. As under effective management, where workers with the necessary skills are informed of the task— the desired result—but given the freedom to figure out how to accomplish it. Unless, of course, a particular worker needs to be told *how* to do his job. Then (but only then) would a more constricted and directive circle of control be required. Likewise, a focus centered on, say, tipping the ski, activates more body parts than a focus confined to a particular movement of a knee or ankle, and it allows those parts freedom to figure out *how* to tip the ski. But if a person's ankle cannot move effectively unless consciously told how, then a narrower and more directive focus for only the ankle would be called for.

In the same vein, a focus on the ski might not, for some tasks, be as freeing or as useful as a larger focus on the terrain, which would engage the entire body, as well as that elusive, complex relationship between the skis and snow. If a focus gets too broad, however, there is no draw to summon the resources available, like when a fifteen- year-old mogul champ says to his unskilled buddy at the top of a bump run, "Hey, just relax and point 'em!" Maybe true for him but useless advice for his friend.

Children have an uncanny ability to pick a focus that is just the right size for the job. Walking around on skis, most five-year-olds don't think, *I want to lift this thigh and extend this foot six inches forward....* No, they say, "Go *to that tree!*" and then they allow thighs, ankles, knees, shoulders, head, all the necessary body parts to act, unencumbered by useless orders of exact weight percentages and measurements of bilateral muscle oppositions. It might sound like I am exaggerating, but techno-teachers obsessed with dissecting movements into the most minute and irrelevant descriptions do their damage in almost every adult ski school. And although this techno-talk can sound impressive and erudite, it is actually very crude compared to the subtle, almost mystical precision kids (and many athletes) display when they pick the perfect size composite for a focus.

Sally had been "victimized" she said by exactly that kind of teaching. She was wary about the idea of *any* focus. In the past, lessons had made her feel like an automaton.

"I couldn't do anything 'cause I was skiing with my head. I

forgot I even owned feet. Oh man, the last guy, he told me—what was it?—to match the angle of my lower leg, my shin, match that to the angle of my upper body. I was supposed to ski down thinking that?" Her hands came together to form an angle. She squinted hard while she made miniscule changes. "89 degrees, 89.6 degrees, oh damn."

"What'd *you* say to him?" I asked, wincing, knowing Sally was the quintessential smart ass.

"No, I was very polite," she said, "I excused myself. I told him I forgot my protractor."

Since Sally had learned to ski as a child, she didn't want to lose the feeling of freedom skiing offered. She stopped taking lessons and was almost resigned to her growing fear—she would just avoid demanding terrain. "I stopped trying anything that looked fun. 'Cause I knew I'd get there and get stuck," she said. "I'd go blank."

Her back helped her to change her mind. She loved to ski bumps, but whenever she did, even on easy terrain, her back ached. She had to choose: either stop skiing the bumps forever or learn how to ski them without bouncing. That was her predicament when she called me.

Knowing that Sally did not want her attention confined, I started with the broadest focus possible that would still aid her aching back: keeping her skis glued to the snow. But that focus was too broad to call Sally's skills into action, as useless as saying to your self-conscious partner on the dance floor, "Just become one with music." We reduced the focus to the slightly more localized but still ski-oriented *whole*: pushing the ski tips down as she went off the back of the bump. She tried it very slowly at first and then gradually, throughout the morning, she built up to her normal speed. She loved it. She still felt free. And she looked free as well, without any of the abrupt, robotic movements we often gain when learning something new. Without her ordering her legs to stretch and flex, they did so naturally, motivated by the focus to match the changes in terrain. "I'm de-bumping the bumps," she said. "it feels so smooth." Best of all, her back didn't hurt. The focus was doing its job, until that is, she looked down and saw a tipped-up, bumped-up Mississippi stretched out before her.

Sally's awareness, which had so effortlessly extended out to the terrain, was now constricted by fear, numbing her ability to sense what lay beyond the borders of her body. Her antennae no longer received any data and she was thrown into the felt isolation of a blank slate. The breadth of the previous focus had relied on her natural feel for the terrain to awaken the agile responsiveness of her body. As soon as her awareness constricted, the focus no longer worked.

Let's go back to rock-and-roll. You're dancing, you're into it, you're not self-conscious about *how* your body is moving, not bending your knees or rolling your hips in any contrived way, your body just shakes and grooves to the sound that speaks directly to it. Then something lifts you from your immersion—a new partner, someone's eyes—suddenly you think, *How do I look?* You're no longer within the music. You are stuck in the dull, ordinary confines of your self-consciousness. How do you transport yourself back? Although feeling the beat might have been all you needed a second ago to stay fully submerged, it is now too broad a suggestion, almost as useless as being "one with the music." You need to start where your attention is—the body—and from there, be led in to the music again. So you backtrack, maybe just rock from foot to foot for a minute or two as if you had just stepped onto the edge of the floor to test the waters.

The same is true in skiing. When the awareness constricts into the body, we need to start there—exactly where we are—and let our focus lead us out of ourselves and into the mountain, the music, again. When my nag piped up at Snowbird, I had to acknowledge her presence and even interview her to glean what information I could. Sally's nag was not "speaking" to her at the moment; she froze into a purely somatic, blank state, but she still needed to acknowledge the presence of that state, to begin where the fear had taken her attention. She had two options. She could lower the task until she felt comfortable again or she could try a restricted, body-oriented focus. I suspected she would be more willing to try this last option and that was my plan, but...

A Stubborn Robert Causes a Detour

Sally didn't wait. She was determined to take off again with the same focus despite (and to spite) her fear. She didn't want to change a thing. But now, because her focus was too broad to hold her attention, it no longer signaled her legs to stretch and flex. She started bouncing more, which made her lose control—faster and faster, bouncing higher, landing harder, onto the backs of her skis. Her arms flailed as she tried in vain to recover. She hit the snow hard; both of her skis released, and flew into the air. Her body bounced from bump to bump until finally she came to a stop about two hundred feet below. I held my breath, but then she raised her head and slowly lifted herself up onto her elbows, moving first one arm, then the other, one leg, then the other, the testing that people do after a fall: Does it hurt? Can it bend?

"You OK?" I yelled as I skied toward her. She nodded and I began to gather her skis, poles, goggles. As I pulled up next to her, she tilted her head and tried to make a joke. She got out "pogo stick" but then burst into tears. I needed to stay just above her, in view, because she was hidden by a mogul and people were skiing by fast, with less control than I was comfortable with. This was no place to dally. She pushed herself up and I squatted to wipe the snow off her back and out of her collar.

"Let's back up, Sal," I said, "Get near the trees." I spotted a cozy, out-of-the-way place under a large maple, its branches overhanging the trail. "We can sit down over there." Her thighs were shaking uncontrollably. "Here," I said, handing over her poles as we began to move. "Lean on these. I have your skis and goggles."

"I feel woozy," she said as she carefully lowered herself under the tree. I plopped down beside her. Her thighs were still shaking. "We're gonna take a break here," I said as I rubbed her back. "Your body needs some time to recover." Sally just nodded, swallowing hard to hold back more tears. "I'm speaking now as your guide, OK?" She kept nodding. "Try to cry a little. That was a wicked fall you just had there."

"What do you mean *try!*" she said and burst into tears. I put my hand on her shaking shoulders.

"I don't know why... I get so emotional..." She talked in bursts between crying and sniffling, trying to stop her nose from dripping. *Damn!* I thought as I fingered through pockets with lip balm, a sharpening stone, Tampax, cough drops, *I never have a Kleenex when I need one.* "I mean I'm OK," she kept on. "I didn't die...or anything... I make such a big deal out of everything... I mean it's only skiing... I just lost it... See?... What happens? I know I should be able... to do it... Everybody says... I *can* do it.... but, but this is what *always* happens to me. I lose..." she wiped her nose with the back of her glove. "...everything."

"What you lose is your ability to listen, to acknowledge the reality of the situation," I said as I cleaned snow out of her goggles with my chamois cloth. "Remember up there where your mind went blank?"

"Too well." She smiled weakly through her sniffling.

"You think that qualifies as fear?"

"Panic."

"That's what your guide is for. To figure out, right then and there, what to do."

Sally just kept shaking her head, looking down, wiping her cheek. "I'm too old for this," she said. The quivering of her thighs slowly subsided.

"You're right," I said, smiling, "too old *not* to listen. You were dazed up there. Did you feel that? Before you took off again?" She nodded. "When your mind goes blank, your body..."

"It totally froze. I was like a board."

"Well, now, you can keep an ear out for that. As soon as your mind or your body freezes, it doesn't matter which 'cause they're connected, it means that you've pulled back from feeling anything—the bumps, the snow—all your attention is trapped inside your body. *You can't just pretend it's not happening.* That's too dangerous. As you know now I guess, huh?" She took off her glove and I saw her hands were still shaking hard. "Your guide can figure out what to do but… and here's the rub…" She looked at me. "You *have* to listen. You had two options there, right? Either lower the task or narrow the focus down, bring your concentration back to your body."

"I did *not* want to lower the task," she confessed. "I was determined… and I am so stubborn, I just thought I'd throw myself down and get it over with. Quick before you would tell me to lower the task." Her face relaxed, her mouth half-smiling, her eyes shiny and beautiful. "Which I certainly did, huh? I certainly got it over with quick. Only now I'm stuck half way up. No! Two-thirds of the way up." Her whole presence started to feel stronger.

Two teenagers on snowboards stopped to ask us if we needed any help. We had taken one of their spots. Both of us looked up and shook our heads. "Only drugs," Sally said and the kids were taken aback, looking a bit puzzled.

"I guess I really *am* getting too old," she whispered as they took off. "I make a joke and they don't know whether to laugh or say 'Yes, ma'am.'"

"We probably look just like their mothers."

Sally sprang up as if those kids had, by their mere presence, given her a shot of adrenaline. "Hey, you takin' off?" I asked, incredulous at the change. "Well, hold on 'cause I don't trust you. *I* am gonna act as your guide for the rest of the run."

"I'm OK now, I really am. And I got it. I know. I gotta listen." She placed her skis side by side on the snow and talked as if she hadn't fallen but I could see her hands still trembling even though her gloves were back on.

"How about we lower the task for a bit," I said, "OK?"

She frowned. "Why not just narrow the focus like you first said?"

"You certainly *are* a Robert," I said, smiling. "Changing the focus would have worked before, when you first panicked, that was my plan. But now, after *that* fall, your body is shaken. I think we have to backtrack a bit more. But we'll get to the focus. Eventually."

Sally snapped into her bindings. I had to click into my own skis quickly. I could tell she was about to take off and she was far from ready. The worst of the trail was ahead. "I'm fine now," she said. My mere mention of backtracking provoked her—she was going to prove me wrong.

"Your body still needs a little time. You need to ease into it so you don't get defensive again. "

"But—"

Knowing I was facing a Robert extraordinaire, I said, "OK. We'll start down here," and pushed across into the trail ahead of her. I made my way down a few bumps as if I were looking for a good place to start, side-slipping down the back sides, then pivoting on top of the next, in slow motion as if I were thoroughly happy to feel (at a crawl) every inch of the trail. Sally followed, her legs still stiff as boards, side-slipping, then slowly pivoting on a flat ski or stepping to change direction. As she got close, I'd yell out again, "Down here," and patiently negotiate five more bumps. Slowly, her legs got both stronger and softer.

"Tricked ya!" I said, as I let her ski up next to me. "We just lowered the task and it didn't kill you, right?" She started to take off again. "Wait one moment," I said but she didn't. She pushed off with her poles right into the fall-line. *Damn*, I thought, seeing her torso fold and her legs stiffen. I jumped around and swooped below her, stopped smack in her way. She pulled up, taken aback. "Now you listen to me," I yelled. "Your body was shaky when we started up there. But would you listen? NO! And now it's *still* shaky. You are one goddamn stubborn Robert and *I am leaving* unless you start listening to your body. We are *not* in a place to screw around trying to pretend you are still twenty-five! You got that?" Sally nodded and I kept on, "Because we just schlepped down here, your body eased up, your joints got more relaxed, your torso straightened. Until you took off right there, head-strong, and it froze up again! Now, are you ready to listen?" She nodded. "We are going to carry on like this, schlepping, saunter-ing, and I want you to slowly let it out— *very gradually* move into your own skiing—but *only* as your body relaxes ... this is impor-tant... your poor, whipped, tortured, captive, aging body..." She started to grin. "And if I think, at *any* moment, that you are trying to bully your body, I'm going to yell STOP! and if you don't, I'm leaving. Gone. Out of here. Got it?"

She nodded. "I just don't want to ski like an old lady the whole way down. When I know I can do it..."

"You don't *have* to ski like this the whole way down. Only as long as your body is still shaky. When you, or no, *all* of you really *wants* to go, then go a little faster, a little more continuous, look a little farther ahead.... But don't just charge off after three side-slips. Ease into it, *sneak up* on your really hot skiing."

And, to my astonishment, she did. After five or ten bumps of easy sauntering, she gradually intensified the activity of her legs, until she was making short, consecutive turns down the fall-line. She never terrorized her body by charging ahead and losing con-trol. And her body rewarded her.

Dynamic Relaxation

Like the majority of skiers, Sally confused relaxation with slack squishiness and tension with stiff and braced rigidity. In ninth grade biology, we learned that some muscles tense and contract while others relax and extend. Relaxation and tension exist as necessary complements rather than as oppositions. Ski teach-ers sometimes use the phrase *functional tension* to describe the appropriate tautness needed in some muscles while others stretch or remain uninvolved. We have all felt the airy ease of shoulders that carry no weight, but we have also felt those same shoulders contract into reservoirs of useless tension and worry. The art in sport lies in the differentiation between tension that is functional and tension that hinders fluid movement. For the athlete, functional tension is an exquisite concentration of energy, powerful in its stillness but ready to move freely at any moment.

By reinterpreting tension, Sally was also redefining aggression. When the terrain became intimidating, her first reaction had always been to attack and "muscle it out," which only made her movements jerky, hasty, and stiff. Shlepping or lowering the task gave her, in a sense, a psychological Valium, softening not only her attitude and expectations, but also her joints. But to Sally's amazement, as her skiing became more relaxed, it also became more dynamic. She continued to intensify her movements while her joints remained soft and springy. As she backed off from her original knee-jerk style of aggression, she replaced it with what she later called "a soft, fem aggression." As she skied to the next ridge, she eased into an aggressive route down the fall-line, feathering the edges of her skis from one turn into the next without any abrupt or harsh moves, as if the bumps were always exactly where she wanted them. Although she was not de-bumping the bumps as she had on the easier pitch, I could hear the voice of one of my mentors in my mind: "She's not harming the snow one bit."

This time Sally grinned when I pulled up beside her. "You should yell at me more often," she said.

Changing the Focus (Finally)

When we got on the chair, Sally squinched up her freckled nose like a little kid asking for an ice cream cone. "Can we go back?" she asked tentatively.

"I think, *finally*, you stopped being your goddamn stubborn self and listened to your body," I said. "And see what happened?"

"I did enjoy how I just skied that, *but…*"

"Here comes the but…"

"I want to try what we did in the morning *there*. On Outer Limits. Is that asking too much?" She still had that mischievous, pleading look. "To feel like the bumps are disappearing under my skis?"

"No, it's not. Now your body's ready. It's primed. We can start with the morning's focus *but…*Ready? This is a big but, a gargantuan but." I waited for her to nod. "You have to be ready to adjust the focus as soon as you need to. Be willing to change your agenda at any moment. If your mind freezes, if your body freezes…" She was still nodding. "We'll start and if you actually *listen…*"

"Not *that.*"

"Listening is your new job."

"My new *career.*"

Sally started down the trail with the morning's focus, pushing her tips down the backside of each bump. Her torso, shoulders, and arms stayed relaxed. Her legs stretched and flexed with a generous measure of grace as the terrain changed… until she came to that same spot where the trail opened up. Then, because the body holds more mass and memory than our wishes and dreams, and because skiing is a slow and thorough teacher, she froze again. Her mind went blank. This time, however, she stopped, turned to me and said, "OK, now what?"

"You're blank, right?" She nodded. "You're pulled back into your body so you can't feel the terrain. So your focus, pushing the tips down, won't work anymore."

"OK," she said nervously, the adorable and occasionally annoying cockiness drained from her voice.

"We're going to try a new focus that will start *in* your *body.* That's where your attention is, so that's where we work from. Can you remember what you felt, in your legs especially, back there when you were so smooth, de-bumping the bumps?"

"Yeah, they were scrunching," she said, her voice still weak, "up over the top of each Volkswagon here, then they stretched down to fill in.."

"...the trough."

"The huge, gaping void." She managed a smile.

"Before we start," I continued, "just to anchor the feeling and focus, we'll try it *across* the hill. Right here. These three bumps are perfect. Then we'll head down." Sally picked up on what I didn't mention.

"Thank you," she said softly after the third bump, "for lowering the task for a moment." There was no hint of facetiousness in her voice.

"You're very welcome," I answered. "Now when you start, command yourself, consciously tell your legs to lengthen into the valleys between the bumps. Your legs like to flex so they'll do that on their own but you must tell them *when to lengthen*. Don't expect it to happen naturally like it did before, at least for a while. OK?"

Sally skied across three bumps as I yelled "Stretch. Stretch. Stretch." Narrowing the focus sharpened and strengthened her attention, like diffuse light concentrated into a laser beam. The body-oriented focus elicited a cruder, more mechanical movement than the ski/terrain focus, but it was power that Sally needed now, not sensitivity.

"An automaton can at least function," she said, grinning.

Using Cue Sounds

In order for the focus to take hold in Sally's body, she needed to use a cue sound each time she wanted her legs to lengthen. We used "Str-e-tch" but although we used an actual word, its meaning was not as critical as its sound—its length, rhythm, forcefulness, and feeling. "Stretch" would not have worked for this particular movement if it were spoken abruptly or fired off in a quick rhythm.

"Come on, yell it out," I said to her after the first three bumps, "in a loud, calm, commanding tone. Like you're talking to your dog and you're not pissed but you really mean it. Really elongate the sound. Give it the entire breath. Like this." I skied the bump directly below us. "Str-e-e-e-tch." I called back to her, "Really draw it out."

Sally yelled "*STR-E-TCH!*" as if her guide had been given a bullhorn.

When a cue sound is spoken aloud, the nag's influence is completely negated. No matter how insidiously she tries to interfere, she is no match for the projected voice. The body seems to listen to the command that carries the most authority. Loudness works. The nag cowers in the corner of the mind and leaves us alone. "I feel like a jerk," Sally said, "and jerks aren't scared!" However, that freedom from the nag only partially helps. To be fully effective, a cue sound must trigger the desired movements. It translates the mental focus into sounds the body responds to, language that often eludes the everyday logic of the intellect.

Sensory Language the Body Understands

When we use words as cue sounds, they should be specific and sensory. Then the body will hear. Techno-teachers are baffled when they hear my students yell out a word only slightly elevated from a grunt. Rather than a breathy "Go!" or an elongated "Str-e-tch," they would favor some ornate cue like "Move your center of mass in such a way as to balance in accord with your forward momentum." Needless to say the body could easily acquire ADHD.

The body, like the imagination, disregards abstractions. Imagine an old *man*. Who springs to mind? Instantly I see Popsy, my grandfather, spit onto the dirt outside his barn. A sensory, singular noun bears a specific image. Now try to imagine old *men*. When the noun changes to plural, it becomes more abstract, less immediate. An image might emerge, but it often appears out of focus, the details vague. We've moved from Popsy or the neighbor walking his dog to old-man-ness. Now skip to a greater level of abstraction like *center of mass* or *forward momentum* and the body takes a vacation.

Abstractions are like huge, largely empty halls that are sometimes useful, especially for weddings and graduations. But too often, they mean nothing because while my point of view might be from the south corner, you see the hall from the very different perspective of the north. Just take the word *character* which can become so overused in political, especially Presidential, campaigns. Certainly the concept means something very different to a working mother in Harlem trying to feed and educate her three kids than it does to a glad-handing oil executive in Texas. Seeing how vacuous these great words become, it's a wonder they are still used as cornerstones of our culture.

Abstractions sneak in everywhere. I just reviewed a manual addressed to snowboarders as well as to skiers. In its all-inclusive spirit, it created the term *snow-tool-user*—double hyphens should immediately be suspect—a word so formless and bland, it slips immediately from the mind. Being raised a Catholic, I couldn't resist planning an appropriate penance for the author: a hundred slow but rhythmical repetitions of the evocative word *tit*. Certainly a cue to inspire the body.

Sound Carries Energy

The sound of the cue rallies the body's energy. As the sound travels into the air, it carries with it the particular energy it has summoned, soft in some cases, loud and strong in others. *The body responds directly to the emotion carried in sound.* But too often, we don't hear this response because we are dominated by what we see.

When my son was five or six, I took a day off so we could take a train ride he had wanted to go on. When we got back, I overheard him say to our neighbor, "Well, it started out really cool till I said I was hungry and wanted to eat and then the rest of the way, Mom's tone was changed." I was stung, but it was true. I became annoyed at his hunger and what I had interpreted as lack of appreciation, but I thought I had disguised my reaction. Not from this kid! He could read anyone's mood after a quick hello.

We need my son's sensitivity to tone when vocalizing our cue. The body instantly reflects the tone's emotion, not the dictionary definition of the word. The fantasy of the guide becomes important here. We, as the doers, may be frightened but our guide is not. When you tell your best friend how to handle her obnoxious boss, you speak firmly, with savvy—because you don't have to do it yourself. The guide has the same advantage because he only has to direct, to coach. So his tone can accurately elicit the necessary response from the body.

Sally was surprised to find this was true. "You're right. My guide is speaking out the cues. *That's* why I can be so—"

"Loud," I finished. When Sally's tone was both calm and forceful, her legs responded with an unhurried but well-defined movement. When the bump trough was deeper and scarier, she yelled "str-e-tch" louder and for longer, and the tone's extra energy summoned from her body the necessary intensity. "How simple is *that*," she said, shaking her head at how effectively her legs reacted.

"The power of fantasy," I answered.

"And also," she said, grinning, "as they hear me descend, they scatter. It's like watching kids play hide-and-seek. I get an empty trail in front of me!" No minor benefit at Killington, a notoriously crowded place.

Letting Go of the Focus

By using a focus, Sally placed her own limit on Killington's Outer Limits and the large expanse of possibilities it presented. Her focus formed a boundary around a narrow band of experience where she felt safe. When I skied STH at the tryouts, my focus served the same purpose. I confined my attention to executing the command to keep the pole swinging down the hill which engaged my arms, elbows and wrists. Within this contracted spectrum of experience, there was no room for fear of a second failure. And as one of my personal cues, the focus helped me keep my upper body stable, allowing my legs to keep working the skis. So it worked both psychologically and technically. Five turns into the run, however, the focus had served its purpose. I had established a comfort zone I could work from. It was time to loosen my attention and allow my awareness to spiral outward into a wider sphere. I sharpened my feel for the skis first, working like they were supposed to. From there, I began to sense more fully the snow that the skis were in contact with... and then the terrain that held the snow...

If we gradually loosen our attention, it will spiral outward into a wider sphere around the initial focus, from a part of the body to the skis, and finally to the snow and terrain.

Without coaching, Sally followed a similar process. As she grew more comfortable with each turn, she softened her cue from a loud command to a breathier "Str-e-tch," almost, at times, a whisper that allowed for a more fluid response. A few more bumps and she repeated the cue word "out loud in her head," which was all that was required to keep her body's attention and stave off a possible harangue from the nag. Her Robert-like tendency to blow through the moment was well in check. She was listening to her body and paying attention to each suggestion of her guide. As she quieted the cue, her tight hold on the focus slowly loosened.

As soon as Sally reached the lower third of the trail, she let go of the narrow focus entirely. She no longer needed to tell her body *how* and *when* to move. Her mind naturally expanded to the broader, previous focus and its corresponding cue: over the back of each bump, she pushed her ski tips down. Now Sally could feel the slope again. She could reopen her conversation with the mountain, showing a responsiveness that included both a give and a take, a receptivity to the changing terrain as well as a responding action, exactly what is needed to ski the bumps smoothly.

In fact, near the bottom, she even let go of the ski-oriented focus. "Oh shit!" she said. "All I felt were the bumps. I didn't remember the cue sound or anything. I was *just skiing.*" This is entirely different from the earlier time when her mind went blank and her attention retreated into her body. By the end of the run, Sally's awareness was fully absorbed in the terrain and her legs kept responding with a free and easy elasticity.

"That's the point," I said, "You let go and let your body *just ski.* How'd it feel?"

"Ah." She smiled. "Ah." But we both knew.

CHAPTER 14

Relaxing the Focus

*... when our perception is oriented wholly toward
what is before us, our body is at ease, and we are not
occupied by any other thought or emotion... This act
of attention requires that we move out of ourselves
and enter fully into the heart and depth of what we
attend to.*

— Robert Sardello

Every single day of skiing, we can hear in line or on a lift the language of battle, a call to conquer the double black diamond. But there is also, every day, the wish to be conquered, to be taken by surprise, taken by love, momentarily captured in the motion of the mountain. When we ski, we can travel almost as fast as we do in a car, and yet we are privy to a moment by moment feel of the ground, subtleties of the mountain we cannot possibly foresee; we remain caught in a state of awe. These two mentalities, to take and be taken, are entwined in each run we ski, as close as the two lovers, Ares and Aphrodite. Ares, the god of war, has for his battle cry, the focus. But Aphrodite counters with her welcoming eyes, a broadened and softened awareness.

Sally had trouble holding her focus in the presence of fear, but others have trouble allowing their attention to relax into a broader, more fluid awareness. The focus keeps their awareness under siege, dictating with an iron will what narrow spectrum of the world they will experience. It becomes the personal equivalent of a centralized government's strict censorship—nothing can enter that has *not* been certified and approved.

Although the hard focus, with its intensified, controlling beam, exists within a wider awareness, a tension exists between these two ways of perceiving. We're intent on our breakfast conversation, while the kettle boils furiously away on the stove. We argue on the cell phone while driving... The more channeled our focus, the more depleted our awareness of the surroundings, and conversely, the broader our awareness, the less we can maintain a focus.

Of course, we need both. As Sally learned, the ability to narrow our attention and intensify its beam gives us power. But the ability to relax that attention, and thereby let go our *in*tention gives us touch, a spontaneous response to what the mountain has to offer. As our awareness is allowed to scan a wider field, we are taken by what we have not personally planned or predicted. *We respond to a world that is alive.*

So how do we learn to let go a focus without being haunted again by the harangues of the nag? Can we relax the concentration without just spacing out? Relax it and still maintain the alertness we need in order to negotiate our way through the moment?

Bruce was a 55 year-old pathologist originally from Brooklyn who had moved to Vermont twenty years before. When I heard his fabulous accent, I asked, "Which part of the city are you from?"

He looked disappointed. "You can still tell?" He had a soft, open face. *Kind*, I thought to myself. He leaned toward me. He needed to tell me something right off and then I could choose whether or not to quit "his case." "I have developed obsessive compulsive disorder over skiing." Then he lowered his voice to almost a whisper, "And, and, and, I think you need to know this: I *sleep* with my skis."

"What are the other symptoms?" I asked, smiling. Even his hands had a fabulous accent.

"You wait, everything you say, I'll write down five hundred times. And I'll record it, too, listen to it over and over. I'll get brain implants that function while I'm sleeping—"

"With your skis."

"Yeah," his eyes lit up, "and I'll call you up after each day and give you a minute by minute, no, a turn-by-turn report—"

"I'll need an 800 number."

"What an idea!"

Bruce delighted in fictionalizing, but like all good fiction, his told many truths. He radiated joy, or rather, an unabashed love of pleasure. And he took almost infinite pleasure in skiing, a sport he adopted after he moved from Brooklyn. He drove an hour to Killington every day after work. He got up at five o'clock on Saturdays and Sundays so he could be the first one up the lift and ski the groomed slopes while they were still smooth. He had enjoyed moguls and ungroomed terrain, but then he suffered terrible back spasms and for two years couldn't ski. His bad back kept him virtually immobile as well as severely depressed. "When I recovered enough to ski Snowshed again, I was ecstatic." Those few, slow, round turns he made each day on the beginner hill convinced him it was still worth being alive.

I asked Bruce what he was working on. "Maintaining contact with the fronts of my boots," he said as if he had rehearsed for that exact question. A teacher suggested the focus during a previous lesson and the balance it gave him made him feel secure. "And I like security," he said, his hand making a fist. "Well... no... but... maybe... actually actually... I hate it. I hate security!"

"You're my kind of student," I said.

Bruce would have looked picture-perfect in a still photograph. Moving, however, he locked into a static position, leaning against his boot tops. In fact, his boots were holding him up.

"Are you calling me anal retentive?" he joked. "Obsessive compulsive, anal retentive." He lifted his hands up by his head. "How will I ever be a real skier?" Then he got serious. "No, actually that's why I'm here. That's why I called you. I don't feel… Oh, I'm looking for a better word, but I guess it's just, it's just… free. I don't feel free anymore."

I didn't know how to begin. Bruce was a consummate feeler. Few, if any, experienced skiers would so thoroughly enjoy skiing on a beginner hill. Here was the prince that could discern the odd wrinkle in the pea. So why couldn't he sense much of anything beyond his boot cuff?

Bruce's attention was locked and so were his ankles. And because his ankles did not flex, his torso folded at the waist abruptly, making his head and shoulders bounce with each change in terrain. This is brutal to the back, *anyone's* back. He had become so obsessively focused on feeling his shins against the fronts of his boots that he reduced all the sensation of skiing to those few measly square inches. His focus was stuck like a broken record, leaving him no feel for the ski or terrain, and therefore no elasticity.

Suggesting to Bruce, "Just forget that focus" would not work. Even if he could, the focus would be replaced by an unsettling vacuum and cause him to grab randomly at scattered, unhelpful sensations and thoughts: a pole swing here, the tail of his ski swishing over there, *Is this right?*, the sound of a snowboard on his left scraping across ice, a tightness in his chest, *Damn, my wallet's in the car*, his hand squeezing the pole grip, his uphill leg pushing against the hill as he started a new turn, the woman erratically cutting in front of him…

Unlike Sally at the end of her run, the process of gradually losing the focus would not come naturally to Bruce. He had to be coached. He not only needed to know *where* to encourage his attention to go but when and how to let it move back and forth between his body movements and the larger composites of the skis and terrain.

No, Bruce would not be an easy student. His fear was not caused by the pitch of the slope, dangerous conditions, or lack of visibility. We were, rather, in trickier territory: attempting the Yikes! zone of the mind. But of course, fear in the mind can express itself in the body. In Bruce's case, it distorted his physical balance, cauterizing his receptors to the terrain.

Balance as a Noun or Verb

Bruce, like many skiers, conceived of balance as a noun, as something you *get* and clutch onto by freezing in a static position, the ultimate micromanagement of a control freak. But there is actually no such thing as balance while skiing. It is only an illusion we keep swinging toward. We constantly adjust. Sometimes the adjustments are so small and subtle, they are invisible, but we are nonetheless permanently in motion. Balanc-*ing* is inherently dynamic, always a verb.

Each time Bruce pushed off, his awareness immediately fixed itself to the point of concentration his focus provided: the shins in contact with the fronts of his boots. This small area of sensation had become, in a very real sense, his comfort zone. As he locked into position, he felt safe even though his back was actually in greater danger. Nonetheless, *this feeling of safety was where we needed to start.*

On the chair, I asked him if he had ever worn heels.

"Honey!" he said, "How'd you guess?"

"*I* just wore them," I said, "Three-inch heels."

"You? I'm shocked."

"I had to go to a wedding, a fancy one. And as I was walking across our driveway to get in the car, there was this little patch of ice and I was scared! I had no ankles! They were locked in a position where they couldn't work. I took these tiny tentative steps and my back, my shoulders were all tight. I thought then, *This is like having an injury.* I felt so top-heavy, with such a tenuous sense of the ground, way down there."

"How long did it take you to recover from this trauma?"

"As soon as I put sneakers back on, my shoulders dropped

about a foot. But I had a new, or renewed—a thorough appreciation for the subtlety—the sublime subtlety—of the ankle joint."

He laughed. "You could almost call yourself a survivor." But then he grew serious. "Let me guess: I need ankles."

I nodded. "You need ankles that move. And I have just the solution. We can start right here on the chair..."

As Bruce learned how to use his ankles, I could see the relief in his torso, shoulders, and arms. They were looser and more relaxed because his ankles were engaged. And he had a greater command of his skis; he didn't let them drift about. But the biggest change was in Bruce's balance. He no longer held himself up by leaning against his boot cuffs. Rather, he kept a light contact there but his balance was stabilized through a firm, yet *adjustable* ankle.

After a few runs, he became so excited, he waved his hands around, "I love it. It's like, it's like, it's like...being grounded but ready, at the same time..." he paused now and lowered his voice reverently, "being ready to *spring*," he said and his chest opened upward. And I felt it, the magnificence of being able to spring into the air. Hearing Bruce's voice (and hands), I began to understand the magic of a true epicurean: no small pleasure will slip by unnoticed.

Moving the Awareness Outward

Tackling the ankles solved Bruce's technical problem of balance. But more importantly, Bruce's awareness had been lowered to his ankle, foot and bottom of his boot. From there, it is an easy jump to work and feel the skis. Attending directly to the skis is the first major breakthrough for the skier's awareness precisely because it is *not* a body part. I can often spot it when it happens—the body-sized sigh of relief.

With Sally, it was possible to say, "Push the tips down" and she could respond. But with Bruce, it was necessary to go step by step. He needed to feel *the effect* of each body movement on the skis. Standing on the side of the slope, I asked him to lean against his poles as he worked his new-found ankles to rock his skis back and forth, onto edge, then flat again, then onto the other edge. He switched his focus back and forth between ankles and skis, creating a groove for his attention to follow once he began to move.

"With the ski focus, you're giving the body a job but also its freedom. Security and freedom both," I said.

"Quite a promise," he answered. "Are you one of those bleeding heart liberals?" Then he grew serious again. "But I don't get the security part. Security for who? It's frightening as hell! If I think only about the skis, I'll lose control over my ankles! I'll fall apart!"

"Let's try it, back and forth between the two focuses, in a rhythm, and we'll just see if your ankles forget who they are and start floppin' around when you let them go a little."

Bruce gradually learned to knead his awareness, to press it outward through the bottom of his boots and into his skis. He had to return many times, however, to his new comfort zone, controlling the ankles. "Just to make sure they're still there." But as his awareness stretched and became more elastic, it developed a greater range. He did not turn fuzzy, or scattered, nervously clutching at random sensations. And he certainly didn't space out. He remained highly alert *within* the territory we had carefully specified.

When Bruce was able to maintain the larger, ski-oriented focus, his awareness could expand to include a wider range of body parts—ankles, knees, hips. If the skis continued to work well, he could continue pressing his awareness outward toward the skis' contact with the snow, beginning even to sense the variation of the ground. But if at any time, his skis resisted turning or slipped sideways, he could retract his focus back into his body and find the recalcitrant part. His ankles, of course, were always the first suspect. After he made and stabilized a correction, his attention could move back to the skis, once again broadening the territory of what he felt. Like breathing, the awareness can pulsate.

Our awareness may be highly elastic in one endeavor but rigid in another. For many years, I helped ski school trainers speak in front of groups. Some were accomplished athletes, able to leap off a knoll onto a windblown slope and sense exactly how much give to expect from the snow. But when these athletes stood to speak in public, their attention immediately locked onto the scripts they had memorized. Their fear did not manifest in trembling hands or a faltering voice, but in a shrunken awareness. They would lose all sense of the audience, unable to respond to even a friendly outburst. And as with Bruce on skis, I couldn't say, "Just forget the script, honey. Wing it." Each needed the suggestion of increasingly larger spheres—stepping stones—to help his awareness expand.

Starting from the speaker's comfort zone, memorized sentences, we stretched his sensibility to, perhaps, a friend's face, or the shoes worn by the people in the front row—whatever seemed do-able. When the speaker's attention could comfortably travel back and forth from his words to the edge of this slightly larger range, he attempted another leap, say, to the person next to the friend, or perhaps a face in the front row. At each expansion, we watched that the speaker did not space and lose his train of thought. Each took as long he needed to extend his awareness to the next sphere until some, without faltering, could include the inevitable wise-ass standing cross-armed in the back.

Just as Bruce learned that by attending to his skis he could oversee his body without micromanaging it, the speakers learned that by attending to the audience, they could stray spontaneously from the script. As the speakers' sensibilities grew more elastic, they also grew more subtle. They could respond not only to outbursts or laughter but also to what was inaudible—impatience, boredom, or pleasure. And they learned, like Bruce, to retract their awareness when necessary so they could adjust their delivery.

At each new level of expansion, the speakers reported a

similar fear of losing control. They might "lose it entirely," "not be able to think," "go blank." One man said, "Each time I 'spread' farther into the audience, I feel like I'm going to disappear. But then there I am, still talking. But I was also listening along with the audience, listening *through* the audience." A few even learned aloud, "saying things I didn't know I knew," allowing their previous knowledge to grow into a new form, shaped by a synergy with the audience. In a sense, we *do* disappear as we hear our words through another's ears, or feel our bodies through the skis' point of view.

Awareness: a Difficult (and Frustrating) Prize

But as Bruce was to remind me, more awareness does not mean more happiness. The next morning, he looked glum and said, "I don't want you to take this wrong. I mean I am pleased. *So* pleased, so don't take this wrong but..." I got very nervous and it seemed to take him an eternity: "But, well, well, well... one turn feels better than the other."

"That's all?" I said. "That's great."

"What do you mean *great*? My turn to the left, it it it it," his hands were up around his head again bouncing in rhythm with his words, "It it... doesn't feel right. I'm chattering sideways on that side."

"That means you're getting very astute."

He cracked up laughing. "Oh man, I love a teacher who can speak in euphemisms, but *that*... I suppose next, you're going to say I'm getting more *sensitive*. Soon I'll be a sensitive New Age guy. Makes me want to go buy a truck with lots of NRA stickers pasted on the back—"

Bruce always made you feel free to butt in. Actually, he made you feel free, period. "No, actually Bruce, I *am* serious. I *want* you to feel when one turn is rough, when a ski's not working well. Now that you've moved your compulsiveness from the few square inches of your shin to the ski—

"To a razor-thin edge, a few lousy millimeters, you mean."

"But at least the millimeters are moving. Travelling across the snow."

"Don't talk like that. I'll start salivating again. No, it *is* great. But, today—"

"We'll check out that bad side."

"Phew." He was visibly relieved.

Once Bruce's awareness was oscillating between his skis and his ankles, I assumed he would enjoy learning to detect problems *on his own,* so he could correct them when they inevitably arose again. All he needed was a little time and a few hints.

After a couple warm-up runs, Bruce stated with absolute certainty, "I rush that side 'cause my ski sticks a bit. It doesn't roll as easily as the other."

I smiled. He *was* getting very astute. "Wow, you're developing the awareness of what's wrong, what's *not* working. That's important before you can fix it."

His face twisted. "I don't give a shit about awareness! I just want to get it right!" He stabbed his pole into the snow.

"This is not about *just getting it right,* Bruce," I said.

"GODDAMNIT! I *do* want to get it right!" He kept smacking his pole onto the ground.

I had misjudged the level of his frustration. "You're really pissed, aren't you?"

"Yes I'm pissed! I want perfection! I don't want to screw around sliding sideways! Feeling bad! I want to get it! Once and for all!"

"OK," I said. "I'll give you a quick superficial fix but you won't be able to tell *any* difference between the fix and the problem, and tomorrow you'll come out and do the same goddamn thing all over again. And you'll have missed—totally wasted—a major opportunity. You have just passed through a crucial stage of learning. And learning has *nothing* to do with feeling good."

"Nothing?" I *did* get his attention.

"No! And neither does skiing."

"Oh, so you're gonna tell me skiing is for misery, huh?" Bruce had at least stopped banging his pole.

"Yeah," I said. "It *is* for misery. You have one good feeling that you've never had before, which of course you can't hold onto, so you spend months trying to get it again and by the time you do get it consistently, you don't care. 'Cause, you see, by then you've had another *best* feeling that you lost just as fast. Maybe you should just quit *now*, stay in your cozy little comfort zone and save yourself a lot of agony. If all you want is a bunch of good feelings."

"Does the marketing department know about you?" he asked.

Scott Lenzi, the Okinawan karate teacher, had been working on a particular kick every day for seventeen years when finally, he showed his master. "That is not it. That is awful," the master said. Scott asked, "Do you think I will ever get it?" To which his master replied, "I do not know. If you get it, I will tell you. I am not here to please you."

And neither is skiing. Or making art. Or writing a novel. Or working on an antique truck. My friend gets goose bumps when he hears motors from a certain vintage. He bangs on metal in his garage, *"damn shit piss..."* frustrated nine-tenths of the time as he both works toward and waits for a solution. But when he emerges after a few hours, black with grease and smiling—*ah!* he loved it. Deep desire is a merciless disciplinarian; it drives us hard— beyond what we would normally call fun, beyond self-congratulation, beyond our limits and our comfort, and into the travails of not-knowing, of learning, the push and pull of the moment.

I remember being downright grumpy when, training for a certification exam, I felt my right ski's errant tendencies. It took hundreds of frustrating turns to get to the point where I could feel it clearly *not* work in concert with my left. Refining the awareness always takes time—months, years, decades. And although the assiduous detection of our screw-ups is usually *not* what is celebrated at the end of the day, it is what proves most useful. Once the problem is detected, the correction is simple, almost inevitable, and, what is best, repeatable. *Awareness*, rather than perfection, is learning's difficult but valuable prize.

| Uncomfortable sensations | ▶ | Awareness of skis and body | ▶ | Enhanced or replaced movements | ▶ | New comfortable sensations |

Developing awareness is a sensitive but
crucial stage in learning.

"Well?" I asked. "What do we do now? You want a quick, superficial fix or you really want to learn something?"

"Are you a pollster?" But then Bruce smiled. "No, I got upset, I'm sorry. But actually, actually, I still am, upset, sort of, I'm starting to calm down, but this is not easy. Does it have to be so frustrating?"

"Well… yes! When you are as caught up with perfection as you are, yes! Then this awareness phase is a bitch."

"My mother would love you. OK, I'll give up perfection. But only for about ten minutes. Shit, not only do I have a bad turn but my guru ends up being a liberal. But you still eat sugar, right?"

"Lots." I started to relax again.

"OK, I can take it then." There was a silence and I thought the conversation might be over when he said, "Meat?"

"Now I do. I love it."

"A carnivorous liberal. Almost bearable."

Even though Bruce laced his seriousness with a wacky levity, I knew the pressure was on. How to proceed? I had wrongly assumed Bruce would accept this aspect of learning, the awareness of failure. Now, in light of his resistance, the fine line of learning seemed suddenly slippery. On one side of it loomed a mire of frustration, on the other the shallowness of a quick fix with nice, but all-too-ephemeral feelings, "unproductive success" a mentor once called it. Still, I knew I better lean toward the fix.

"Let me ask you, Bruce, you felt that left ski kind of stick, right?"

"Yeah, that side just won't—"

"Turn as *perfectly* as the other. You know it's the *perfection* of the other ski that's causing your frustration?"

"Now you're going too far," Bruce said, his face soft and smiling again.

"Can you feel the difference between these two movements of your foot? Let me move your foot around so you can both see it and feel it." I knelt down and pulled his downhill foot out in front of him so he immediately felt out of balance, and then I placed it back underneath him where he could still roll it to tip the ski. "I hope your foot isn't an erogenous zone or this could be sexual harassment."

"Everything you do is harassment. But yes, I feel the difference. So this is my big hint here, huh? I shove that foot out in front, but when? When do I do that?"

"When you're just starting to make the turn on this sticky side. But you don't do it all the time and you don't do it at all on the other side."

"You might have to institutionalize me if I screwed up both sides."

"But now, lovey," I said, "start with the focus on the ski and then if it screws up, check out that foot. And *thank, congratulate, praise* yourself if you feel that foot poke out. It's a big step." And I winked at him.

He smiled. "I'm going to be a big boy from now on, I promise."

The Temporary Role of Feedback

We easily attach inaccurate labels to our movements, especially those involving our basic sense of balance. We tip backwards or forwards, feeling with utter certainty that we are standing straight. It was perfectly normal for Bruce to feel that his foot stayed underneath his body when it did not. So I skied behind him, close enough for him to hear me when he needed concurrent feedback. Then he could realign his inner gauge so it accurately reflected the physical reality. But that done, he had to be gradually weaned from needing this external feedback.

Students like the kinesthetically unconscious Carol with a vague, fuzzy sense of their bodies continue to demand: "Tell me if I am doing it right." Encouraging such dependence by continuing to provide feedback precludes a student from developing the awareness necessary for self-correction. However, I had learned as a teacher never to take the weaning process for granted. So I was relieved when Bruce began to self-correct, alternating back and forth between the old habit and the new, replaced movement. Each time his foot and ankle popped ahead, he pulled it back underneath him.

"And you know, my attention *is* starting to move back and forth," he said, looking almost dumbfounded. "Between my skis and my ankles."

"Yeah, your awareness is starting to pulsate..." I brought my hands in like they were holding a ball, then out and in again. "... between the whole of the ski and the parts of the body."

"Pulsate! Pulsate! Whoa!" He started wiggling his torso. "Pulsate! Are you allowed to use that word? I mean the Christian Right might have a warrant out for your arrest! Corrupting innocent skiers with words like *pulsate*. My awareness pulsating! Yeah, pulsating between frustration and ecstasy. Oh man, no one warned me about you," he shook his head, "...a Catholic dom—"

"But Brucey darling, you *did* manage to reach a bit of perfection there and it was icy, too! I don't want to risk the possibility of you screwing up again and having a tantrum so maybe we should airlift you out of here."

"Airlift me right to a cocktail!"

"And a toast!"
"To pulsation!"
"To exhaustion!"

Over the next week, the larger ski-oriented focus gradually became Bruce's default mode. After he reminded his ankle/foot to stay under him and roll, his attention naturally returned to the ski. And he needed to remind his foot fewer and fewer times. Slowly, instead of *pushing* his attention outward, he began to relax and *allow* it to shift to the ski.

Bruce's body felt the freedom. Turn after turn, he began to release his skis into the fall-line with his ankle firm and his body perpendicular to the pitch of the hill. He seemed suspended in the air for an infinitesimal but memorable moment. And his skis responded. The tips engaged. Then each ski sliced down and across the hard surface like a perfectly sharp carving knife, what a ski is born for. Bruce's face opened, "Ahh, ahh..." the involuntary sounds of the awe-stricken suddenly aware of their luck.

"I'm connected to the ski," he said. "It feels almost *instinctive*."

"With most people, that would be great," I said. "but with you, I'm worried."

"What do you mean?"

"Well, if it feels natural to *you*—" I started.

"It means it's sick," he chuckled. "Deeply flawed."

"Deeply," I said, nodding. "Obsessive. You' re beginning to fixate now on your ski. But at least that means your body is freed up."

He grinned. "You mean there is more to the world than my skis?"

CHAPTER 15

Body... Ski... Mountain

Rather than petrifying things as does the stare,
the glance graces what it looks at, enhancing and
expanding it...

— Edward Casey

Although Bruce was able to feel the connection between his body and the skis, it would take a long time for him to sense fully the skis' interaction with the mountain. For someone who learns to ski as an adult, it can often take years before the slope itself becomes the attention's natural resting place. Like an artist who offers her technique to the will of the painting, so we offer our technical skills to our relationship with the terrain. As the brush bends to the canvas or the skis bend to the slope, we become intermediaries. We feel part of something larger, something both cryptic and inventive.

This is the final stage of letting go of our personal focus. We no longer need it. Our resources have been activated. Now they must become subservient to the task at hand. It is time to give ourselves away.

...Throw yourself like seed as you walk, and into your own field...
Leave what's alive in the furrow, what's dead in yourself,
for life does not move in the same way as a group of clouds;
from your work you will be able one day to gather yourself.

—Miguel de Unamuno (tr. by Robert Bly)

This poem would be heresy to sport psychology, whose language is bloated with words that begin with *self*, self-confidence and self-esteem being the most ubiquitous. No matter how it is marketed, the message remains: inflate yourself into a huge, misshapen balloon. "Become the best *you* can be." I was told probably a hundred times to use positive self-talk, as if I had an intentional, determinative relationship with myself: "Ms. Blakeslee, you are fantastic," whether I believed it or not, whether it was true or not. Did I even *want* an external construction to control my inner reality? There is an insidious materialism in the counsel to "smile and you'll be happy." And how exactly would pumping myself up help when what I was attempting involved *surrender*?

Sports psychology does not acknowledge the surrender that is necessary to create something new. It envisions the athlete as a machine with conditioned responses. The mind, or worse, the heart—both troublesome nuisances—just gets in the way. But no problem: trick either with a few distraction techniques and bravo! the machine will function as designed.

Rather, let's imagine the athlete as an artist. Then our language can change. A novelist I know said the other day, "It took me about a month longer but it's what the story wanted." What a shift it would be to hear: "It's what the mountain wanted" rather than "I nailed that sucker!" Artists are accustomed to being engaged with their art almost to the point of self-obliteration. There is little interest in one's personal best. Rather, there is a consuming hunger to go beyond the merely personal and fall under the force of the painting or the garden or the poem: the mind, heart, and body all thrown into the vortex of the muse. One's personal *ability* becomes just another tool, useful, but not central and certainly nothing to obsess about. One of my mentors said to me while I was writing my first novel, "Hurl yourself onto the paper." Each day, we can throw ourselves into our jobs and whether we are good enough at what we have never done before is not for us to judge. A question we cannot afford the time or energy to ask.

Likewise, athletes immerse themselves in the experience of their sport, oblivious even to pain. That is why many of them do not relate to the puffy language of sport psychology. "You'd do better if you blew bubbles through my head," one said to me. I understood because just then the sun spilled onto the pitch with three feet of light powder and gravity tugged at us to respond with whatever we had. There was no room for the language of self-promotion:

> *Why question*
> *Just ride*
> *The horse don't come that often.*
>
> — Jim Bultman

When will we learn that this is not a horse that can be told *when* or *where* to come? We can only be ready for its arrival.

Different Emphases in Skiing

As a young ski racer at Burke Mountain Academy, I trained four hours a day running gates and doing drills. Talk was minimal. We watched, we tried, we repeated again and again. Feedback came only if we continued to fail. Years later, training to be an instructor, I found myself in a group that skied maybe ten turns, then stopped and talked about each and every movement from their fingers down to their little toes. I thought, *Wow! How'd they feel all that in such a short time?* I was impressed at their body awareness and the intelligent articulation of the skills that went into their skiing, but I was also disturbed. Although it took me a while to understand, my apprehension was this: *How am I going to maintain this relationship—this friendship—I've had with my skis for twenty years if I get obsessed with each body movement?* I was afraid to begin their minute dissection for fear I might sacrifice my connection to the ski.

That can happen. A ski teacher has a very different job than a racer. Teachers not only need to know how to explain the fundamental movements for their students, they also serve as images to imitate. When demonstrating at a much lower skill level than their own, instructors cannot rely on sensations coming from their skis. Their first priority is to develop the body awareness that will make sure they are, say, initiating a wedge turn without a sloppy shoulder rotation or a left elbow poking up sideways. Many are not trained to be sensitive to the ski, so they do not understand what each movement actually *does*. If their catalogue of movements remains ungrounded by experience of the skis' response, they will be at the mercy of the latest buzz from the latest training clinic. That is why the ski teaching world itself suffers from Bruce's obsessive compulsive disorder, collectively fixating on the current movement in fashion.

A racer, on the other hand, just needs to get her skis to go as fast as she can down a twisting, turny course. All her skills become subservient to that end. Form follows function. She has learned to feel exactly what her skis are doing through each turn: sliding sideways, moving forward, a combination of skidding and carving. Is the pressure too heavy? Too light? But ask that racer to describe the body movements that go into making the skis work and her answer will usually be simplistic. Ask her how to develop in a less coordinated, weekend skier the skills he needs to ski in control and… well, that is certainly not *her* job.

I've heard many condescending race coaches joke about ski instructors who they say suffer from "paralysis from analysis." But some of those same coaches are at a loss when trying to help young racers develop fundamentals. A kid would come flailing through the gates only to hear a useless, even detrimental truism like, "Don't rotate," or "Don't get back." The racer would ski away, determined on his next run to follow his coach's advice. I often fantasized that one of them would spit back, "No shit, Sherlock! You think I'm *trying* to rotate! Tell me how not to, damnit!" But most kids are too polite to their gurus.

So it seemed simple. We need both: ski awareness most of

the time, body awareness to correct ourselves when necessary. I spent years thinking the equation was complete, and that the perfect teacher or coach had a healthy dose of both. Race coaches (usually ex-racers) needed more training in isolating fundamental movements so they could *develop* skills in their young skiers. Instructors needed to pay attention to the ski to bring some life back into their own skiing. The coaches did have a point: constant analysis could make instructors numb to the ski, the very reason they were on the hill in the first place.

Then I went to Austria and met another breed of skier entirely: off-piste skiers, many of whom were mountain guides. What was always in the foreground of their awareness was the snow and the mountain. Their body movements and their affinity with the skis had been formed by the terrain with all its variable conditions.

This was the "whole focus" I had witnessed in children who tell themselves merely: go *there!* rather than the endless minutia of how to accomplish the task. But these were grown men. The *there* of their awareness was textured by years of experience, observation, and discipline.

In Austria, my understanding of skiing and teaching was stretched. I understood that the move through the moment involved transcending our technical skills. But I hadn't gone far enough. Not only our disciplined body movements, but *also our feel for the skis* was part of our total offering, subsumed by our relationship with the terrain.

I realized then that while it was easy for me (due to my training) to give up a body focus for the larger whole of the skis, I had difficulty giving the skis over to a predominant connection to the mountain. Whenever I was intimidated (in places where sensitivity to the snow and terrain was not only useful but often essential), I could feel my awareness shrink back. Just like Bruce micromanaging his ankles, I tried to micromanage my skis. Letting go of such a learned comfort took a while, but it took even longer to understand the process thoroughly enough to teach others.

Of course, there is no end to this. It is a process we constantly revisit and reinvent. Every time I am about to descend what one my friends calls a "toe-tingler," I think, *Here it is again. How uncomfortable I feel—but how alive.*

We fear that if we follow that feeling of the ski to where it meets the snow and mountain, we will leave behind all the various *hows,* all our skills, those fundamentals we have so dutifully acquired. We worry, like Bruce, that our ankles might forget, our skis might not even turn! A ski teacher wrote me:

> *It was hard skiing, crusty, wind-packed snow. My first run down [the trail], my legs were so stiff. I had to go back there and try it again. My legs still stiffened for about half the run and I thought, This is no use. I wanted to get the hell out of there. But then I zoned into my ankles like you showed us and I felt for a second the skis cutting through the snow and I said to myself, "Come on, come on." The snow was so heavy and stiff, normally I would've been freaked. But I just kept asking, not in words, I just stayed open to what was in front of me. It was as if I kept my attention nearby the ski, my feelers out in a sort of exploratory mode. It was not easy! It took every bit of concentration I had not to pull back and try to hold a position. It sounds crazy but I ended up skiing both really loose and super precise. I knew my legs were moving to the terrain but I never told them to or even worried about it. Now, coming from me, Ms. Anal, is that a miracle or what?*

Yes! A precisely monitored miracle we used the following method to cultivate.

Soft Eyes, Soft Attitude

The first time I went mountain biking, I noticed that as soon as my attention locked on the front tire, or the next rock, my legs would stiffen. I couldn't keep pedaling and the bike would not have enough forward momentum to keep it balanced over all the obstacles. Still, I couldn't let go of my fixed vision. I did not trust the bike's almost mystical ability to handle this terrain. I rode like I was on my old Schwinn three-speed. I gripped the handlebars harder and tried to muscle my way through. That familiar friend again—the grit-your-teeth-bite-the-bullet approach. It didn't work. I stiffened more. My (experienced) partner told me to look ahead, but of course I thought I was. Then I remembered a technique I learned while riding a horse.

In Sally Swift's book, *Centered Riding*, she discriminates between "hard eyes" focused intently on an object and "soft eyes." She writes:

> *With open eyes... encompass everything that comes into your field of vision... taking in the largest possible expanse... The more area you encompass with your eyes, the more you'll be aware of your seat. Glazing or making your eyes fuzzy is not your objective; that would most likely reduce what you feel with your seat... Soft eyes are much more than just a way of looking... it is like a new philosophy. It is a method of becoming distinctly aware of what is going on around you, beneath you, inside of you... You are aware of the whole, not just separate parts.*

I gradually softened my locked gaze on the tire as I faced the log in front of me. As soon as my vision broadened, my legs loosened and I could sense the bike negotiating the log *as if on its own*. I was finally allowing my body to respond without constant meddling. I said to my partner, "Oh, I got it! You don't mean 'look ahead.' You mean 'don't look anywhere *but* ahead.'"

What Sally Swift suggests her riding students do with their eyes, we can do with our attention. The body can respond quickly and accurately to variations in the terrain if we do not consciously attempt to register each and every sensation. We must let the body feel on its own. The experience is inherently paradoxical.

We can see more if we don't try so hard to see. Similarly, we can feel more if we don't try so hard to feel. By trying to feel, we narrow the attention down to a plodding perception of one kinesthetic "object" after another. That sequentiality is too slow and robotic for the ephemeral, spatial relationship between the body and the mountain. We need to soften our attention just as we soften the eyes, slowly expanding our circle of awareness around our original focus. We take in more and more until we ourselves are taken.

Often, the sheer difficulty of the situation can force us to transfer control from the conscious mind to the body. The terrain or the conditions demand that we give. We struggle and struggle, then suddenly we forget and a moment of inspiration comes. Ms. Anal needed the specific challenge of wind-packed conditions to force her to push her awareness out. Appropriately prepared, she happened upon the perfect level of difficulty necessary for her to break through her controlling mindset. If the difficulty is too great or we are not prepared or appropriately guided, we end up just frustrated, or worse, in danger.

Reliving one of those subliminal (and sublime) moments in skiing, I can remember the precise texture of the snow, each suggestion of the steep slope. At the time, however, I did not attempt to feel what was beneath me. My attention was not fixed on any particular. Rather, it was taken by the entirety of the experience. I floated in a sea of snow. There was cold, there was sun, there was the rhythm of each turn: dropping, then being held, dropping again, a perfectly inspired roller coaster that moved in a sweeping, godlike rhythm. Although these sensations were highly differentiated, they did not stand apart. No *one* claimed my focus. Together, they created the color and texture of a woven whole.

> *O body swayed to music, O brightening glance,*
> *How can we know the dancer from the dance?*
> — W.B. Yeats

Feeling Beneath, Seeing Ahead

A softened attention becomes very fluid, flowing back and forth from what we feel beneath us to what we see ahead of us. We can discern the different quality of each experience without one disrupting the other. Our response to what is happening now under our feet does not disturb our vision of what we are moving toward and likewise, what we see ahead does not snap us back into the sequential registering of each feeling.

These two experiences, seeing ahead and feeling beneath, call forth a different response from the body. Skiing is both the magnanimous motion of sliding forward into the immediate future, and the miniscule adjustments to the present beneath our feet. We release the skis' grip on the mountain and send our bodies forward into what feels like the open space of the future. But we also flex and extend to what lies beneath us right now. We learn these as separate movements, but they can begin to seem barely distinguishable, like the interwoven strands of a perfectly spliced rope.

My son, Hansen, was a small ten-year old when fifty-four inches of snow fell at Windham. We were skiing the woods just west of the Wedel where we faced all sorts of drifts and wind-blown pockets. At first, his little skis were tossed about. I saw him struggle as he tried to manage them. I said, "Don't care about your skis. Just go where you want to go." He stared at me for a moment and then said, "Oh" and took right off. We could barely catch him the rest of the day even through bouncy, tracked-up snow until he landed in a drift twice his size and we had to dig him out. Later, I heard him say to another kid, "You can't care when you ski real snow. It's like learning to ride a bike."

He was right. Hansen had been trying to find his balance on a steady ski on firm ground. By attending *only* to where he wanted to go, to what was just ahead, he had learned to balance on the momentum of his center travelling forward. His legs immediately relaxed. They were free to respond to the wildly erratic undulations and densities of the snow. His attention softened and he could feel without trying to feel.

Although it isn't always so easy for us adults, the idea of "just going where we want to go" can still work, and not only for advanced skiers but also for beginners. In skiing, epiphanies happen at every level.

Jill, a reserved, intelligent woman, had signed up for the fear workshop early in the fall. She had tried skiing only once years before and wanted to try again. In late October, Jill's sister, dying from an aggressive form of cancer, came to live with her. She died two weeks before the workshop, but Jill didn't cancel. It would be her first time out "since." I was both surprised and daunted. I wanted to tell her, "Go home. Take time to mourn. Don't bother trying to learn to ski now. You have something much more important to do." But this woman stood in front of me and said, "I don't know why I didn't cancel, I just didn't." I couldn't say a word. Instead, I nodded.

The conditions were awful, especially for a beginner. The base resembled not so much the icy hard-pack you find in your driveway as the ice on a pond. And a series of thaws and freezes turned the snow on top into dense piles of a sand-and-gravel-like substance. So a skier starting with minimal friction underfoot would pick up speed only to be rudely stopped and thrown by this unnamable stuff you could have built a road with. In fact, it would have been easier to ski on a construction site.

In the workshop, there is usually a blessing hidden in such horrible conditions. Groups bond. People no longer feel like vacationers but fellow soldiers; they tell each other secrets, get very silly, laugh hysterically at nothing as if drunk from the ridiculousness of their situation. But there were no other beginners in that particular workshop and Jill and I were alone without the buoyancy and humor of a group. The two of us rode the beginner lift through the damp grayness, gray sky, gray earth. The gray seemed to cover every part of us, seeping beneath our clothes and behind our weak smiles, seeping even into our words.

Security in Motion

It was important for Jill, especially on her first day out, to be able to ski very slowly. She could wedge and turn on the flat but she didn't like any form of speed: not in a car, not on a bike, not even as a viewer in a movie. Yet a little momentum would help her navigate the conditions we faced. Picture trying to drive up a hill through a gritty pile of frozen slush the plow just left. The gas pedal is essential. I needed to get Jill to use the concept of momentum while still travelling slowly.

Jill didn't like being up "this high" on the mountain and began in a tentative wedge. I spun around to ski backwards in front of her so she could see my face and we could talk. At any time, she could ski into me and grab hold of my arms. (Neither of us had poles. Poles often cause beginners to tighten their shoulders as they try to control the skis with their hands.) In front of her, I was her buffer, her safety but I was moving down the hill. Unconsciously, she was learning that she could find safety only by continually moving forward. I was pulling her down using the same kind of psychological vacuum I used with Lorraine, the woman who after a knee injury hadn't "felt adrenaline in six years."

Jill would grab hold of my arms and while still moving, I would massage her shoulders, arms and hands, gradually loosening her hold until she was barely touching me. Then, as casually as I could, I would free myself. I often use touch while teaching, especially in fearful situations, but over layers and layers of clothing, it is not intrusive. This was important for Jill. Sensing her grief in the lodge, I had wanted to hug her but felt instinctively that she would take it as an imposition that was also presumptuous: I did not know her, I did not know her sister, I did not know her very particular grief. She seemed extremely reserved, a classy, well kempt woman, one who would rarely speak too loudly or say the wrong thing. Now with our skis two *V*s one inside the other, we moved down the hill like a couple in a bizarre Halloween costume. I continued to work with Jill's taut muscles, but I was also massaging the edges of her comfort zone, the contracted sphere where she felt safe, pushing and letting off, pulling and letting off, stretching her toward increasing independence.

Slowly, I created more distance between us, careful not to break the psychological suction that kept her moving down the hill. Finally, I was able to spin around and ski with my back to her for a few turns.

I had used this same strategy with other beginners. But for Jill, who was so raw, the metaphor of skiing was becoming more and more transparent. We were approaching a little knoll she couldn't see beyond so I spun again to face her, to look her in the eyes and reassure her to keep coming toward me, toward my eyes, but I saw her face start to contort so I pulled up and she grabbed hold of me.

"The slightest little bobble, I pull back," she spit out in a half-whisper, half-cry. "I can't, I can't…" I just kept nodding and holding. She started squeezing my arm. "I *have* to keep moving forward." I kept nodding as if my nodding were holding her up. "Slightest little thing…. throws me. I want to clutch…grab hold of something… the ground…but I can't… slightest little thing, I pull back, I get so thrown."

I knew she was not talking about skiing, but skiing was there for us now—offering us a transparent, but essential buffer. I said, "The only balance you can have now is in moving forward. There is nothing solid under foot. No security there. Don't even try. What you want to grab onto beneath you, the ground, that's the present just past. If you try to find balance there, you'll easily get thrown. You have to keep moving forward to what is just ahead. Anything that happens, the slightest little bobble, throw yourself forward. Toward the future, the immediate future."

She kept swallowing and nodding, squeezing, nodding, swallowing. "I rode a bike once," she said. Her eyes were green, full and glistening. My eyes were full, too, and careful.

"The immediate future?" She smiled.

I nodded.

"That would be... now. The now just ahead of me."

"Just ahead," I said.

"Just ahead," she repeated. "Help me start. Then I can do it. I really can."

"You already have," I said as we started to move again. "You're doing it. You're moving. Just like that. Forward and forward—"

"And forward." It seemed more a mantra than a cue word.

"... and forward."

Each time she hit a pile and was about to bobble, she did not clutch me, she did not even clutch the air, she extended her hands and her body into the vacancy in front of her like it was a gift. Her face was soft; her shoulders, arms and legs no longer rigid but responsive. She wedged here and there freely, over and through the piles of crud. She understood. She was feeling something that took me thirty years of skiing to get: keep your center moving so you can balance on your momentum. It feels as if the ground could dissolve under your feet, and you would still be skiing.

When we got to the bottom, she said, "Now I know why I didn't cancel." Then she gave me a hug. "I got it," she said and then pulled her head back so she could look me in the eyes. We were both crying. "The only security is in motion."

"You really did get it," I said, amazed at the idea she had just expressed.

"Not *too* far ahead though," she added. "It's the now just ahead. Immediately ahead."

"You were *really* skiing," I said, swallowing and nodding.

"I was. I was *really* skiing."

CHAPTER 16

Sensation Hunts

We must be highly receptive to what we encounter,
approach it without assumptions or judgements,
letting the reality reveal itself to us.

— Robert Sardello

My older sister, Kathleen, blindfolded me when I was young and took me on a walk. She wanted to introduce me, she said, to my other senses. I remember touching the ragged, intricate bark of the white pine outside our kitchen and being so intoxicated by its smell, I didn't want to leave. I felt the consistency change under my feet when I stepped from the lawn into the spongy soil of the garden. I fell to my knees the way kids do, quick and carefree, and the dirt seemed to take some care to catch me, as if each knee were held in the cupped palm of a hand. Toward the end, rain began to fall softly, and I didn't shy away from it, I stuck my face out to feel its drops. Later, lying in bed that night, I had the thought that I'd met the pine that day and the soil and the rain, too, and that it was like meeting new friends, friends I knew would always be there. And I still remember how my little body squirmed with so much joy I could not fall asleep.

I take my students, beginners and experts alike, on what I call sensation hunts, and although their eyes are open, I ask them to keep their "feelers" out. These hunts give everyone the chance to leave behind any obsession with personal performance and enjoy the various shades and suggestions of the mountain.

Reacting to the Past, Anticipating the Future

As both Jill and my son experienced, when we release ourselves to the immediate future, we can adjust quickly and accurately to the present. But the converse can sometimes be just as relevant. If we do not make the miniscule adjustments to the present, the body, as a unified entirety, does not move forward. Our legs stiffen, and we are thrown back. Some part of us retreats from what lies ahead. Franz Krickl, the director of the Snowsports school at Windham, imagined as a child a big bowl of water in his belly, and as he skied down the hill, his legs did whatever they had to do to keep the water from spilling out. Our legs must relax *when relaxation is needed* in order to keep our bodies moving forward over our skis and into the welcoming space ahead.

Skiing, of course, takes strength to resist the pull of gravity and the forces of a turn. And because skiing is part of a machismo world, muscle power is talked and written about endlessly. But skiing demands an equal but more tricky aspect of muscle use: the ability to give and soften. We often overlook this. The dictum "keep moving forward" will have no effect if a skier stiffens either in reaction or anticipation.

If we allow our attention to move *too far* into the future, we can stiffen in fearful expectation. The result is that we do not even experience the particular patch of ice or gnarly bump or gloppy crud that frightened us. Our bodies have already shut down and become rigid. Likewise, if we allow our attention to slip into the *oh shit!* mentality of the past, our bodies retreat. By worrying about how bad that last turn was, we ruin the next, and the next. In both cases, either reacting against the past or fearfully antici-pating the future, we lose our chance: the moment at hand can-not imprint itself upon us.

I had just turned fifteen when I skied my first downhill race at

Sugarloaf, Maine. Each training run, I became scared at the same place: after three long turns, the course turned over a headwall and onto some bumps below. What I saw in front of me from the top of the headwall was the woods. Trees. Big, solid trees. I would begin to stiffen coming out of the last turn in anticipation of the headwall. The coaches actually laughed each run as I flew off it, my inexperienced legs so rigid I bounced against the bumps like an egg on its way to becoming an omelet. I got worse each time. I was not picking this up naturally like some of the other girls. But luckily, I was in love. With a downhiller who had a penchant for esoteric thinking. He told me what he did whenever he got scared. As the ski traveled cleanly forward, he felt *through* the ski to the snow below it.

Fear intensified the power of my concentration. I can still feel that snow like I just touched it, as if I were touching it now with my fingertips. And I heard the sound of my ski running, too, like a large being breathing. I felt I was gliding in slow motion. My legs softened, stretched and flexed to match the undulating bumps. With a smooth, elastic contact I did not normally have with the terrain, I carried my speed onto the flats beneath my coaches' incredulous faces.

If I had been told to "just move forward" or "not care about my skis and go where I wanted to go," those statements obviously would not have helped. The convolutions of real life consistently resist a pat formula. Not only did my case involve a speed event demanding great precision, I was also prey to a particular brand of anticipatory worry compounded by my increasing number of past failures. Focusing on the present was necessary to pull my awareness back from the too-far future. By fully experiencing the snow beneath my feet, I softened and responded to the present. I was then *able* to "keep moving forward." I had localized my attention *only* to that moment where the present meets the very imminent future, the now just ahead.

By experiencing skiing as a sensation hunt, skiers can also

begin to attend to that moment immediately at hand. Remember what Ms. Anal, the ski teacher who skied the wind-pack wrote? "I just kept asking, not in words, I just stayed open to what was in front of me…my feelers out in a sort of exploratory mode. It was not easy! It took every bit of concentration I had not to pull back and try to hold a position." This is a moment full of paradoxes. We concentrate hard to let go. We soften our attention, which then spreads into a non-particular awareness of an extremely localized moment. In short, our attention broadens spatially, but localizes temporally. We no longer pull back into what has already happened or jump too far ahead in frightened anticipation. This is not only a precisely monitored miracle, but a hard-earned one as well.

> *Miracle doesn't lie only in the amazing*
> *living through and defeat of danger;*
> *miracles become miracles in the clear*
> *achievement that is earned…*
>
> *…Take your well-disciplined strengths*
> *and stretch them between two*
> *opposing poles. Because inside human beings*
> *is where God learns.*
>
> — Rainer Maria Rilke (tr. by Robert Bly)

Different Levels of Skill

Novice skiers on a sensation hunt explore changes in terrain and snow by following tracks children make. Children, especially when roaming in bands, still have the uncanny knack of making the most boringly groomed, clear-cut slope into a thing of interest. They dip behind snow-making barrels to fly off the lip of the trail. They disappear into neighboring woods wherever an opening invites, then shoot out from under a fat, snowy tree. These resourceful jostlings form the small, harmless illegalities that make up our Eastern off-piste. Usually quite safe, these routes are rarely difficult for even new skiers, some being made by kids barely five years old. As I take my new students through these paths at a slower pace, they begin to understand instinctively that different snows and terrain demand constant adaptations; no single position is possible. I am trying, right from the start, to skew their taste away from the bland homogeneity of the monoculture created by grooming.

Experts can probe for more subtle diversity by refining their kinesthetic sense. One of the best ways for normal-sighted skiers to do this is to ski blind, using, of course, a partner for direction. (Close the eyes for a moment or pull a hat down that can be easily raised.) Blindness, at first, presents so much sensation to process that it can make us dizzy or nauseous. Another world—a universe!— bombards us. We realize that our vision is a very greedy sense, overriding internal feelings of moving through space as well as the constantly changing intricacies happening beneath our feet. Without visual reference, we greatly misinterpret speed in a rudimentary effort to process what we feel. We think we're moving when we've stopped or that we've stopped when we're moving. Vertigo causes us to wobble backwards. We grab for our partner. This is certainly not an adventure for everyone. But the experience of blindness can deepen even an expert's understanding of snow and terrain. In the darkness, we feel them from within, overwhelmingly close, immediate, undiluted by other stimuli. When the apparent border between us and the world is erased, we no longer live on top, outside, at the comfortable distance we have grown accustomed to. We are caught inside the world's touch.

By refining senses other than sight, we discern the distinct and sometimes dissonant sounds and textures of snow—its graininess, its density, its liveliness. When testing skis, the card used to record reactions always leaves a space to report the conditions. Working for K2 a few years ago, Scott Schmidt, the great and original extreme skier, described the snow simply but precisely as "old." Age is indeed significant in the hundreds of permutations of snow: compacted, month-old snow; snow that fell in the last five hours in a still, shady glade; sun-baked snow; sun-baked then refrozen snow that is losing its life. Only real snow feels alive. It has body, or as experienced skiers say, "it gives something back." That phrase always delights me. It's reassuring to know that we cannot truly "make" snow. Because real snow is alive, it can also rot and become like quick sand, dangerous and unpredictable. But even the inert, unresponsive machine-made snow is not all the same. There is the light and airy (almost real) stuff shot out on a zero-degree night. But there is also the base snow made in late fall at marginally warm temperatures that feels frighteningly close to frozen water, and occasionally, there is "porcelain" or other strange mixes that conjure visions of Dr. Seuss's oobleck.

Then, of course, there are bumps of every shape and size, and crud checking in at every weight. There is ice of all degrees of slipperiness, from "grippable" to "waterfall," which needs no translation. There are "death cookies," a name marketing departments across the country have tried to euphemize but to no avail. You might as well be skiing over ice cubes made for giants. There is avalanche debris to watch out for as well as breakable crust and "karton" and then, suddenly, there will be a surprise—snow of the most feathery softness imaginable. There is any and every variation on a mountain from delicious to lovely to vaguely discomfiting to yucky to downright dangerous. The dangerous is absolutely necessary and keeps us human—in our place: animal, mortal, and careful.

It is not, however, experts or novices that benefit most from sensation hunts but skiers stuck on an intermediate plateau. They often find the hunts difficult at first. Accustomed to groomed terrain, many have become tame and anesthetized, obsessed with maintaining a static, picture-perfect position. They feel, if not entitled to safety, at least *insured*.

When faced with new (and therefore uncomfortable) sensations, I ask them to reserve judgement, as if they were eating a meal in a remote country. They wrack their brains searching for non-judgmental descriptions. This is the beginning of a skier's sensibility: the delay of judgement in favor of perception which, with time and practice, can become highly differentiated.

We are all captive to our quick and dismissive opinions, but fortunately, we can be wrenched free in the sneakiest ways. One bright, spring morning, I took a five-year-old boy down an intermediate slope that had been groomed into the spongy consistency one expects after a thaw and freeze. By the woods, however, a snow cat had left a trail of deep, frozen tracks. I started down the soft, packed snow expecting my little student to ski behind me. Instead, he followed the frozen cat tracks that shook and tossed his body every which way, bouncing his skis on and off the snow like he was riding a mechanical bull. I looked back and yelled, "Over here, honey! You can ski over here, behind me, where it's smooth!" To which he replied, his voice vibrating, "NO! I LOVE THIS!" There I was, caught! My prejudice exposed: the sensations were much too messy *over there* while this was a smooth ride, a good and righteous ride. I had fallen prey to the great sucking power of the mono-culture which was as interesting to this little boy as white Wonder Bread is to me.

Eventually, even for groomed-slope diehards, judgments soften. Even concerns about position—whether the arms are well placed or the skis are parallel—begin to fall away. Something else is awakened, a sensibility that has been asleep for years.

Knowing nothing shuts the iron gates; the new love opens them.
The sound of the gates opening wakes the beautiful woman
asleep.
Kabir says: Fantastic! Don't let a chance like this go by!
— Kabir (tr. by Robert Bly)

Susceptible to the Elements

When I arrived in Alyeska, Alaska, it was clear. I could see the mountains rise deep green and white out of the sea, their shoulders rolling with proportion and flair into well-defined lines that curved and peaked against the sky. Clouds here and there both hid and revealed, pulling and pushing my eyes. It was so grand, so intimate that I hurried into my friend's basement apartment, closed the curtains and took a nap. Such excruciating beauty! I needed to let it in slowly or I might splinter into a thousand pieces. After sleep, I would try again.

Those of us who are easily overwhelmed by our environment have what I call a long embryo time. We rise into our new world slowly. If we rush, we feel weak and small. Those with thicker skins and a shorter gestation period do better. They adjust easily. They go forth and quickly conquer. Usually, in the world of sport, it is our lot to envy them. But at times, they should envy us. When we finally do emerge, fully formed, but still susceptible to the grand imprint of the world, it is a surrender that, like love, carries just a hint of pain.

This is the purpose of sensation hunts. To allow the elements in the world of skiing to make their mark upon us. Rather than resisting the peculiar nature of each element, we mesh our intentions with its strengths. We participate, even play with each, but on its own terms. And now I think it's time for a bit of play, a brief interlude…

play…

GRAVITY, The Great Door.
> Double-headed Janus who welcomes as he says goodbye.
>> Inspires both fear and thrill. Loves to hold down and send flying. Predictable but charismatic.
>
> Most compatible with split personalities, the very old, and children.
>
> Incompatible with no one.

ICE, Arbiter of Compromise.
> Master of Indirectness. In cahoots with gravity and all things frictionless. Lover of speed and noise. Trickster. Great sense of humor.
> Compatible with politicians, card sharks, and rock musicians. Incompatible with administrators, aromatherapists, and accountants.

FLAT LIGHT, Mate.
> Grounds spiritual love. Demands communication. Apparent sameness hides both pitfalls and magical moments. Introverted tendencies.
> Compatible with forest rangers, plumbers, and philanthropists.
> Incompatible with playboys and -girls, star wanna-bes, and groupies.

CRUD, The Maestro.
> Adds gravitas to every conversation. Tames the young and premature. Lover of finesse and sensitivity. Known to be intense.
> Compatible with chefs, oceanographers, and blues musicians.
> Incompatible with positive thinkers, mechanical engineers, and sportscasters.

BUMPS, Clown.
> Party animal. Understands there is always another way to do… *whatever.* Lover of the young and marginalized. Street smart. Quick wit.
> Compatible with Elvis impersonators, pot heads, and race car drivers.
> Incompatible with corporate lawyers, fundamentalists, and consultants.

GLADES, Domestic Homebody.
"Small is beautiful" activist. Lover of beauty and a sense
   of place. Makes even the most scattered learn to focus.
   Unwilling to compromise.
Compatible with artists, troubleshooters, and brain surgeons.
Incompatible with claustrophobics, UN negotiators, and
   CEOs.

WINDPACK, Strict Disciplinarian.
Destroyer of Innocence. Smashes illusions.
Makes adults out of children. Loves paradox. Can easily
   deceive.
Compatible with polytheists, short-order cooks, and the
   police.
Incompatible with therapists, advertising agents, and hair
   stylists.

CORNICE, Sculptor.
Wizard of sudden, unforeseen changes. Playmates with wind.
   Loves sleight of hand. Emotional. Can have a temper tan-
   trum without warning.
Compatible with stock brokers, actors, and meteorologists.
Incompatible with behaviorists, fortune tellers, and middle
   managers.

FOG, Shaman.
Poet. Shapeshifter. Transforms the ordinary into the mystical.
Lover of solitude and revelation. Deep and mysterious. Not
   for the inexperienced.
Compatible with the blind, recluses, and gardeners.
Incompatible with bank presidents, political pundits, and
   programmers.

POWDER, Geisha.

Musician. Weaver of epicurean fantasy. Lover of atmosphere and sensuality. Intolerant of Puritans. Adolescent tendencies. Hates to be misunderstood.

Compatible with massage therapists, wine tasters, and florists.

Incompatible with workaholics, personal trainers, and toxicologists.

CHAPTER 17

The Group: Moving Through the Moment Together

Be kind, for everyone you meet is fighting a hard battle.

— Philo

Last April, I worked with an advanced group at Snowbird that was frightened of deep snow and narrow steeps. For a couple of hours, everyone had been preparing to attempt their Yikes! zone, a difficult chute near the top of the mountain. It was ten-thirty in the morning and they felt ready. As we headed down toward the narrow slice that folded and dropped steeply into the bowl below, the sun was nowhere to be seen. The light grew increasingly flat. The undifferentiated white of the snow matched the equally indistinct sky, making us queasy with partial blindness. All we could see was where we could not go. Two bands of rock lining either side of the chute jutted out, black and sharp, from the bland mass of sky-ground.

This would have been a sensitive time for any group. Under pressure of the impending moment, people can lose conventional politeness and social grace, acting like they are with siblings. A few go off to be alone and let no one, *I mean no one,* talk to them. Others chat away and cannot, will not, shut up. Some cry and want to retreat. Others get antsy and want to rush. Some stall. Some make dumb jokes. Others want to hit them.

This was a particularly motley collection of skiers. Not only were they spread out all over the slope above the chute, they would have been spread apart on *any* map, whether it graphed technical skills, levels of fear, or general temperaments. I brought them into a huddle under the ruse of "discussing the plan" but actually I was trying to protect some of the weaker, more fearful skiers who I sensed were feeling psychologically stranded. There had been some friendly pairings over the last few runs, but now we needed to gather in close proximity so each skier could tap into the others' support.

Just when the group seemed primed, one of my more insensitive colleagues pulled up nearby and joked, "So you guys the fraidycats?" then took off skiing fast and carefree out of sight. It was as if a hypodermic needle had pierced the invisible membrane that contained the group's energy. We had to start over. I wanted to kill him.

That membrane not only contains but also animates the group's energy by reflecting it back on itself. The resulting magnification is the double-edged sword that can either strengthen everyone in the group, or isolate and threaten particular individuals.

My own Achilles' heel is skiing with *Rowdy. Male. Peers.* Change any one of those words and I'd relax and wax expansive. But lump all three together and I begin to rush, stiffen, and grow defensive. I withdraw into myself, ski worse and worse, and finally cry. I used to avoid those groups so I wouldn't be "caught," but I couldn't when I was part of a team made mostly of vibrant, athletic men. Although I had been teaching group dynamics for years, it was by examining my own failures within the team that I began to understand the elements that encourage or inhibit individuals within a group.

Valuing Negativity

One of the first things that happens when we feel at odds with a group is that, as with other fears, we turn inward and begin to contract. We trap ourselves in self-absorbed inwardness. Other's positive energy often exacerbates this contraction, by excluding those of us who are not feeling so jolly.

You can witness this on a powder day, especially when the snow is deep but not easy—heavy, and perhaps tracked up. People are excited because *there is snow!* Or, some people are excited, others feel that they are supposed to be, but they are actually struggling and full of fear. The leader (looking just wonderful) skis down to a group of, let's say, nine, pulls up and exclaims with a huge grin, "Wow! That's fantastic! What a great day!!" Five people dance in agreement. The other four back up a step, look down, and sink into a guilty slump. But the happy five don't notice because they have already taken off, hooting and hollering, caught either in the day's euphoria or its pretense.

The blinding light of positivity has a well-defined shadow: *it is negative toward negativity itself.* Only by valuing negativity, giving it a place, can we gain value from it.

If that same leader had skied down and (looking just as wonderful) exclaimed, "That's not easy! It'll take me some time to get used to my skis bouncing around." If he had milked, even flaunted the least bit of difficulty or apprehension he might have had, all nine would have drawn closer, each one thinking, *Maybe I didn't do so badly after all... Maybe I'm not the only one nervous...* He would have included and absorbed the inevitable negativity, an especially important act when that negativity involves fear.

Simply by making room for another's discomfort, we reverse the tendency to withdraw. As each person expands, she allows for exchange, becoming, in a sense, permeable. Feelings flow freely, in and out and between ourselves and others. They are no longer just our own feelings, imprisoned behind impermeable walls.

Negativity carries the added burden of shame. We do not brag that we are flailing in the low-lying swamp of fear, sadness, loss, jealousy, guilt, not-belonging... Our culture loves the hard, reflective light of happiness. Happy is normal. Death is not, sickness is not, injury is not, sadness and fear are not. If we are acquainted with any of these, we instantly feel marginalized. We begin to contract. And the cultural bias toward positivity actually steepens the descent as we slide into a state of self-absorption.

I once saw a story on the evening news about a woman who was paralyzed from the neck down. Even so, she still felt a great deal of pain. The reporter called her condition a "cruel twist of fate, " to which she replied, "No. I'd rather feel pain than nothing."

Although it seems obvious that we would not exchange our fate with *Star Trek's* Data, our culture seems to favor numbness over pain. The legal, prescribed, day-time drugs might be, in the long run, the most insidious. If we drug ourselves to maintain a functional evenness, what heights and depths are we losing? What stories? What moments that could flash before us when we wake at night for a time of reckoning? When do we, coveting "normalcy," begin to resemble well-preserved mannequins posing on a flat plain of existence?

Is it possible to value the intensity we find in negativity (and in our lives) rather than judging whether such messiness is acceptable? Can we hold negativity before us, investigate it with care and without castigation? Could we perhaps crack it open for its peculiar gift? By excluding negativity, we lose the chance to mine the rich, intricate layers of our lives. We shut out the most fertile conversations.

I skied at Jackson Hole with a group of ski teachers who were learning to enjoy deep, heavy snow. Katie was a graceful skier who did not waste one movement, the type of student who needed no remedial fix, only a gradual, steady increase in difficulty to stretch her skills. She negotiated the heavy snow so well that I was thinking of raising the task specifically for her so she would receive enough challenge within the group. Then we reached a band of breakable crust half-way down the Hobacks. She had "done in her knee" on precisely this kind of snow. As soon as she felt it, she turned up the slope and stopped. She tried to go again but couldn't; her legs shook. She began to cry and breathe rapidly, shoulders rising and tensing with each breath. I pulled up beside her and began to breathe along with her, making a lot of sound on the exhalations which included and eventually absorbed her crying. Finally, she was ready to continue through the crust. When she reached the group, Katie felt ashamed. She could not look anyone in the eye. We went up the chair together and after she finished crying, she started swearing at herself, full of both self-castigation and shame.

It was the group that helped Katie accept her tendency "to suddenly just goddamn freeze." They were able to see it as a valuable enigma in her life, a part of what made Katie an interesting, unpredictable presence. "What would we talk about," one woman joked, "if we weren't all so neurotic? There's nothing more boring than a bunch of *healthy* people."

"Can you imagine a party like that? Everyone healthy?" someone asked, turning her mouth down into a *yuck!* expression.

Another extended her hand and smiled like a talk-show host. "Hi! I'm surrounded by nothing but the most communicative, open, honest relationships, how about you?" to which someone else answered in a sappy, lifeless tone, "Oh yes, especially my *family.* We love to nourish each other and support and guide..." her smile turned to a toothy grimace, "guide... and advise... and instruct and manage and berate and kill!"

I continue to be surprised by laughter let loose after a dark emotion is acknowledged, as if when the fortress of acceptability comes tumbling down, not only the lucky humans but the emotions themselves feel the freedom.

If we keep the walls up, either inside ourselves or between members of the group, we cannot engage. We cannot contribute. We can't even say what we need. I was never able to say to my demo teammates who were also my friends, "I love you guys, but for some screwy, inexplicable reason, I don't do well skiing in a group like this."

In this silence, we may feel our presence is benign, as if we are invisible, but actually, we have become a black hole, sucking energy and giving none back. Every group necessarily attempts to neutralize those holes by ignoring them. A mutually imposed exile with a common but paradoxical twist. We feel rejected by the group we were the first to reject, which compounds our fear of reaching out.

One woman came up to me after a lecture and described a bump lesson she took at Steamboat. She had felt agitated about "being thrown in over her head" and was relieved when her instructor asked the group, "Do you want to try concentration?" Believing this man had magically intuited her fear, she was the first to shout, "Yes!" not knowing he meant the double black diamond named Concentration. About a quarter of the way down, she froze completely and could not move.

"And when I freeze," she said, "I get very very stubborn. I don't take advice from *anyone*. You know the mood, don't you? Please-help-me-Get-away-Leave-me-alone!"

We want the group; we hate the group. What we really want is to be ourselves *within* the group. And we want the group to help us be ourselves.

It is common for exiles to attempt to attach to *one* person in an available or stolen moment of privacy. (Many a haven has been found in women's bathrooms.) We single that person out as a protector, perhaps even a bridge back to the group. When I skied with the team, I'd usually end up riding the chair with either Terry or Dave, both close friends. A heap of neediness, I'd burst into tears. But all that did was put them in an awkward position because my needs, by that time, were at odds with the energy of the team which had already been functioning without me.

When we break down, we want to spin out of our self-con-straining spirals. We reach, which is the right instinct, but we rarely reach beyond ourselves. After one of our team get-togethers,

I found out that a vibrant athlete with a tough, bouncy exterior happened to be having a horrible time, too. She had carefully disguised what she called her "impending breakdown." I'd had no idea she felt that way. I hadn't asked.

My neighbor once said that she picks herself up by "visitin' people worse off 'n me." We know we would not feel so poor if we could give another even the small gift of our attention. But how do we get to that point when we are able to give?

Curiosity and the Ego

If we cultivate genuine curiosity toward others, we will discover something to respond to. As our resources awaken, we reverse the tendency to contract. When I was skiing with the team, my guide was usually drowned out by louder voices, as if the nag had brought along a few friends. But once, in desperation, I turned to my guide, ready to listen. Knowing that I was not in the mood to follow advice, she asked just one small question: Why don't you find out how the *others* are feeling?

Curiosity is not only a form of generosity, but also respect. It meets a story on its own terms without judgment. By being curious about the stories of others, we begin to tear down the established walls of acceptability. And as we show that form of respect, the feelings trapped within us begin to move, too, suddenly released from our repressive rulings. And when feelings move from one heart to another....skiing, that emotional girl, can dance again.

What stands in our way? Even the smallest gesture of generosity demands a sacrifice. And the ego— brittle, wizened survivor— suddenly gets nervous. But not too nervous: it has won before. The ego is confident that we are not capable of chucking it onto the coals. In the past, my guide has asked ineffective questions like "What are you going to lose if someone sees you ski badly?" To which my ego abruptly answered, "Quite a lot, thank you."

There is a tricky way to stimulate our curiosity and bypass

the ego's territory. We can imagine the particular situation as an experiment, our guide being the researcher who studies the group including, of course, ourselves—our reactions, our feelings. What we see and feel become *data*, impersonal phenomena that do not need justification, just further research. This way, we tend to treat ourselves more kindly. At the same time, we become less self-involved, our eyes open to the border between ourselves and the world. We observe how the world affects us as well as how we affect the world. The obsessive, inward direction of our energy begins to turn.

Anne, an excellent ski teacher, became a "nut job" whenever she tried to get certified. "I'd be doing fine," she said about past exam experiences, "and then all of sudden I'd be in a mine field. At any moment, something could be said, the light could change, or we changed the order we skied in. I'd see a face that reminded me of my grandmother, anything! and I'd lose it, my confidence would be gone, puff!" *Should I try again?* she wondered. We both knew she was technically ready.

"Take the exam as an experiment," I said. "Study your tendencies. Study each and every event that affects you *that way*." A researcher does not shout, "Oh my God, you idiot! How stupid to be thrown off by that guy skiing ahead of you!" Rather, she looks more carefully, continues to ask, "What is it about that guy? Is it just when you follow him? Is it his particular skill level, his style?"

"If an examiner says anything that ruins you, something rude or careless or even quite benign, study exactly how it makes you or the others feel. Take mental notes. Bring everything under your study, especially the group dynamics. *You* examine it all."

Her scrutiny lowered the examiner from his authoritative pedestal. This freed him as well. By not carrying the full responsibility of Anne's fragile mindset, he no longer felt prey to her inevitable rebellion. The question might be "Why did that bit of friendly feedback kill me?" rather than the "Why me?" of the bitter victim.

"It was still horrible," Anne said after the exam, "but I never totally lost it. In fact, I helped a lot of the others. I saw so many things that hit me, but by looking at them carefully, taking notes, I wasn't knocked over... I kept bending instead of breaking..." In fact, Anne did break into tears a few times but she stayed connected to the group. She never fell into a self-imposed exile.

Supporting Others Strengthens the Guide

In any group, tensions arise between our selfishness and our altruism. And the peculiar nature of the moment aggravates this conflict. A leap into the Yikes! zone demands from us a unique, often idiosyncratic response: a lone soul attempts to pass through a highly individualized moment. And yet at the same time, we often crave, even drain the support of a group. This sets up an obligatory equation. We must, in turn, offer support, which is rarely asked of us on our own time schedule and can oscillate between being a minor inconvenience and a royal pain in the ass.

By "support," I mean the simple availability of one's presence, not giving patronizing advice. When it came time to choose a few people to be at my son's birth, a wise friend told me: "Pick *only* the people who can bear to see you in pain." When we support those about to pass through the moment, we cannot interfere, we can only stand at the gate ready, allowing each to endure whatever is hers to endure.

Medicine men test you by fire and heat. The women...watch
to see how much you can listen to, how far down their road
you can go without finding an answer.
— Sallie Caldwell

In offering support, we find an unexpected boon. "I even helped the others," Ann said, an act which strengthened her own guide. In a fear workshop, people often have a breakthrough immediately after responding to another. When asked what taught her the most, one woman said, "Helping M. on the Wall. That's the

moment my guide really flowered and became... well, a guide."
Another answered, "When J. got stuck, I stayed behind her, waiting. I didn't want to go past her in case she needed me. I felt that I knew exactly what she should do. So when it came my turn, later, my guide felt strong."

Sometimes it is not possible or constructive to confront our well-protected selves directly. Supporting others can open a back door. This is especially true for Roberts who tend to avoid self-examination, those who do not wake up in the night plagued by demons of doubt and regret. One woman said, "By listening to what the others needed, my guide found out what I needed." When I asked for an example, she took a while, then said, "I never would have guessed that lowering the task (which meant, of course, my expectation) could apply to me. But then I saw it work so well for K."

I kept probing, "Was it important that it was K.?"

"Yeah," she answered, "'cause we were similar. At least skiing."

By listening to another, this Robert was able to learn what she didn't want to know she needed.

Established Groups

Although being in a new group often adds a dreaded unknown, established groups can be even trickier. They are comfortable, often familial. But the fixed patterns and hierarchies that create their comfort can, in turn, cause limitations.

Remember Sharon, the gifted ski teacher who warmed up slowly but still wanted to rip with the hot guys in the morning? That particular group was driven by mutual expectations, including Sharon's. She, upholding her entire gender, had to keep up with the boys. They not only had to duke it out among themselves, they couldn't let a girl out-ski them. Until Sharon risked slowing down for her first run or even for only half a run, everyone felt required to rip. They all tried to keep up, not with each other but with their conceptions of each other, conceptions that were never articulated or acknowledged. No one stopped to think through what was happening. It was as if they were hypnotized by a subliminal drum. Sharon broke the spell. Once these hidden notions were exposed, they lost their power to run the group. Everyone was not only relieved, they also started skiing better.

Acknowledging the Group Situation

Back to Snowbird, back to square one... The group had been disrupted, the invisible membrane pierced, leaving everyone deflated above the two rock bands that lined the chute we would take to the open bowl below. The first thing I did was to acknowledge what had happened. Without such acknowledgement, eight spirals of self-blame would have spun inward, as if the sudden depletion of energy was each one's personal fault. In fact, the nags had already found their point of entry: "How silly to be so sensitive..."

After acknowledging the setback, we *as a group* could rally to remedy our spirit. Without a hint of embarrassment or shame, each person matter-of-factly stated his specific fears. A woman with a bright red parka hated how the rocks closed in on either side, "that tiny narrow alleyway"; she wanted space, just space! some width! Whenever Bill, the sixty-three-year-old, was not able to see, his stomach started to "do a number, especially here, with the terrain falling away like that, you can't see where it goes! below you!" Another could flip at the sheer pitch. He was from Pennsylvania. Another man with smile wrinkles and crow's-feet felt this was "just like the place and the exact conditions" where he got hurt. Jill, a small, fifty-five-year-old woman in navy blue did not say a thing. But she had skied well since we started and she listened, nodded, and smiled.

Then there was Peggy who was scared of everything. The flat light had added another unwelcome variable I hadn't counted on. She would need extra care. And of course, there was one (there is always one) who was "not actually scared at all." He just wanted to reach his "full potential," to "ski as well as I know I can." The others bristled. This man had been overrating himself all morning. He drove everyone crazy with his patronizing instruction. (He was silently but collectively dubbed *Asshole,* which I will call him from now on.) Opposite him was Dwight, who wasn't frightened of anything in particular but felt a "generalized discomfort." He was the heart of the group, supporting everyone all morning with authentic admiration for their abilities and efforts.

No one stamped their poles in the snow or in any other way showed impatience with the comments. It was as if all admissions were part of the team effort to get everybody down in one piece, *as if safety were more important than the protection of their egos.* It was starting to resemble a miracle. My insensitive colleague had actually helped the group by creating a mini-crisis. I decided that once I finished lecturing *at* him, I'd buy him a beer—a cheap, tasteless one.

With everyone so open, my mind began clicking out a plan that resembled a puzzle, dovetailing one person's fear with another's, and using all the gifts of a group: *diversity, order* and *proximity.* First, we needed a human chain.

Diversity, Order, and Proximity

I sent Asshole in first, an important role only a strong skier can handle, but this had an added boon: no one had to listen to him anymore. He was thrilled, his self-admiration flaming up toward the invisible sun. I told him that I was scoring his turns which should be "very clean and very round." In truth, I didn't bother to look. I was giving him a task as I would give all the others tasks. I told him exactly where to stop: the number two position in the human chain, using him for simple mammalian presence. There, we could just barely see him. His arrogance out of reach, he performed his role perfectly.

Dwight was next. Technically, he was not the strongest skier but he had enough skill that he could negotiate the terrain and still have psychological energy left to give.

"You're my key man, Dwight."

"Me?" he said with a surprised smile.

"Go only one turn down, close enough so everyone can see your face. Back up against that rock."

Bill, the man whose stomach was doing a number had to go or he might vomit, which is never good for a group. He now had a reference; he could see two people, enough to get him "in". I was counting on him having enough momentum (plus the added aversion to stopping by Asshole) to move to the next post farther down and be number three on the human chain. Others would ski below him so he could refer to the chain for visibility the rest of the way down.

Next came the woman in the red parka, Carey, who wanted space. "Doesn't matter how steep it is as long as it's wide." Setting Dwight and Asshole diagonally apart from each other created an illusion. The chute appeared wider, almost the normal width of an Eastern trail, especially since the light offered little depth perception. Friendly and outspoken, Carey had rallied the support of the group behind her. They set up a comfortable rhythm, a rhythm she had been practicing. *Now. Now. Now.* I motioned to the group to lower the volume so Carey could hear her own voice emerge from their chorus. She pushed off repeating her cue. The group went silent but their heads still moved in rhythm with her turns. She made it past the rock bands… phew! Number four on the chain. She skied better than I'd thought she would. She was steady enough that I knew I could now use her.

Next: the man with the joyful face who'd hurt his knee. When he got scared, he stiffened and sat as if lowering himself onto the pot. With his hips back, his skis didn't readily turn and he picked up speed. This put pressure on his quads as well as his weak knee. I told him to stem his first few turns which would absorb his fear safely by keeping his body in balance. Till he got past Asshole. Then he had free will. Dwight had been paired with him a lot. "Come on, Buddy. Just like we've been doing all morning. Stem up! All right!" he shouted, "Another!" I heard Dwight continue under his breath, "Stay forward, come on, stay forward." Buddy did, his knee was safe. He vanished out of sight. Number five.

Now, I thought, *the real work begins.* We needed to send Peggy. Even though she couldn't see, she knew what was there: steep, increasingly heavy deep snow, narrowness, rocks on either side. She hated it all; she was trying to hold back tears. She had the human chain to support her as well as examples of her peers who made it in. But it wasn't enough. She looked like she wanted to drop into the center of the earth. *I should have sent her earlier,* I thought. I made a quick decision to go with her. And leave the next two, Jill and the Pennsylvanian.

The Pennsylvanian would be fine. He was actually the best technically, even better than Asshole. He was just not familiar with this pitch combined with this length. But the human chain is one of best ways to shorten a trail for Eastern or Midwestern skiers, the distance from one skier to the next feeling just like that steep knoll at home. Even without stopping, the rhythm of human presence is a comfort.

Jill would be fine, too. She always skied in control. And Dwight, the leader, would be last from the top. Then Asshole, the overall strongest skier, could sweep, making sure the others stayed below him. He could take care of himself.

"Peggy," I said, turning to look her in the eyes, "we're going together."

"I feel like I'm going to faint," she said, swallowing.

"That's good," I said. "That's adrenaline. Which you need right now. Once we get going, the adrenaline will make you stronger, quicker, more powerful. It's a great friend. Preparing you just for this. Don't worry about that queasy feeling. It's just the dues you gotta pay." This was important knowledge for her guide although some might call it a partial truth. Perhaps she did have too much adrenaline pumping through her for the task at hand. But that questionable fact would only pit her against her body. She needed, at this moment, to feel that her body was on her side, that she could trust it.

"Really? All that helps?" she asked as she stepped forward, looking at me.

"Yes," I said, "your body is there for you." I wanted to keep her moving. "Let's side step down here by Dwight. We'll start *across* the hill. Like this." Very tentatively, she lowered her ski off the lip.

"How about a stem step?" I asked.

"I don't know. My mind's totally blank," she said.

"You did that beautifully this morning. You were able to turn in a really cramped space, right?" She nodded. Peggy tended to pull her head back when she hit the fall-line, and her skis would take off. By the time she regained enough balance to finish the turn, she'd be going mach ten and needed to run out her speed across a wide, wide slope. Which we didn't have. The cue word had to get her whole body to commit to the fall-line, especially her head, the heaviest part of her body. Or she would speed right into the rocks. "What's the cue that worked the best?"

"Stem and yes," she squeaked out.

"You need to really yell it out. Stem and yes! "

Dwight joined in, gradually raising his voice with hers. The *yes!* didn't sound like a word so much as a loud, blown out breath which helped her body to flex forward.

"I'm going to stay right in front of you. I'm your cushion," I said. Very deliberately, we stemmed our uphill ski and YES! she committed with her whole body (head included) to finish the turn. It worked. No pulling back, no runaway skis. And another. And another. Three, now four turns in a row, the others joining in with her cue as we skied by. Finally, Carey's red parka came into view. Number four. I pulled up. "You're golden now, honey," I said to Peggy as she stopped beside me and smiled. "Follow Carey now. Just down to Buddy. See him below us?" Buddy waved his arms and yelled, "Come o-on, Baby!"

"Peggy, you stay with him. Your task then is to breathe and

smile." But she already was. And Buddy, with the knee injury—
her presence would help him, too. (He was not actually named
Buddy, but he invited the nickname. Was it his eyes, his crow's-
feet?) Supporting Peggy would keep his mind off his injury. Peggy
was a new friend drawing from him a new response, reminding
him this was a very different time than the infamous "before."

"Carey, you go one link farther down." We were below one of
the rock bands so although it was just as steep, it was wide enough
now for Carey to feel OK. Plus her parka was easy to spot. That
would solve a few problems. The chain would continue to extend.

I was too nervous to go any farther. If someone got stranded,
it would be a nightmare. Because of the pitch and the heavy snow,
no climbing was possible. I yelled to Dwight, "OK. You can send
Jim now." The Pennsylvanian. I heard Dwight's voice which carried easily. Jim was obviously *not* wanting to go. Dwight told
him to breathe in through his nose, all the way into his belly, out
through his mouth. Just like we practiced that morning. *Dwight's
perfect for the job*, I thought. "Do a stem turn right here by me."
He had the knack, a psychological dexterity you cannot teach. He
followed his suggestion with, "Just to set yourself up." He intuited
Jim's fragility. "Just to get your rhythm," meaning *no mark against
your skiing that your first turn into a chute is a stem.* Jim went and
you could hear the excitement in Dwight's voice. "And again!" he
shouted. "And again!" Jim came into view, skiing each turn with
more relaxation than the last, as he began to understand that the
snow held him back, that pitch without ice can actually be quite
friendly. "Keep going!" I yelled, not wanting to break his momentum. "As far as you want!"

Fog was starting to mix with the flat light. I had to get Bill
with the unsettled stomach out of there before he couldn't see a
thing. "How are you doing, Bill?"

"OK," he said in a voice that meant he wasn't going to be for long.

I waved my arms. "Can you see me?"

"Barely."

"Come to me," I said.

"Right now?" he asked.

"Yeah. Use your cue sounds." Which he did. "All right, Bill. You're doin' great. Buddy and Peggy are right below me." I turned to them, "Hey guys! Bill's comin'. Wave your arms so he can see you. See 'em?" I asked Bill. Their movements changed vague darkness into familiar human shapes.

"Almost," he said, but his voice was stronger now.

"Carey's below them. Stay with her. Then, you can follow her all the way down." *Thank God for bright, shiny parkas,* I thought.

"OK," he said, blowing out a big breath before he pushed off. I heard Buddy and Peggy below me cheering him on.

Only one more to go. "OK, you can send Jill down," I yelled to Dwight, suddenly realizing I didn't know what to expect. She was such a quiet, unassuming person, an unknown. *How'd she end up last?* Her skiing—controlled but without zip—like her personality drew no attention to itself. Navy blue. She had no blatant problems, no defensive movements. I grew increasingly uneasy. She was *not* going and I didn't know if Dwight knew what to do. Perhaps his ebullient nature made her retreat. It felt like minutes were going by. I heard nothing. "Jill?" I yell up. Dwight answers, "She's coming. She just needs to take her time." That's good, I think, he's protecting her. I begin to shake. I want to climb but it's useless here—you climb up, and slide down all in one move and end up where you started.

I start to talk to myself: "Let go, Mermer, you can't control everything." Maybe her ability tricked me, I think. She's a Jane, that's why her body doesn't show any erratic behaviors. Damn! "Come on, Mermer, you've prepared them well." I repeated the words I used when my son went off to college and I worried he'd miss his connection: "Let go."

Still nothing. Finally, I decide to ask, as quietly as I can and still be heard, "What's her task?"

Dwight yells down just as quietly, "We got it covered." They're a little lower. He must have gotten her to step in sideways like I did with Peggy. Then I hear him say, "Let it out, let it out." She's crying. Shit! Jill mumbles something but I can't hear it. "Where?" I hear Dwight say. "Your shoulders? Your thighs? OK, clench them, clench your whole body…a little longer, harder, harder, just a little longer…" Perfect, I think. He's doing the muscle contractions we practiced: tightening the shoulders, the thighs, whatever is shaking or frozen, then the whole body as hard and as long as you can, then releasing all at once.

I start to coach Dwight in my head: *Do a few of them and then, just as she releases, pull away, carry her along with the vacuum before she freezes again.* Timing is so crucial. And the energy link, too—her eyes, some form of touch or proximity. *But he's got that, Mermer. He's right with her. They're on their fourth contraction.* That's fine, I think. It sometimes takes quite a few before you pick your moment. *And only you can pick it, Dwight.* If you pull away and break the link, you have to start over.

I hear Dwight say, "Longer, harder, OK, release…" They're moving. "I'm right with you. I'm right with you." She can lean on his voice, the tone calm but strong. "OK, Jill, right with me, right now. Step and turn." Dwight makes an involuntary noise. She fell. She must have pulled back. Shit!

"OK?" I yell.

"We're OK."

Asshole says, "You sat back!" *Oh shut up!* I think.

"Take your time," I yell. "We have loads of time." I try to climb where it's tracked. I make it up about three feet. I hold my breath: "Got both skis?" No answer. I realize they're digging. Asshole is helping, too. A perfect job for him. Let him be a hero and find the goddamn ski. He does!! Thank God. He's not so bad really, I think. It was a big deal for him to come to the fear group in the first place.

"Here. Lean on me," I hear Dwight say. Jill must be trying to step into her bindings.

I yell down to the others who have been waiting too long, "Go on. Group up on the flat." I hear Asshole now who thinks he can take Dwight's place. He starts giving Jill advice: "Don't sit back now." That could be a last straw. I yell to Asshole, "I need you down here." When he approaches, I say in an important tone, "Ski from one person to the next and tell them to group up at the flat. You sweep. Make sure everyone's OK." He accepts his job with aplomb. Thank God for inflated egos, I think, they can come in so handy.

I hear Dwight above me, "Breathe deep, dee-eeper. Push my hand out," which I know is on her belly, encouraging her diaphragm to drop, expanding her lungs. "Yes, let the shoulders drop, yeah, there." The fog is so thick now, I can barely see my skis. "Breathe in through your nose, all the way into your belly, now out, let it out, there you go, in and let it ou-ou-out."

I go back and forth, talking to Dwight, talking to myself. *Let go, Mermer, they can do it on their own, they practiced this. You shouldn't have left her last. Good, Dwight, stay with the breathing a little longer. Never put an unknown last—what were you thinking?* I wasn't worried about Jill. I thought Peggy would be the big IF. Dwight's voice, "Stem up… there, good… and GO!" Jill made it through one turn! She stopped. Damn. "Perfect!" Dwight yelled, "you came right to a stop." The man was gifted. "Such control! If you can stop after every turn, you can ski a goddamn tree. Let's do one more. Ready? OK. Step and GO!" I hear her tiny voice chime in, "Go." One more. "I'll go just a little bit below you," Dwight says. He's stretching her, pulling her down. *Not too far, Dwight, I worry, don't break your link.* "Come right to me. Am I crowding you?" A brilliant question.

"No!" she almost shouts. "Stay right there." Good. She knows what she wants now, that's a big step.

"One more," Dwight says.

"Where's Mermer?" I hear her ask.

"Just below you," I say into the fog, hoping my voice carries, "two more turns. You're doing the perfect thing."

Dwight doesn't lose the momentum. "Breathe out, louder,

louder. Follow me, stem and GO!" We all yell the cue word. She stops again. Is that dark shape Dwight? No. "One more." They start: ONE (*keep going!*), TWO turns! They come into view. I want to hug both of them. Instead I say, "It's OK from here." Actually, it's about the same but now Jill has skied two consecutive turns, which is an entirely different animal from having skied one. Two easily runs into three, which is a few that becomes many. "How do you want us?" I ask Jill, wanting the guide in her to come out.

"You ahead. Dwight behind," she answers.

"OK and what helps the most?"

"Dwight's voice."

"You got it!" he says.

The three of us take off: One. Two. Three. I look back. She's going to make it through a fourth turn! She stops.

"What is it that happens to me?" Jill asks. Her face starts to twist. She's about to lose it, shifting into a post-crisis mode. She can't fall apart now. We have too far to go.

"Five more turns!" I yell, my voice hard, not acknowledging even a hint of Jill's questioning. "Let's go! The first one a stem. It doesn't matter what they feel like. Come on!"

I call this necessary non-receptivity the *metaphorical slap* after the story an Austrian friend once told me. She was next in line down a steep couloir when the person before her fell and slid out of sight. My friend had begun to go into shock when the guide, still calling for help on the radio, walked over and slapped her. "A most essential slap," she called it.

"Stem and go! And go!" I mouthed along with Dwight's voice. I looked back. Jill was no longer stemming. She was skiing like it was easy! Even though the snow was stickier down here where the sun hit it—homemade mashed potatoes with lots of lumps. I started to hear the group on the flat below. I didn't let her slow down after the fifth turn. "Come on. Right down to the group!" The snow was becoming like glue, tugging every which way. But the others' proximity pulled like a magnet. "All right! Jill!" I yelled as they cheered us in. I gave her a hug. She was shaking like a leaf and smiling. "Oh my God!" she kept saying. "Oh my God!" Dwight and I exchanged looks before I grabbed his arm, mine full of gratitude, his full of relief. We both knew: that was no small feat. "You have the knack," I said very quietly.

"I never thought I could do something like that," he said as his eyes began to tear.

As the group huddled, there was not a solid, defined individual among us. Everyone dissolved into a teary euphoria of relief and collective accomplishment. Each story got told, retold, framed, and reframed, everyone very much themselves and everyone wrapped in a circle of love. And of course, Asshole reminded us that he, in fact, found the ski. *Yes we know, and yes, Asshole, we can love even you.*

Reflecting

CHAPTER 18

The Landing

...First, 'soul' refers to the deepening
of events into experiences...
— James Hillman

One of the trickiest portions of the workshop is the last afternoon of the final day: after the moment, after the Yikes! zone. Spirits are high, bodies are tired. "Coming Down from Heaven" is one of the names the Chinese have given to the time after sex, but it could also be given to this time after the moment. Both call for delicacy and intuition. The surrender, and hence the danger, is past, but there is still no friction under our feet. It is an easy time to slip.

At the end of each leap into the Yikes! zone lies a different landing. After some leaps, a full let-down is possible and perhaps even required, but after others, where the landing is partial and precarious, we must often continue to perform at a level just shy of another leap. In order to negotiate our way through this time without harm, we need to respond appropriately to the type of landing we are offered.

Full Let-Down and Restoration

In 1988, Professional Ski Instructors of America hosted an educational trip to St. Anton, Austria. I had skied there the year before and knew that I could not miss this. I signed up.

We were graciously received by the late Professor Hoppichler in St. Christoph, the home of the Austrian Education and Certification Programs. Groups of ski teachers were led by both American and Austrian Demonstration Team members. I became one of ten in an infamous group—competitive, fast, macho, even dangerous because we would not say give— a group dominated by a survival-of-the-fittest mindset. And, I am ashamed to say, it was a group I belonged in because I was too proud and too stupid to leave, although I was full of trepidation from the moment we were handed our avalanche peeps. Our Austrian leader, inspired to show his own Darwinian tendencies, delighted in presenting us the most challenging and spectacular terrain the Arlberg could offer: chutes, cornices, peaks.

Over the course of four days, I became more frightened, rather than less, as I became increasingly aware of the fragile dependence we called our safety. Our connection to the guide in fog, the correct track "or we come and get you in the spring," two skis staying on, contacts staying in (I had lost both off-piste my first time in Austria), bones and joints remaining intact…but especially, the Question, like a tiny child might ask in the face of a mighty army: "Will the snow hold?" Its continuous voice ran beneath everything we skied. We would traverse single file, thirty or forty feet apart, in silence, because the vibration of a particular tone at the right decibel could make "the whole thing go." During one traverse, I remember seeing above me a mountain goat perched on an outcropping the size of a dinner plate. My eyes teared. I wanted to stop. In such starkly gorgeous, barren, inhospitable terrain, this fellow mammal felt close as kin.

At the end of the fourth day, I was on the verge of a breakdown. I walked into my room, took off all my clothes, crept under my duvet, curled into a fetal position and held my breasts. Hours later, my husband (visiting from another hotel) discovered that I had missed dinner and came into the room to find me. When he lifted the duvet, a shaft of light pierced my dark haven.

"Protect me!" I yelled. Eric quickly restored my cover, sat down and offered the pressure of his arms and hands on my back. He waited as dusk descended, and then carefully, very gradually, he pulled down the duvet as my sweaty head emerged into the dim light.

Eric finally broke the silence. "Are you OK? What happened?"

"I don't know," I said. "I wanted, I needed total darkness. And to curl in. As curled in as I could get."

"You're tired."

"No… I mean, yeah, I am, but I'm shaken. Or I was. I thought I would never come out. Not ever again…No! Don't turn on the light yet."

"OK. You're really hot."

"I wanted to be held in. Real tight."

"Did something happen? Today?"

"No. Or, just… more of the same. We hiked a lot. I'll show you on the map where we went. And actually, I skied, not great, but OK. But it wasn't just today. It's the accumulation…the last four days. I was over my threshold—the environment is so different, so foreign, I never know what to expect, or if I'll be up to it… but you can't say, 'OK that's great, that's enough! I've had my Yikes! for today.'"

"Yeah, once you start down a valley, you can't exactly turn back."

"No! And you can't let down. There's always more to come. More that you don't know anything about. I did everything I could—and my guide held up pretty well. Into one chute, it was so narrow, and lots of avalanche debris, big ice boulders you couldn't see beneath about three feet of heavy—real heavy—snow."

"Glad I wasn't there. Was Franz with you?"

"Yeah, and I went right after him. I knew if I followed him, I'd be fine. Then in some places, I stemmed for a little to get in. On a few traverses, the scary ones, I did some deep breathing—oh God, I made noises, too."

Eric smiled. "Did anyone hear you?"

"No, Jeez, they'd think I was nuts. Bernt was already laughin' at me. 'Another crazy American...' he said. 'Cause I was yelling cues to myself skiing the breakable. It was thick, but it wouldn't hold, it was awful. I managed to figure out some focuses that worked pretty well though."

"You need a real good sleep."

"Yeah, my Yikes! tolerance is spent, depleted, gone, zero. But I had to keep going, I couldn't let down. Not until I got back."

"And I guess you can't say, 'What's the worst that can happen?'"

"Yeah, there were quite a few places where you couldn't make a wrong move. I just needed, finally—"

"To recover."

"Yeah. I actually might want to, maybe, get up. What time is it? I came in early. Around three."

"Almost eight."

The next day, I skied with great freedom and almost no fear even though the circumstances did not change. Only then did I realize how contracted I had become over the past days. If anyone just pointed out a narrow chute or peak, I would grow scared because I knew whatever we saw we would eventually ski, so, in a sense, I stopped myself from looking. I didn't want to see even a postcard of the Alps.

That was when I first became aware of the power of restoration. Though of a relatively short duration, it was effective because of its intensity, because *its inward pull mirrored the outward expansiveness of the Yikes!* A simple idea. Nevertheless, many of us tend to be frightened of the restorative pull—its forcefulness, its introversion, its predilection toward the dark—so we stop short of a full recovery. The heart could lie ragged and exhausted from a roller coaster love affair, yet we force ourselves up and out into the glare of the city to meet people again.

One of the frightening aspects of restoration is the recognition of what we just accomplished, and what is now possible in our lives. While only seven, my son followed me down a steep, narrow trail full of icy, irregular moguls. I slowly increased our speed because I heard him right on my tails. Halfway down, we were skiing quite fast. In fact, the one time I glanced behind me, he arced his skis down the backside of a knoll slicing a much cleaner line than I had. When we got to the bottom, being the surprised and elated mother, I said, "Look at what you just skied, honey!"

As he looked back up the trail, he immediately burst into tears and said emphatically, "I never want to follow you down there or anywhere ever ever again!" Later, when we talked about it, he said, "It made me feel like I couldn't just be comfortable anymore."

It can be difficult to see a flash of what we are capable of, because at the same time, we know what it takes, the energy it demands. As one woman told me after a similar glimpse, "I hate this! I just want to hibernate and never come out." We will, of course, rise when our spring comes, but at winter's nadir, it is natural, though certainly disturbing, not to be sure of that.

If we don't allow for the complete restoration required, no hunger emerges for another leap. We begin to live in an unsettled limbo, no longer able to extend ourselves fully. Duty or pride or competition might still drive us, but our hearts? We have shunned the depths where desire is rekindled.

Partial Restoration

Sometimes, however, we should *not* fully let down. A partial restoration is called for, and although the intensity of a full restoration can be difficult to absorb, the lack of intensity of a partial one makes it trickier to negotiate. Gabby (the kayaker who was driven by the Puritan work ethic) mentioned that she often screwed up on easy gates immediately following a difficult transition. I was not surprised. In ski racing, it is common for a kid to ski flawlessly through a tricky combination, where his coach stands biting her lip, only to lose concentration as soon as he has made it to the flats.

Once we are no longer carried along by the heightened sensibility of the moment, we need to return to the lifeline of a specific focus in order to keep our attention from dissolving. In a sense, we backtrack through the steps that brought us to the moment in the first place.

Pamela, one of the women I ride horses with, had a hard time jumping a complete course. She would collapse on her horse's neck after each jump, causing her horse to lose his forward motion. Trying harder didn't seem to help. She would grit her teeth and go into the jump with a specific and forceful focus and then, in the air, her mind would go "totally blank," for which she castigated herself. When we talked, she had a detailed memory of how the horse felt as he gathered energy and curled beneath her, as he lifted and stretched through the air, almost as if it had happened in slow motion. "Yes, *now* I do. But at the time I'm blank, I can't keep my focus," a focus that happened to be narrowed to her heels, a specific body part. This blankness was not, as Pamela first thought, "a state of unconsciousness," but rather a keen, highly charged openness where she felt, in her own words, "susceptible to everything." She was passing through the moment. Forcefully keeping the focus throughout would not only be inappropriate, it would be detrimental; it would constrict her attention so she would not be able to feel the horse actually jump.

I suggested she stop meddling with the moment. Rather, she should grow attentive to the exact instant "the moment let her go," when she was no longer suspended in that heightened susceptibility. Once she took note of that time—as soon as her horse's front feet landed—she was able to cue herself with a new, appropriate focus that carried her into the next jump. By regaining her lifeline, Pamela could keep herself and therefore her horse moving forward. "I can actually land instead of going splat."

Micro and Macro Patterns of the Wave

In most of life, the Yikes! zone is complex, a conglomerate of moments difficult to differentiate. A moment can be as compressed and isolated as the release of our skis into a turn, or it can span the entire run, day, year... Our simple sine wave follows micro and macro patterns at the same time. Within the larger wave, undulations arise, just as the sustained language of a novel compresses and relaxes according to an internal rhythm.

Before riding a jump course or speaking in public, we might feel anxiety that remains with us until the event is over. But within the larger Yikes! of the entire time frame, we encounter mini-Yikes! we need to prepare for, both as we take off and as we land, for it is during these moments when many of us falter.

Bob came to me with a problem he wanted to discuss over lunch. Even though I had lectured on fear in skiing, he saw a parallel in his work, which involved public speaking. I was intrigued (and I love a good meal) so I accepted the lunch date. Bob was a biologist who gave talks to both environmental groups and corporations. "Some of my audiences are friendly. But some... they carry, not tomatoes, but daggers." He grew gradually into public speaking as his job description expanded, speaking first to students, then small groups of the like-minded, finally branching out to large, politically diverse audiences. He was nervous before his talks but that was "normal" and never really bothered him. "I'd just begin and after a few minutes, I'd be sailing..." In short, he had always felt he was good at his job, confident and successful. Until about six months ago.

So, of course, my question: "What happened then?" He paused, looked down, his face flushing a deep red. His conflict was palpable: he had asked for this, even arranged for it, but still, couldn't he just drop through the floor and forget the whole thing? Luckily the waiter interrupted. We backed away to make room for plates of mesclun salad, mine with roasted pecans and warm slices of duck, his with oranges, sesame seeds and marinated beef. We both made a lot of hoopla over our dishes, partly out of hunger and partly to deflect attention from the imposed intimacy. I let him take his time, hoping that time itself would prepare a place to receive his obvious pain.

"Well," he began, "where do I start? My wife of twenty-five years, a great woman... she is *still* a great woman..." admitted that she did not want to stay with him, and that she hadn't for a while. And that she had had other lovers while he had been on the road. On and off for a couple of years now and... he was wrecked. "Therapy, the whole thing..." They were still trying to work it out. "In some ways, it's better than ever. We're really learning to communicate but... BUT..."

He kept stalling, his eyes fighting tears. "I can no longer speak. I mean to an audience. Really speak, the whole audience right with you and you're saying things you hadn't even planned, like a fantastic conversation. I can't do that anymore. I get up there and I feel like a fucking robot. Before, it's what made me different, as a scientist, you know, an egg-head; I made it a point never to read from a paper. Maybe a paragraph here or there but never to read a whole paper. That's different than a talk. A paper's exactly the same to every audience, and to be a talk, it has to be different. Or you're not connecting. But now, I can't connect. I just don't have any... confidence, I guess, to let myself go."

I chewed on slices of duck, remembering for an instant what my son said as a kid whenever he ate meat: "Thank you [duck] for being killed so we can eat you." I chewed. I listened. The only thing I could say seemed both obvious and useless: he was living his whole life in the Yikes! zone. The macro wave. He couldn't handle any more. Was time off possible? No. What would I do if he were my student? I thought. Would I tell him to go have a Scotch instead of ski? No, if he were out there on the hill, I'd begin *where he is now*.

"Do you use notes?"

"Now I do. After I had a disaster. It was the first time I spoke *since*... I got up and nothing happened. My mind was... like jelly... it was... well, a disaster."

"Jelly? Did you eventually speak? At all?"

"Yeah, I did bumble through, barely making sense, jumping around. I kept thinking, 'How did I get *here*? What am I doing talking about *this*?' People were walking out, or looking at their watches. There was a lot of shifting in the seats. It seemed to go on forever. It was supposed to be an hour and fifteen minutes, plus a Q & A. But I cut it short. It was probably forty. Forty minutes of mostly unintelligible rambling. I'm lucky it didn't ruin my career. So now, yes, I use notes. I'm glued to 'em."

"What happens when you first face the audience? I mean *now*."

"Well, actually, when I get up there, I'm not that nervous. Not any more than before. I just can't leave my notes. I can't think spontaneously. I might as well be reading a goddamn paper."

So the hour-long wave was relatively unaffected, I thought. It was the mini-Yikes! that stymied him. It felt the most drastic, and it was the easiest to avoid.

"Why don't you go ahead and read your paper?" I asked. He looked at me, and stopped, mid-chew, like I was either being intentionally dense or hard of hearing. I continued, "Why not read your paper, but leave big blank spots interspersed through-out where you could, if you felt like it, begin to jump off, elabo-rate, improvise, just if you felt comfortable? Or you could keep going..."

"Plodding along like all the others."

"Maybe their wives hurt them, too." *Shit*, I thought. *Did I go too far?*

But he nodded. "Touché. I can be very arrogant." He smiled. "Or that's what my wife tells me."

"I know the feeling of connecting with an audience. When it doesn't happen, it's just awful. Each moment feels—"

"Like an hour. And I still want to cringe when I think—"

"You need to start where you are now."

"You mean reading. I'm at least capable of that. But you say to give myself a few jumping off points, a few opportunities to… talk."

"Yeah. When you work out your paper beforehand, give yourself a smooth, an irresistible lead in, about something you're really comfortable with. Like what you talk to yourself about when you're driving. You do that?"

"All the time."

"Nothing too new. Something you've already discussed, maybe ten, a hundred times with close colleagues, your buddies—" Mid-sentence, I remembered the metaphor of skiing and my mind clicked in: the landing! Don't forget the landing!… "But when you plan it," I added, "after the blank spot where you let yourself improvise, give yourself an easy way back, an easy entrance back into your paper."

"A way back in?"

"Yeah, you're gonna be out there floating around in who knows what kind of abyss, you have to give yourself some phrase that will pull you back from anywhere. A few words that will ease your way back into your paper. No matter how far out you've gone."

"A bridge," he said.

"Yeah, plan that part well. Take extra care."

Dessert was very fine, a lemon tart. Then my favorite: a cup of hot water, cozy and clear after a meal. Bob was a cappuccino man. No dessert. His next talk was Friday. He would swallow his pride. He would read his paper. He'd create the perfect springboard.

"Maybe not a springboard," I said, "something gentler."

"Like a wheelchair ramp."

"Yeah, and don't forget the landing."

He called me a week later and said, "Well, actually, all things considered, it went pretty well, but… the landing!" He hadn't prepared enough for the landing. "But *now* I know what you mean.

Once I felt that chemistry, that synergy again with the audience, I was *so* elated—I was floating—which is exactly what you knew would happen, right? You start floating and you forget where the hell you are. I was doing so well and then suddenly, I was about to fall from a great height and I heard your words, 'Don't forget the landing, Idiot.'"

"I never called you idiot!"

"You did then."

"What happened?" I asked.

"Well, I floundered for a while and then I just said to the group, about a hundred A+ types, 'OK, I guess it's time to get back on track.' So instead of a seamless entry into the rest of the paper, it was more like a stall, jerk, and start."

"At least you started again."

"I didn't try jumping after that. But tomorrow, I'm talking again. And I have the same take-off ramps but better landings planned out."

"Just remember a few key words that can bring you back from wherever you go."

"Yeah, Idiot!" he added.

During his next few papers, he jumped and landed three or four times. Each time, his jumps got longer, his landings sometimes so graceful, he bragged on the phone, he could barely pinpoint when he returned to his paper. He switched back to notes within a few months, and after a while, barely used them.

He began to mentor young scientists who often slip into shock whenever they have to open their mouths in front of a group. "But now I know what they're feeling. I'm there with them." Helping them jump, but especially, helping them land.

Accepting Restoration

Each year, I continue to be surprised at the number of women who come to the workshop because they have a lower tolerance for the Yikes! zone than the rest of their circle, whether it be spouses, children, siblings, or friends. Because they need more restoration time and less Yikes! than others, they express various forms of shame, often blaming the patriarchy, their mothers, or the lack of Little League for girls.

Just as we all have different libidos, we all have different appetites for Yikes!, which *continue to shift through our lives.* Notwithstanding the pressure around us to conform, it is *we* who must learn to respect the unique ratio of restoration to Yikes! our lives demand. This is especially so after a trauma. We cannot judge the penetration into our souls caused by even the smallest leap, never mind a major intrusion. Therefore, we also cannot guess the depth of restoration necessary. Just the other day I heard a recent widow say, "I used to be able to jump right back on the horse." Yes, but that was a different horse, and you are now a different rider, and no one, not even you, knows where that horse could take you. Or perhaps, what you might find just sitting on the grass.

We must not only give ourselves permission to restore ourselves, but we must also accept the ways that restoration manifests itself. Without a collective inheritance of established rituals, we must turn our ear to what the soul might need. Often, it is not what the culture condones. And it is rarely welcomed by our pride.

The idea itself—*restoration has value*—can help us. No set program exists for it, nor could one. Following a program would contradict the nature of this time, which demands not only intuition, but often the relaxation of a collective code of behavior. As people recognize a purpose in their tears, or swampy inertia, or sudden reaction against an extra project, they not only feel they have permission, but even an obligation, to protect that purpose. "I started to schedule post-Yikes! on the calendar," one woman said, "just to keep that time open, not fill it all up. I'd even drive more carefully. It's a weird time, things can happen. You're not all there." After any Yikes!—at work or on the hill or in the family —we need to slow down so we can be vigilant and attentive, on guard against the inertia of productivity.

Deepening Our Lives

Restoration can take many forms. The unique recovery each Yikes! necessitates can occur anywhere on a continuum from conscious examination to physical, fetal regression. All the forms, however, arrest our forward movement, directing us both backward and inward, serving as a necessary reflection, a looking back upon the original Yikes!

One student, Randy, told me that when she was diagnosed with breast cancer, it was as if a wedge had been driven between her and her body, cleaving their partnership. "My body was no longer on my side." She drew a parallel to torture victims who, after a certain period, experience their bodies as the cause of pain rather than the torture itself. From the moment the victims turn against their bodies, the torturer gains control.

In the workshop, Randy's Yikes! zone involved making rhythmic turns quickly enough to bypass her thinking which was predisposed to managing each movement. She had to rely on her body "being there for her." Which it was. She felt elated. But it was not until the next morning that she fully understood what had happened. Lying with her eyes closed in bed, she realized that her body had, once again, become her partner; she would take care of it, and it, in turn, would take care of her, an alliance that had not been renewed since her cancer ten years before.

By examining what took place in her experience, Randy deepened her understanding and furthered the conversation with her body. Otherwise, she would have merely improved her skiing. After listening to stories of restorative moments, I realized that it takes this last phase to complete the surrender into the Yikes! zone. Without such inward turning, a Yikes! experience does not necessarily deepen our lives. In fact, it can merely serve to inflate the ego.

This realization pointed to a question I have asked for many years. In sport, it is occasionally acknowledged that surrender is involved. When Michael Jordan said, "I wait and the game comes to me," everyone nodded. In the same way that artists allude to the muse taking them into unknown territory, athletes often experience a similar visit as they become part of a larger pattern. Even if they don't articulate it, they recognize an unexplained energy that fills the body *as if from the outside.* So why, after such moments of surrendering the self, is there so much ego-inflation in sport?

Without the necessary reflection, we mistake that inspiration— "the divine breath"—as our own. It is no wonder we inflate. "I need to own it" is a common phrase. We are a people that possess everything from land to emotions, to our spouses' schedule, and even time, which we spend, waste, buy or kill. Is it any surprise that we want to possess our successes as well? But as we turn inward, allowing our reflection to fall upon our reduced selves, we pierce and puncture such illegitimate ownership.

Artists and athletes alike are often humbled by the mercurial nature of inspiration. Because we seldom understand that humility, we can mistake it for lack of confidence. Rather than shellac over these feelings with platitudes about self-esteem, we should learn to place such authentic humility in a context where it can help—deepening our understanding not only of sport or art but of life. John Logan, a great American poet, once talked about the sadness that comes after writing a poem: *This poem is the only one that was or ever will be, and it will never come again.* Like the Pieta, he said, when Mary looks down on her son. What is divine came through her, as if it belonged to her, but as it was given, it was taken away.

When we understand the inward pull of restoration in context and accord it honorable status in our lives, we no longer feel it as a threat. As we grow more familiar with its nature, the delicate strands of intuition stretch and strengthen. We know how to take proper care while we wait to be at the mercy of the next pivotal moment.

CHAPTER 19

Fear, Our Teacher

Show me a hero and I will write you a tragedy.

— F. Scott Fitzgerald

In 1990, I planned a third trip to Austria. The Professional Ski Instructors of America were going back. I would be smarter this time: I would join a supportive group, I would slow down and learn. The trip was planned for April, but as early as December, the nagging thoughts began. About avalanche. I decided to talk to my friend, Franz Krickl, the director at Windham and an Austrian mountain guide who had been with me on both previous trips. (As part of the infamous group on the second trip, he dug many of us out of the snow.)

"Have you ever been frightened that something was going to happen to you?" I asked.

"You mean like a premonition?"

"Sort of, maybe..."

"Yes," he said, "when I was seventeen, right before I crushed my right leg in a downhill accident." That was not the answer I was looking for.

It was the unbidden thoughts—small, nimble stowaways that hide between presentable, well-clothed deliberations— that were most disturbing. "Well, if I'm alive in May..." or "Before the avalanche..." Sometimes the sudden glimpse of my son, alone, without a mother, would pop up while I was driving, or resting, or just after waking. The possibility of no longer being here, on this earth, caused even the worn, familiar shapes and colors of my home to take on sharper angles, deeper hues. Some moments, I would stare at my kitchen—the handed-down dishes, the woven rug unweaving itself at each edge, the dog's water dish with drops surrounding it on the floor—as if all were suspended, caught in a photograph, as if these temporary things did indeed contain a numinous permanence: those water drops are here, were always here, will always be here. And this single moment, pressing itself upon me, was all there was, and it was not only enough, it was too much, it was excruciatingly beautiful.

In March, my mother, Josephine, famous among family and friends for her uncanny intuition, called me and, without bothering with any hello, said, "Mermie! Have you made out your will yet?" I didn't answer but it didn't matter because she continued without missing a beat, "What about Hansen? If anything happens to you in Austria…"

When I started having dreams, I talked to my husband (who would be traveling but not skiing with me) about canceling the trip. But we didn't. The plan was to leave Hansen for ten days with my parents, Grandma and Granddad, where he could be spoiled with all his favorite foods and best of all, TV, which we didn't have at home. I was down on my knees hugging and kissing Hansen goodbye, both of us crying, when he, barely eight, yelled out, "It'll be so long since I see you again. The next time I see you… you'll be in your grave!" I broke into a sweat. But I still got into the car.

On the second night in Austria, a talk on avalanches was introduced into the schedule because a skier in another group had been caught in a small slide. Everyone sat through the presentation with apparent ease and even inattention, as if watching a flight attendant deliver for a worn-out safety message. Not me. I looked like Woody Allen in Annie Hall when Annie's crazy brother is driving, the one who's just confessed that he has the urge, often, at sixty miles an hour, to veer across the yellow line into the oncoming lights.

It was very different from the last trip. The fog and avalanche danger kept us lower. We were learning more. The group was supportive, enthusiastic. But then the sun came out along with the Austrian Demo Team. It was time to be taken on a tour. Our group combined with another so there were two guides and twenty of us, a large number considering the fragility of the snow. The peeps were handed around, all part of the routine. Everyone was laughing and excited: the sun was out! But I was thinking, *Is today the day?*

We began on top of the first Schindlerspitze chute. I had skied it on both previous trips, but that year, it had been closed due to avalanche danger. Until now. The snow was still heavy and breakable. We stood in line on the ridge. I was fifth. "We go in one at a time," the guide in front said. I knew this already, the weight of two might cause…The guide continued, "You do not stop. You do not fall. And when you finish, you pull out and stand under the rocks, in case…" I knew the words, those same words, "…the whole thing goes."

The first of our group went in. "Not easy," the second guide said, as he watched the man ski down. I looked over at him, one of the greatest skiers in the world, smiling, relaxed, at home on his rock perch on the far side of the chute. "Not easy," he said again. The second went; then the third, Peter Palmer, my good friend. We waited. It took a long time for each to finish. Dave Alonzo, just ahead of me, was about to go. But for a reason no one knows, the first guide stepped in front of him and traversed in. He stopped before making a turn and whispered something in German to the guide on the rock just above him. He did not make another move. The second guide immediately gestured to us with his hands: "Shh! Shh! Quiet!" Dave whispered back to me, "He heard a crack." The second guide, after securing himself, reached down and took hold of the other guide's arms so that as he stepped up and out of the chute, he would put as little pressure as possible on the snow. We all turned around. "Crack. Unsafe to ski" rippled through the line. "We'll meet the others at a junction below." I knew right then: that was it. I felt a thousand pounds lift off my shoulders and suddenly disperse. And with the lightness that followed came the realization of how much more weight that dark, tenacious warning had gathered in those last moments. I hadn't felt so light, so free in months. I could move, I could ski again, the rest of the day, the rest of the week, with respect, but free, finally, from that instant on, of fear.

I still had questions. If it had been my turn to ski that chute when the guide went in, would those foreboding voices have gathered enough force for me to listen? Would I have been too stubborn? Was that voice a protector? A sign that said, *If you go this way, watch carefully*?

Fear Refines the Wave

Fear is constantly lambasted for inhibiting us, but its restraining nature refines our interaction with the surrendering moment. In a risk sport such as skiing, this becomes more evident as our skills improve. The large oscillations of a beginner's wave as he leaps into his Yikes! zone become, with increasing skill, a suggestive ripple. Our conversation with fear warms with the friction of intimacy as we negotiate the nuance between 99.9 and 100.1% Without such refinement, we could die. Remember the intrepid Hermann Maier at the Nagano Olympics? He flew headlong (and too far) into his Yikes! zone when he tried to take an impossibly aggressive line in the downhill and was flung full speed into the nets. He, like many great downhillers before him, know the importance of riding the finer line.

Bode Miller, an articulate, imaginative athlete, has been America's most gifted ski racer, and he has done his best to stay true to the original spirit of the sport. Notoriously defiant, it was his way, no matter the stakes of the race, to ski all out, continually pushing his limits into unknown territory, where he would either fail (sometimes brutally) or force his body to respond in dazzlingly innovative ways. He has been our avant-garde, pushing the sport along as well. (In his earlier years, he was either on... or not. When he tried to pull back from the edge, he looked uninspired, his movements no longer as instinctive and catlike.) In his honest (and thankfully, unscripted) interview with Tom Brokaw before his glorious 2010 Olympics, he described how, as his skills grew, he had to stop transcending his limits—not necessarily for the results, but to stay unhurt, to stay alive. Contrary to his nature and habit, he had to force himself to ski up to and along the edge, not beyond it. Over the span of Bode's career, you can clearly track the refinement of these undulations into the Yikes! zone, from his earlier dramatic swings and ensuing erratic performances toward a subtle, cultivated, and highly attuned relationship with the edge.

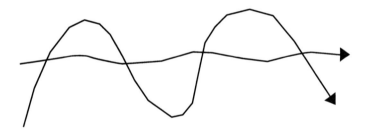

As one's skills improve , the large oscillations
of a beginner's wave become a suggestive ripple.

Fear's Teaching

Releasing the skis' hold from a cornice is a moving and spectacular event. We fall into a momentary abyss until our skis meet the snow again. But there is another cornice we can jump off, the cornice of what we have learned, the hard-earned investment of our acquired skills, our technique. The layers of learning add meaning and force to our leap as we attempt to create what is not yet known. This can be a far more difficult jump. Like a doppelganger, its height mirrors our desire for control. And like a shoreline, its edge constantly recedes.

As we enter the intangible realms—intellectual, emotional, political, spiritual—the jumps become more complex and continuous, the gradations less obvious. Fear itself can move us to this different quality of jump, deepening our encounter with the moment.

Often it can be frightening to approach fear as one does a teacher, with respect but without awe, and receive its penetrating, wise directive. But fear finds a way to make us listen, even if we are stubborn.

I had climbed up the side of a hundred-foot waterfall near my hometown many times—sometimes once a year, sometimes three or four—since I first followed my brother up when I was twelve. I had even carried my son up on my back five, maybe ten, times. There is one difficult overhang but the rest is straightforward, careful scrambling up the rock face on all fours. When I was twenty-eight, I was about a third of the way up, beneath the overhang, when I *saw* the danger as if for the first time: from there to the top, I could not slip without dying. And once I saw it, I couldn't *not* see it.

I had begun to wrestle with the fear, out of habit, when suddenly, I realized that this fear had a different quality. It was severed from the moment. There was no moment here for me, no point my soul would turn upon, no surrender necessary to carry me further into my life. To continue up this climb would be like walking into an abandoned building where I had expected to find my home.

There had been a shift in my life, which I knew then to be my conversation with the world. I had grown, each year, more in love and I wanted, above all, to stay. There was a lot I had to do, but not here, not on this climb. This fear was telling me to turn back.

I climbed down. I knew I would never ascend the waterfall again. There were other moments waiting that would be of a wholly different nature. They weren't mine to choose, I thought. Would they choose me if I approached? Would they push and pull me under their magnetic influence?

The next day eating breakfast in a local diner, I heard that a man had fallen from that waterfall and died a few hours after I turned around. I closed my eyes. *There but for the grace of fear...*

It is fear that presses, from our limitations, the aged wine of humility as we face the implacable givens of the world.

Glossary of Ski Terms

binding: The highly technical gadget that hooks your boot to the
  ski and usually, if set properly, releases when you fall to prevent injury.

black diamond: The standard label for a trail that is *most difficult,* or the trail itself. (There is no national standard for
  the degree of difficulty so the label is relative to each resort.)
  A *double black diamond* is even more difficult than a single
  black.

bump run: A trail designated for bumps or moguls (see moguls).
  A bump run resembles a large quilt from a distance. It is
  almost always more demanding than a groomed run with the
  same pitch.

carving: Turns that utilize the skis' design with little or no skidding or slipping sideways. Each ski, tipped on edge, bends to
  match the arc of the turn, the tail following the exact track of
  the tip. A carved turn presents an indescribable feeling with
  disparate qualities of directional control, frictionlessness,
  acceleration, and ease.

cornice: An overhanging (and sometimes fragile) ledge of ice or
  snow at the edge of a steep ridge or cliff made by prevailing
  winds.

couloir: A steep chute or gully on a mountain.

fall-line: The imaginary line that water would follow down a
  slope.

Great Scott: A steep, sensational chute with a tricky entrance
  through rocks at the head of the Cirque in Snowbird, Utah.

groomer: A machine that prepares trails by grooming or
  smoothing the surface. Also slang for a groomed run.

moguls (also called bumps): Irregularities in the terrain, caused either by skiers or boarders traveling the same track, compressing and pushing the snow into clumps, or by machine, in which case they are much more regular. These solidify into rounded shapes varying in size from small boulders to Volkswagon beetles.

off-piste: Areas outside of the designated "piste," a European term for a prepared or groomed trail. These areas are often susceptible to avalanche.

Outer Limits: A challenging bump run at Killington, Vermont.

schuss: A German term for moving straight down the mountain.

side-slip: Sliding down the slope with the skis across the fall-line scraping the snow; a maneuver sometimes necessary to negotiate very difficult terrain.

stem, stem turn: A turn begun by lifting the uphill ski and pointing it toward the fall-line before putting weight on it; a tactical maneuver that can preserve a skier's fore-aft balance in some difficult conditions.

wedge, wedge turn: A position in which the ski tips are pointed toward each other with the inside edges brushing the snow; an updated form of the old snow-plow with less braking or plowing of the snow.

NURSING CARE PLANS
The Nursing Process at Work

SERIES EDITORS

Kathleen M Berry SRN SCM RNT AcDipEd
Will Bridge BSc PhD
Jill Macleod Clark BSc SRN PhD

In the same series

Research for Nursing — A Guide for the Enquiring Nurse
Teaching Patient Care — A Handbook for the Practising Nurse
Communication in Nursing Care

Table of Contents

Foreword

The first edition of this work was welcomed as a very practical guide to the nursing process at work in 1980 when there was little for the English reader. It has been heavily used and now this second edition adds the fruits of experience gained in the intervening six years.

Experience is injected into this work in a commendable way. It is not just an academic treatise, but both authors write from experience in nursing practice which characterises the book. That experience has enabled them to make revisions in this second edition that are most useful. Some readers may question the identification of nursing diagnoses as a stage in the process, having avoided the medical connotation of the word until now. The use of the word diagnosis is not exclusively medical, however – engineers carrying out a diagnostic tuning of engines! Identifying diagnosis as a stage in the process highlights the need to be precise about what it is that nursing care is aimed at and it avoids all the debate about the comparative merits of identifying 'needs' or 'problems' and whether these are nursing problems or patient problems.

This new edition is once again extremely practical in its advice to clinical nurses but it also deals with the implication of nursing process in an institutional setting and for managers and nurse educators. I find it is written with a clarity of expression that makes reading effortless and I believe the book will continue to have its appeal to students and registered nurses at all levels.

McFarlane of Llandaff
November 1985

Preface

During the last decade nurses have become increasingly aware of the need for a systematic approach to nursing care. This awareness results from a number of factors which include a desire to identify and establish 'nursing' as a profession with its own body of knowledge, concern about standards of care, and the need to keep nursing records which will provide an accurate, detailed account of the patient's stay in hospital. At the same time nurses do not want to lose their caring role, for this is central to nursing. Care planning not only provides the basis for this systematic approach but it also emphasizes and helps to develop its caring aspect. The nursing process is the framework within which such care planning can take place.

Since publication of the first edition of *Nursing Care Plans*, tremendous progress has been made with the introduction and use of care plans based on the nursing process, and there is no doubt that the concepts embodied in the nursing process are increasingly being accepted by nurses at all levels and in all areas of practice. However, our continuing experience indicates that despite this more general acceptance, there is still a need for a practical guide to care planning. The aim of this second edition, therefore, is to provide such a guide which is relevant to any system of health care and nurse education and focuses on how nurses can plan appropriate care for each individual patient's needs. In our revision and updating, we have re-emphasized that Nursing Care Plans are a means of putting the nursing process into action, and we have incorporated the experience gained from improved skills, understanding and knowledge of care planning.

The changes which the reader will find in this edition are many. In Section 1, for example, the chapters have all been completely updated and the chapter on Helpful Hints (former-ly at the end of the book) has been moved here because its practical emphasis makes this position in the early part more appropriate. Another change will be found in Section 2, where we identify and describe five stages of the nursing process, assessment, nursing diagnosis, planning, implementation, and evaluation, rather than four. The inclusion of this addi-tional stage – nursing diagnosis – confirms our belief that before appropriate care can be planned, nursing problems must be accurately and sensitively diagnosed.

Section 3 is completely new and recognizes the separate, yet interrelated, parts which nurse practitioners, managers and educators have to play in care planning. Section 4 contains the reading guide and bibliography chapters, both of which have been completely updated to incorporate new knowledge and understanding of the complexities of care planning, as well as the increased volume of literature now available. Both the reading guide and the bibliography contain information and references on such concepts as ideologies, nursing theories, models of nursing, nursing diagnoses, primary nursing and teaching the specific skills incorporated in the nursing process.

Finally, ours is a problem-solving approach which begins with an understanding of what we value and believe about people and uses this as a framework on which practitioners, managers and educators can base their implementation of care planning. We do not claim that this is the only way of im-plementing care planning but we do believe that our approach offers something tangible and concrete to nurses at all levels and provides an exciting and challenging opportunity to assess the effectiveness of our care.

Jennifer M Hunt
Diane Marks-Maran
January 1985

Acknowledgements

We would like to thank all those who have helped us to write this book. In particular we would like to thank our nursing colleagues at The Royal Marsden Hospital and St Bartholomew's Hospital for helping us to maintain progress and at The London Hospital for supporting the research which started us off on our Care Planning Project. Our special thanks must go to all those friends who have helped by listening, discussing and arguing.

Finally, we would like to express our gratitude for the help we received from members of the Editorial Board, from our secretaries who typed and re-typed the manuscript and from all the hospitals and health authorities who have kindly permitted us to use their care planning formats which appear in the Appendix.

J M H
D M-M

INTRODUCTION

What are Nursing Care Plans?

Nursing Care Plans are written for individual patients and are a practical way of putting the nursing process to work. They are not the same thing as the nursing process, although there is a definite relationship between the activity of producing Nursing Care Plans and the philosophy of the nursing process. Producing a Nursing Care Plan involves assessing the patient's needs and planning appropriate care. The nursing care can then be given, or modified and adapted as necessary, using the written record called the Nursing Care Plan; furthermore, care given can subsequently be evaluated. A Nursing Care Plan is, therefore, a practical tool which helps nurses give individualized care to patients.

A Nursing Care Plan has five purposes. It provides an assessment of the patient's needs; nursing diagnosis; details of the planned care; a description of how this was implemented; an evaluation of the outcome for the patient. These steps correspond to the stages of the nursing process. Learning about Nursing Care Plans, and gaining practice in their use, should help nurses towards a clearer understanding of the principles of the nursing process.

It is important that readers should understand the terminology which has been used throughout the book, to avoid the danger of confusion. When we talk about *Nursing Care Plans* (ie. capital letters and preceded by Nursing) we mean the totality of the plan which is needed to put the nursing process to work, including the patient's history, his nursing problems

1

and needs, the planned programme of patient care itself and the detailed evaluation of that care.

However, when we speak of the whole process of decision-making and recording which is necessary in order to produce a Nursing Care Plan, we have termed this activity *care planning* (ie. without 'nursing' and without capital initials). On occasion, particularly in Section 2, we will need to refer to that part of the whole Nursing Care Plan which contains just the written list of the patient's problems, and corresponding actions and goals. We have called this document the *Care Plan*, but whenever we have used this phrase we have differentiated it from the whole Nursing Care Plan.

The purpose of this book is to provide a basic guide to care planning and to give practical help in making the nursing process a reality at ward level. The book is divided into four sections, of which the first provides an introduction to Nursing Care Plans and gives a background to using them and the nursing process generally. In this section, we also introduce the topics of types of ward management and the organization of patient care such as team nursing, patient allocation and primary nursing.

The second section contains a chapter on each of the five stages of the nursing process (assessment, diagnosis, planning, implementation, and evaluation) and discusses how each stage can be fitted into the Nursing Care Plan. The third section examines in depth the changing roles of clinical nurses, nurse managers and educators. We end our book with a reading guide for nurses who would like to extend their knowledge of care planning; a detailed bibliography is also included in this section.

Throughout the book we try to emphasize the practical aspects of care planning, including our successes as well as the mistakes we made. We hope you will find using Nursing Care Plans and the nursing process exciting, as well as practically valuable, in terms of giving good patient care.

Section I

An Introduction to Care Planning

In this first section we take an overall look at care planning, placing it within the conceptual framework of the nursing process. We then outline different methods of organizing care: task allocation, team nursing, patient allocation and primary nursing. Finally, we discuss how planning can be implemented.

Chapter 1

Words and Meanings

Care planning is not new. Over 30 years ago McManus (1952) said:

> 'The unique function of the professional nurse may be conceived to be (1) the identification of the *nursing* problem and (2) the deciding upon of a course of nursing actions to be followed for the solution of the problem in the light of immediate and long-term objectives of nursing'.

More specifically Mayers (1983) defined patient care planning as:

> '. . . systematic assessment and identification of problems, the setting of objectives and the establishment of methods and strategies for accomplishing them'.

Care planning therefore is not new. Its use and usefulness have in fact come about over a long period of time. At first it was used mainly as an educational tool by teaching staff but recent developments have concentrated on its use in wards. What is clear, is that regardless of whether or not it is being fully implemented, the influence of the idea has been immense and has brought about tremendous changes, the most profound being a questioning approach to care which nursing had previously lacked. It is only when care planning is used by all nurses working in hospital and the community that its benefits will be fully realized and appreciated. It is very important, first of all, to define the terms we will be using.

> *care planning* A systematic approach to planning patient care which enables the nurse to provide effective nursing which will meet the individual needs of the patient.

5

Nursing Care Plan The visible and written record of the implementation of care planning. It documents the use of this approach. A Nursing Care Plan has the following components:

- a nursing assessment of the patient;
- details of the care planned to meet the patient's problems and needs;
- evaluation of the care given.

Why we need care planning

Nursing in the United Kingdom has traditionally revolved around a task-allocation approach to clinical care, ie. nursing care is described as 'the work' and lists of jobs to be done are drawn up. Very few nursing actions have been subjected to a close look at what is being done and why it is being done; there have been few, if any, scientific principles behind nursing care. Care planning uses a problem-solving approach. This emphasis on problem solving should encourage nurses to develop a much more objective and logical approach to their work.

While the development of the medical profession has been built upon research, with changes and improvements being made as new ideas and knowledge arise, this is not so in nursing. Although an increasing amount of nursing research has been undertaken, the information obtained is seldom put to use in the clinical setting. This may be due to the fact that nurses are unaware that such information is available and do not have the skills to assess and utilize research findings. Also, nursing care is seldom evaluated and continues to centre on nursing activities developed from medical diagnoses, rather than on the individual nursing needs of the patient or on research information. Phrases commonly heard on wards such as 'The appendicectomy in Bed 10' or 'All our herniorrhaphies have x, y and z done to them' or 'Use lotion X because Sister likes it' bear witness to this fact.

One of the factors which allow medical staff to evaluate the treatment of their patients' condition is the medical record, which forms a permanent and continuous picture of the patient's medical treatment. This is particularly true when

Problem-Oriented Medical Records (POMR) are used. Nothing is erased from the medical record as the treatment changes and general phrases, so common in the nurses' Kardex system, do not exist. Research has shown that nurses' records are brief and ritualized. Phrases such as 'slept well', 'good day', 'up and about' are used which give no real indication of the patient's progress, the care that he has been given or how effective is that care.

Care planning and the nursing process   Care planning and the nursing process have become closely linked. Many nurses, however, dislike the term 'the nursing process', because it is seen as being too high-powered or meaningless and use other though similar terms to describe planning care, for example 'total patient care'. Again, this reflects the value nurses traditionally place on the importance of practical rather than theoretical ability; indeed, nurses who do take a more questioning thinking approach are often discouraged from doing so. The development of nursing in a way which will encourage both thinking, and questioning is, however, very important if nursing is to be a true profession and provide effective nursing care. The nursing process emphasizes the importance of practical nursing skills – it certainly does not deny these as some nurses believe, but also makes nurses think more about what they are doing, why they are doing it and whether or not it is effective.

The importance of written records

In order to be effective the planning of care must be expressed in a permanent form. Only if this is done can nurses ensure the transfer of accurate information over a period of time and between members of the nursing and health care teams. Such permanent documentation is achieved through the development of a written Nursing Care Plan, which is a continuous, comprehensive record both of the nursing care a patient should receive and the care he has received.

A Nursing Care Plan should include the following information about the patient:

- relevant information on which to base problem identification

- identification of the patient's actual or likely nursing problems (nursing diagnoses)*
- patient-centred goals or objectives for each problem
- specific nursing instructions to meet these goals
- a report on the patient in relation to each problem
- evaluation of the nursing action in relation to the stated goal.

Exactly how this information is documented will vary. The early documents were very structured (Appendices 2a, 2b, 3, 5 and 6) but over the last few years the trend has been towards a much freer approach, examples of which are to be found in Appendices 7 and 8.

The Nursing Care Plan takes into account the patient's background and environment, his likes and dislikes, his response to his illness and his ability to cope with his illness and with his daily life. A Nursing Care Plan is so individual that it cannot be used for any patient other than the one for whom it was written. Each Nursing Care Plan, therefore, is unique.

A Nursing Care Plan should be in continuous use, being updated as often as any changes occur. It should not be something which is written down on the day of admission and then put aside and left unchanged and unused. Because of this updating the Nursing Care Plan contains all the most relevant information about the patient and therefore accurately reflects his condition at any time. Because a Nursing Care Plan is a written plan, it is available to all those involved in the care of the patient both as an aid to making decisions about future care and in assessing the effect of care already given to that patient. A Nursing Care Plan then becomes the basis for reporting sessions, both nurse to nurse and nurse to other members of the health care team.

What form should Nursing Care Plans take?

The type of format used will vary from one ward or community setting to another according to the needs of the patients. Nursing staff have to be educated to think about nursing care in a more professional and individual way. Part of the problem

---

* Both these terms will be used in the text.

in introducing Nursing Care Plans is the discomfort felt by nurses on having to think about the reasons for the care they are giving and on having to consider whether it is what the patient wants or needs at the time. It also means abandoning some old ideas about ward routine. Such thinking involves change and change is uncomfortable.

Organization of the clinical setting

Nursing Care Plans, however, do not and cannot exist in isolation. Other factors are important, such as the organization of the clinical setting and the nurses working within that setting.

Only the organization of care planning within the hospital setting will be discussed in detail. Other areas of clinical practice such as community nursing function on a one-to-one basis in any case and are not faced, therefore, with such organizational problems.

Within hospitals, the organization of work within different wards and departments varies. Basically however there are four ways of organizing patient care:

task allocation
team nursing
patient allocation
primary nursing.

An understanding of the difference between these methods is necessary, since the method employed has considerable implications for care planning: they are outlined below (see also Chapter 9).

What is task allocation?

Task allocation is the assignment of individual and not necessarily related jobs or tasks to a particular nurse. For example, Student Nurse Smith takes all the patients' temperatures; Pupil Nurse Jones carries out all four-hourly mouth care and Staff Nurse Adams carries out all the dressings. This system is still widely used although it has been shown to be less effective than a patient allocation system as well as causing a high-degree of frustration among nurses (Bendall 1971; Briggs Report HMSO 1972). Task allocation has been perpetuated over the years as the traditional method, and tradition is a very comfortable thing that requires less thought and effort than a new system.

Task allocation has a number of disadvantages. Firstly, it creates a job hierarchy. Jobs such as bathing or feeding helpless patients are considered to be of low status and are frequently allocated to junior learners or auxiliaries, while tasks of a more technical nature are considered to have a high status and are allocated to senior nurses. Thus, activities which enable the nurse to spend time with a patient and to develop a personal relationship with him, and which give her an excellent opportunity to observe him directly, are seldom performed by senior or qualified members of staff. Secondly, patient care becomes fragmented, and is seen as a series of unrelated tasks, each performed by a different nurse. Thirdly, task allocation tends to produce a rigid ward routine, to which the nurses adhere rather than the routine being subordinated to the needs of the patients.

What is team nursing?

In team nursing the nursing staff are organized into teams, each of which is led by a staff or senior student nurse. Each team is allocated a group of patients. The team leader is responsible for planning the care of these patients either by a system of patient allocation or by task allocation – more frequently it is the latter. Team nursing does reduce the number of nurses who care for each patient at any one time; however, unless patient allocation within the team is practised, it does not provide individualized care.

What is patient allocation?

With patient allocation, each nurse is allocated her own small group of patients. If staffing permits, one nurse can act as a 'runner' as well as being allocated fewer and/or lower dependency patients of her own. She can then help other nurses with procedures, such as bed-making and lifting, which require two nurses. Alternatively, two nurses can always work together when necessary, but the nurse to whom the patients have been allocated assumes responsibility for them and is accountable to the Ward Sister. Patient allocation does *not*

mean that one nurse must carry out all the care for her patients, but it does mean that the nurse is responsible for the planning of that care. Trained nurses can plan the nursing care for their own patients. Learners and inexperienced nurses will have to be supervised by Sister or a staff nurse.

The length of time for which patients are allocated to their nurse varies – eg. for one span of duty only, for a longer period such as a week or for the whole of a patient's stay in hospital, and this will affect how and when care is planned, in particular the extent to which a nurse can be responsible for short and long-term planning.

What is primary nursing?

Primary nursing means that one nurse is responsible for the care planned for a patient – 24-hours a day, 7-days-a-week. Thus the primary nurse admits the patient, assesses him, defines his nursing problems, goals and nursing instructions and cares for him whenever she is on duty.

Clearly, not all members of the nursing staff can be primary nurses since they have to be able to accept that level of responsibility. In most cases this will mean that the primary nurse is qualified, in order to ensure that she is competent.

Equally clearly, the primary nurse cannot be on duty at all times and care has to be delegated by her to another member of the nursing team (secondary or associate nurse). That nurse, depending on the needs of the patient, may provide care as planned by the primary nurse or may change and add to the plan if necessary. Patients who are seriously ill, for example, will have problems which change rapidly and therefore every nurse caring for the patient must be able to alter and up-date the Care Plan as and when necessary.

Traditionally, the ward sister has accepted the care planning responsibilities of the primary nurse. Where staffing permits, primary nursing shifts that responsibility on to each and every competent nurse.

How to co-ordinate individual care with ward routines

As previously stated, one of the reasons why care planning is alien to traditional patterns of nursing care is because the latter

involves strict adherence to a rigid ward routine. Lelean (1974) has said 'Adherence to routine could in part be due to procedure-centred nursing, thus the patient's care was never seen in total and her needs never fully met'. The routine, in effect, became more important than the needs of the patient. Lelean suggested that one reason why certain tasks, such as hourly bedpans or two-hourly pressure area care, were not carried out as instructed by the Sister was that nurses were so busy trying to keep up with the routine that anything which interrupted this was regarded as a nuisance and tended to be forgotten or put off until such time as it fitted in. Lelean went on to suggest that as this approach adversely affected patient care, matters would be improved if each patient were to be treated according to his individual needs and not be made to fit into an inflexible ward system.

For example, if Mr Smith is the last on Student Nurse Black's list of bed baths to be done, he may not have his bed bath until 11.00 or 11.30 am. This in itself may not matter. However, if Sister has also said that Mr Smith is to sit out in a chair for an hour in the morning before lunch and an hour in the afternoon, then the morning 'hour' cannot be fitted in. Getting all the beds done by mid-day becomes the important goal for Student Nurse Black, and not the individual needs of the patient.

With patient allocation, routine can be replaced by a more flexible system which takes into account the patient's total needs. Of course, certain fixed times such as meals, treatment and investigations usually have to be taken into account, but since these will be done for the patient by his own nurse she can plan the remainder of his day around these activities.

Advantages of individualized care (patient allocation or primary nursing)

(a) It is more satisfying Task allocation has been shown to be a source of great frustration among nurses. The nurse feels that she is not caring for the patient as an individual but is merely performing a set of unrelated tasks. Although both nurses and patients find individualized care more satisfying many wards still use task allocation. This kind of discrepancy creates a considerable amount of stress.

(b) It expands the role of the nurse   The use of individualized care means re-defining the role of qualified nurses. The emphasis is on their role as practitioners supervising less experienced nurses as well as teaching learners by example as they carry out bedside care.

Because each nurse is responsible for the care of her own patients the Sister's role changes to that of a clinical supervisor, always available for consultation in case of difficulty but relieved of many interruptions, since she can refer many queries to the nurses who are actually responsible for the patient in question. She therefore has more time to attend to overall planning of her ward, to teach, to advise and to develop her own and her staff's clinical skills.

(c) It helps learners (as also does team nursing)   Individualised care (and team nursing) benefits the learner. Both systems help her to gain confidence and experience in caring for patients, yet with supervision. Learners gain great satisfaction from knowing that they are playing a more important role in the planning as well as in the giving of care and that they have been made responsible for 'their' patients. At the same time they know they have support from more senior nurses and are not just left alone to cope unaided. The learner can also get to know her patient better, understand the precise reason why aspects of care should be prescribed and performed, and have the opportunity of raising questions with senior nurses as well as with medical staff. Individualized care (and team nursing) also play a part in better preparation of the learner for her practical assessments by ensuring that the relevant experience has been gained.

(d) It leads to the patient being seen as a person   Although team nursing is a vast improvement on task allocation, patient allocation or primary nursing is necessary to make nursing care truly individualized. The number of patients allocated to each nurse will depend upon several factors:
  - the seniority and experience of the nurse
  - the nursing care needs of the patient
  - the number of high-dependency patients in the ward
  - the number of nurses on duty
  - the total number of patients in the ward.

When a patient is looked after by his 'own nurse' there is a stronger feeling of identity and security: the patient develops a special relationship with that nurse and always knows to which nurse he can go for help. Ward activities revolve around the patients' needs rather than the ward routine. Because there is no pressure to complete baths, dressings and beds by mid-day, other aspects of care, eg. two-hourly turns, can be carried out as prescribed and the work is spaced out more evenly over the day.

(e) It improves ward communication Patient allocation improves written and verbal communication. A nurse who is responsible for the total care of a patient knows more about, and can give a better report on that patient than one who may nurse him for only a few minutes at a time. She is also able to report on all facets of her patient's condition, eg. state of skin, healing of wound, level of pain, mental state, etc. She is the best person to give verbal and written reports about the patient. The ward sister always knows who to ask for information about a patient's condition and progress; similarly, the medical staff can be taught to ask the patient's nurse for information rather than always asking Sister.

Naturally, Sister retains overall responsibility so she will need to hear the reports on all the patients in order to co-ordinate care. However, the introduction of care planning rounds, and 'nurse-to-nurse' handovers should be tried as they provide the opportunity for more detailed discussion of the patients' needs and progress.

References

Bendall E (1971) The learning process in student nurses. *Nursing Times*, 67 (43, 44), 169, occasional papers

Briggs A (1972) *Report of the Committee on Nursing*. London: HMSO

McManus R (1952) Assumption of functions of nursing. In *Regional Planning for Nursing and Nursing Education*. Report of Conference, Plymouth, New Hampshire, 1950. New York: Columbia University Teachers' College Bureau of Publications

Mayers (1983) *A Systematic Approach to Nursing Care Plans*. Norwalk. Appleton-Century Crofts

Chapter 2

From theory into practice

Talking about and writing about Nursing Care Plans is all very well, but it is the translation of words into actions that is the real test of its value. There is an increasing number of hospitals where care planning and the nursing process are being tried. Much can be gained from the experience of others so this chapter describes our experience in the hope that others can benefit from our mistakes as well as our successes. All the ideas described in this book have been tried by ward sisters and learners.

As a preliminary step, we looked at what other nurses were doing or had done in relation to using such plans and the nursing process. Furthermore, since doctors use a problem-orientated format their approach was also studied. The problem-orientated record was developed by Weed (1969) and its use has become widespread in the USA; it is also used by an increasing number of doctors in the United Kingdom. The literature provided both knowledge about the theories and concepts and practical examples of the formats used.

The nursing process became the framework within which the ideas and plans were developed, in conjunction with a model of nursing care (Fig 1) developed by Hunt (1977). Originally, the Nursing Care Plan contained three components: one for assessment, one for the plan and one for the continuing record. In essence the need for these three components remains; however, although the assessment remains separate, the planning and recording of care may be documented in a variety of ways.

For any system to be acceptable it must meet a number of

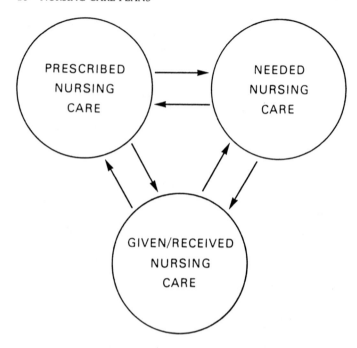

Fig 1 Nursing care: a theoretical model

requirements, i.e.
- be easy for nurses to use
- be large enough
- be standardized and yet meet the needs of different wards and departments

Assessment record   Frequently, this will be called the Nursing History. At first, most nursing histories were very structured, but recently a much more open and flexible approach has been adopted by a number of hospitals, a trend which has been accelerated by the increasing application of nursing theory to care planning. Each approach has its advantages and disadvantages. Certainly upon the initial introduction of care planning a structured format is probably necessary, but as nurses become more skilled and knowledgeable a less structured approach becomes more useful. It has the advantage, too, of enabling the forms to be standardized and yet be used in different clinical areas because they can be used in a flexible way.

The Care Plan   The core of the Nursing Care Plan is the Care Plan itself. A problem-orientated approach is essential. Nursing problems are first identified so that the nursing goals can be established and the care required to achieve those goals prescribed. Continuous evaluation of progress then needs to be documented, although it should be emphasized that this does not necessarily mean that something – anything – has to be written every day. Use can also be made of flow charts, and other kinds of charts and forms. The important thing is that the information should be relevant, accurate, meaningful and used.

Introducing Nursing Care Plans

Getting started   Like most projects which involve trying out something new or different, particularly when the benefits are not immediately apparent, writing a Nursing Care Plan presents the problem of where to begin. 'This is just more writing' or 'I've been planning care for ages, why should I write it down?' or 'I'm too busy nursing patients to write Nursing Care Plans' are all reasons given by nurses for not wanting to start them – these are really just excuses and not valid reasons at all. Anyone can start – all that is really needed is the desire to do so and a willingness to expend some time and effort, especially at the beginning.

Writing a Nursing Care Plan is really a simple procedure once the basic steps are known and understood, especially problem identification and the setting of goals. It is simple because the steps are logical, building upon one another in an organized way. Many nurses think along the lines of care planning, but usually their approach is neither systematic nor problem-orientated. Producing a Nursing Care Plan involves using these thought processes to identify and plan care, to solve or relieve nursing problems, and then putting thoughts down on paper for all members of the health care team to see and use. This is particularly important in situations where learners or inexperienced nurses will be responsible for giving much of the care. By using this method of documentation they can find out easily what care is prescribed, the reasons for specific nursing action and what that action should achieve as far as the patient is concerned.

What will Nursing Care Plans achieve?

There is no such thing as a perfect Nursing Care Plan, nor will one 'cure' an incurable problem. Even the best plan cannot ensure that the patient will receive effective care. Good Nursing Care Plans come with knowledge, with practice and with experience. Mistakes or omissions in one Nursing Care Plan should mean that the same mistakes or omissions do not occur the next time around. Success in solving a particular nursing problem should mean that this approach can be used the next time the same problem occurs. This application of information – the avoidance of mistakes, the use of successful methods – cannot be anything but beneficial to the patient because it ensures that he receives the most effective care. The problem-orientated approach challenges many of our accepted practices and procedures, and in its implementation it is bound to challenge more. It is a challenge we should and can meet, and we should enjoy doing so for it will provide us with the means of enabling nurses to achieve their full potential in caring for patients. Such improved care can only raise the standards of the nursing profession.

Summary

Theory cannot be translated into practice without some effort. It requires not only the co-operation and participation of the nursing staff but also a considerable input of teaching time. At the present time the nursing process is still not taught to all learners so the teaching of care planning on the wards has to include the basic concepts as well as their practical application. Obviously, the best approach is where the school and wards complement and reinforce each other's teaching; positive encouragement from administration is also necessary. It is vital that Nursing Care Plans become accepted as an integral part of nursing practice rather than as something taught in school but too impractical or theoretical for day-to-day use. Their use as a continuing everyday tool in the wards is essential.

Implementation on a wider scale demands a more formal in-service education programme. Each course must include an introduction to the theoretical background, to the uses which can be made of nursing theories and to the practicality of the system that they, the nurses, will be using. Most important, senior nurses and teaching staff should always listen to what the ward sisters and staff are saying. They must be aware of the fears and anxieties (real or imagined) about adopting a new way of planning nursing care and include the ideas and thoughts of the staff on the wards when introducing any changes.

Reference

Hunt J M (1977) *The Nursing Care Project*. Tower Hamlets Health District, unpublished report

Chapter 3

Helpful Hints

In most countries there is an increasing interest in and emphasis on making nursing care more individual, as well as planning it on a more scientific basis. We believe this to be necessary, and that it will have important benefits for the patient; we have therefore set out some hints for nurses, nurse managers and nurse tutors who are interested in implementing Nursing Care Plans or the nursing process, which may be useful before embarking on large or even small-scale implementation of the approaches we have described.

1 Find some people who are already implementing Nursing Care Plans or some form of individualized care planning and talk to them. Ask them to come and speak to others in your hospital.
2 Start small. Do not attempt to create a Nursing Care Plan package to try on a ward and then expect the ward to begin implementation straight away.
3 Try one thing at a time – start with, for example, patient allocation or using individual work cards or, perhaps, nursing histories.
4 Find one ward sister who is at least interested in trying to use Nursing Care Plans.
5 Make sure the new system is practicable under existing staffing levels and workload.
6 Go slowly. Do not rush people or force them into accepting a completely new system straight away.
7 Involve the School of Nursing as soon as possible to provide both ward and school-based teaching.

8   Organize workshops or in-service courses for qualified nurses to teach them the techniques of implementation.

9   Listen to, and incorporate suggestions from wards which are using Nursing Care Plans.

10 Give the nurses as much praise and encouragement as is justified. Concentrate on the patients and nurses and not on the system alone.

Care planning using patient-centred Nursing Care Plans based on the nursing process has a number of advantages over other methods of planning and recording nursing care:

1   When presented and taught step-by-step it is easy to understand and more likely to be adopted at ward level.

2   Nurses at all levels of training and seniority begin to think of the reasons behind the prescribed care, so that care is not given just because 'Sister says so' or because 'that's the way we've always done it' but because it is known to be effective.

3   Setting goals ensures that nurses and patients know what they are trying to achieve, and allows the care to be evaluated in terms of whether or not the goals have been met.

4   It lends itself to a completely new method of teaching learners.

5   It creates further possibilities for multi-disciplinary approaches to care by its easy accessibility to doctors, physiotherapists and other members of the health care team. It is possible to use this type of format as a basis for a problem-orientated patient record which includes all problems, goals and actions (medical, nursing, etc.) defined by all members of the health care team.

6   It encourages learners to take a more active part in planning patient care under guidance from senior members of staff. This involvement will make nursing more stimulating and challenging to learners.

7   It encourages patients to take part in the planning of their care, by enabling them to know the goals towards which they can aspire, and gives them something positive to work towards.

8 Nursing becomes more effective in that care does not continue to be used if it is not proving to be effective. This means that the patient will not be given nursing care which is not working.

The nursing process has been talked and written about at some length. Ultimately, however, the only test of the validity of the approaches described in this book lies in their implementation and the effect that this will have on nurses and the wellbeing of patients. Nursing Care Plans using a problem-orientated approach are tangible evidence of the implementation of the nursing process. They are exciting and challenging to use: they are the nursing process at work.

The Five Stages of Care Planning

Assessment
Nursing Diagnosis
Planning
Implementation
Evaluation

Chapter 4

Assessment

This chapter is about the first step in care planning – assessment – without which effective care planning is impossible. Assessment includes:

collecting information, and

interpreting information.

How assessment is carried out will differ from district to district, hospital to hospital and even from ward to ward. In any event assessment will always reflect the beliefs which nurses hold about people, society, health and illness and nursing itself. This chapter differs greatly from the assessment chapter in the first edition of the book in that there is a shift in emphasis from a highly-structured guide to taking a nursing history towards a look at the wider implications of assessing patients. Each district or hospital will look at assessment differently depending upon its own stage of development in the use of Nursing Care Plans and the nursing process.

Collecting the information

Nurses increasingly use a model or theory of nursing as the framework for care planning in general and for assessment in particular. The information which nurses decide to collect will therefore depend upon their beliefs about man, society, health, illness and nursing. Maslow (1970), for example, identified certain basic needs which he listed in a hierarchical order as a way of indicating that certain needs take priority over the others (Fig 2). Physiological needs must be met first, so people are motivated to meet these needs for themselves

Fig 2

before they are motivated to meet higher needs. In an ideal situation, a person who has reached the stage where he is motivated towards his own self-esteem or self-actualization, does so because the needs in the lower part of the hierarchy have been adequately met.

Henderson's 14 activities of living (1968) and Roper *et al*'s activities of daily living (1980) are essentially based on human needs which have been translated into day to day activities (see Figs 3 and 4). If a hospital or district uses a human needs approach in a practical form as described by Henderson's or Roper's activities of living, they will assess patients in terms of their ability to carry out these activities. This human needs approach reflects certain beliefs about people, society, health, illness, and in some part, nursing. These, or any other beliefs which nurses have, should be well thought out and even written down and discussed in wards and in units within or outside hospital. They will be used to determine what information will be required when assessing patients.

1	Breathe normally
2	Eat and drink adequately
3	Eliminate by all avenues of elimination
4	Move and maintain a desirable posture
5	Sleep and rest
6	Select suitable clothing, dress and undress
7	Maintain body temperature
8	Keep the body clean, well-groomed and protect the skin
9	Avoid dangers in the environment
10	Communicate with each other in expressing emotions, needs, fears, questions and ideas
11	Worship according to his faith
12	Work at something which provides a sense of accomplishment
13	Play or participate in some form of recreation
14	Learn, discover or satisfy curiosity which leads to 'normal' development and health

Fig 3 Daily living activities (Henderson 1960)

The nursing history sheet is the written record of the information which has been obtained upon admission. It may be highly structured, as is usually the case when nurses are in the early stages of collecting information and taking nursing histories, or it may be less structured, as is happening in those centres which began with structured formats but have now recognized the limitations imposed by a structured nursing history sheet. Examples of structured and less-structured nursing history sheets will be found in the Appendices. At the present time, most nursing history sheets in use include relevant information about the patient's past health, present health problems, social history, habits of daily living, personal likes and dislikes, certain physical and emotional observations made by the nurse and a general overview of the patient's condition at the time the assessment was made.

The idea of beginning with statements of beliefs about people, society, health, illness and nursing is a new one to

1	Maintain a safe environment
2	Communicating
3	Breathing
4	Eating and drinking
5	Eliminating
6	Personal cleansing and dressing
7	Controlling body temperature
8	Mobilising
9	Working and playing
10	Expressing sexuality
11	Sleeping
12	Dying

Fig 4 Activities of living based on a model of living (Roper, Logan & Tierney 1980)

many nurses. And yet, without such explicit statements of beliefs there is little understanding of what assessment information is required, why it is being collected and how all the information interrelates. The statement of beliefs need not be high-powered or full of jargon: it merely clarifies, explaining clearly and explicitly to all nurses on the particular ward or unit what kind of information is needed in order to be able to assess patients and to plan appropriate nursing care.

What skills are required to assess patients?   Several important skills are required to assess patients properly, whether on admission or to assess day-to-day progress. Two such skills (communication skills and observation skills) are discussed in this chapter and other skills will be described in Chapter 11.

Communication skills   If nurses are to learn how to assess and how to improve their assessment techniques communication skills must be an integral part of both basic nursing education and of continuing education. Some teaching of communication skills can take place in the nursing school, especially if experiential teaching methods are used, but continued teaching about communication skills must be carried on in wards, units and in the community. The most effective way for nurses, especially junior nurses, to learn good communication skills, in terms of taking a good nursing history, is by observing their seniors. Senior nurses will always be role models for junior nurses. It is therefore inappropriate to expect a first ward nurse to take a good nursing history if she has had no previous opportunity to develop communication skills. Ideally, junior nurses should observe a senior nurse taking a history and have the opportunity to discuss the communication skills involved. This requires senior nurses to have good communication skills and the ability to communicate skilfully during a nursing history interview.

How information is obtained is very important. Questions should be concise and to the point, and only one question should be asked at a time. It is better to ask 'Do you have any children' and afterwards 'Do you have any other dependents'? as separate questions rather than ask 'Do you have any children or other dependents?' The nurse should also use language which the patient understands. Lay terms should be used as far as possible so that the patient understands the question. If the patient is a doctor, nurse or other health professional, however, more technical language might be employed when asking questions. To the lay person one might ask 'Do you need to get up in the night to pass water?' while of a doctor or nurse one might ask instead 'Do you suffer from nocturia?'

Questions may be open-ended or closed. Open-ended questions are those which require the patient to use his own words to answer the questions. Closed questions can merely be answered by 'yes' or 'no.' Obviously, open ended questions will elicit more information from the patient. 'How do you feel today?' will provide more relevant, detailed information on how the patient is feeling than 'Do you feel all right today?' Questions should also be phrased so they do not bias the patient's answer. Asking 'Do you feel nauseated as well?' might make the patient think that the nurse expects him to feel nauseated.

Interpersonal skills are vital to good communication and when taking a nursing history it is important to have the approach and attitude. Remember that the patient may be anxious, nervous or even angry, as well as being unwell. The nurse, therefore, must be sensitive about how much questioning and discussion the patient can tolerate. She must also give her full attention to the patient, both in terms of her tone of voice and manner as well as by her position; the best way to do this is to bring a chair or stool to the bed or chair, and sit in such a way that she has equal eye level with the patient. This lets the patient know the nurse has time and that she wants to listen. The nurse must also try to keep discussion flowing, yet not restrict answers. Too often nursing history interviews come across as interrogations: this is usually because the nurse is in a hurry, the discussion and questioning is chopped and stilted or else she is too preoccupied with going through the history sheet question by question to maintain the flow of the discussion. It is also wise to check with the patient about the information you are receiving – this will ensure that the nurse has perceived the information in the same way as the patient meant it. This can be done occasionally injecting a clarifying sentence such as 'It seems to me that what you are saying is . . .'

Privacy is essential: other patients must not be able to hear what the patient is saying. This is not always easy, particularly if beds are close together or if the patient is hard of hearing, but every effort must be made to ensure privacy. If the patient can walk and there is an empty day room or office on the ward, it may be more appropriate to take the patient away from his bed whilst obtaining a nursing history. The interview should be conducted in peace and quiet and be free from interruptions, if possible. The nurse must not appear to be hurried since, if the patient suspects that the nurse is busy or preoccupied with time, he may try to rush his answers.

Before beginning the nursing history interview the nurse must explain why she has to ask the questions and what will be done with the information. It is a good idea for the nurse to begin by approaching the patient with a warm smile and, by giving her name, introducing herself to him. A simple explanation of why she is asking the questions can follow, as well as some statement that the information will be used in order to plan the best possible care for that patient. As already mentioned, good eye contact and pulling up a chair close to the bed are ways of 'telling' a patient that the nurse is interested in him. This is part of a type of communication skill known as non-verbal communication by which we send messages to people without using words, eg. by facial expression, eye contact, touching and nodding or shaking our heads. Interest in the patient and warmth towards him can each be expressed non-verbally; for example, if you lean forward towards the patient you will give him the additional message that you are interested.

The patient will also send non-verbal messages to the nurse. The nurse should observe the patient's facial expression carefully: for example, she should observe how well he maintains eye contact with her because lack of eye contact can be his way of expressing embarrassment, worry or fear. The nurse can also tell what the patient might be feeling by observing his movements, such as fidgeting or wringing his hands. These non-verbal cues from patients should be checked by the nurse to make sure that she perceives the messages accurately. Making an observation statement such as 'I see you are twisting your ring on your finger quite a bit . . .' gives the patient the opportunity to express his anxiety, if he so chooses, and at the same time enables the nurse to confirm that her perceptions of patient anxiety are accurate.

The information recorded on the nursing history sheet should be as free as possible from judgemental phrases such as 'good' or 'bad'. What is good to one nurse may not be perceived as good by another.

Observation skills   When one mentions the word observations to most nurses, they immediately think of temperature, pulse, respirations and blood pressure. This is a great pity, because it detracts from many of the important observation skills which nurses acquire and use when assessing patients. On admission, there are many things which nurses should observe and record about their patients; for example the one mentioned earlier – non-verbal cues.

Among other observation skills which must be used to assess patients are the following. Observing how well the patient hears, eg. do you have to repeat most of the things you've asked; observing how well he walks or moves around; observing his skin – perhaps while helping him to undress for the doctor's examination or if you help him to wash or bathe.

Physical Condition		Mental Condition		Activity		Mobility		Incontinent	
Good	4	Alert	4	Ambulent	4	Full	4	Not	4
Fair	3	Apathetic	3	Walk/help	3	Sl. limited	3	Occasionally	3
Poor	2	Confused	2	Chairbound	2	V. limited	2	Usually/Ur.	2
V. Bad	1	Stuporous	1	Bedfast	1	Immobile	1	Doubly	1

Total the scores from each of the five categories. Any score below 14 indicates that the patient is at risk.

Fig 5 The Norton Scale (Norton, McLaren & Exton-Smith 1975)

Even the visible areas of skin – hands, arms, face – can provide information about his overall skin condition: dehydrated skin has its own characteristics, as have oedematous skin, a rash or jaundiced skin.

Assessment by observing the condition of the mouth can be very important especially in the elderly patient, the dehydrated patient, the unconscious patient or the patient who is receiving cytotoxic drug therapy. The nurse can use a small pencil torch and a disposable tongue depressor to look into the patient's mouth if he is at risk. The condition of the teeth and/or dentures can also be observed at this time.

Very few reliable assessment tools are available for nurses to observe and assess their patients. The nursing history sheet is a tool for recording some observations and assessment information. The Norton Scale (1975) is another observational tool with which to assess patients: it provides a concrete way of measuring and recording susceptibility to pressure sores in the elderly. The Scale is based on a scoring system whereby certain marks are given in five areas, mobility, incontinence, activity, physical; condition and mental state (see Fig 5). The nurse determines the patient's score for each category and adds the five scores together. A score of 14 or less indicates that the patient is at risk of developing pressure sores and appropriate nursing action must be taken, such as 1-to-2-hourly relief of pressure. Scores can be taken at regular intervals, eg. weekly, to determine if there is any change in the patient's susceptibility to pressure sores.

Observation skills include recognizing many of the non-verbal cues mentioned previously as a way of assessing the patient's emotional state. Other observations, such as the extent to which the patient socializes with other patients or how well he is eating can indicate something about his emotional state.

In summary, many skills must be acquired and developed by nurses in order to assess patients completely and accurately. Two such skills have been discussed in this chapter: good communication skills allow the nurse to create the right climate for information to be obtained from the patient, and good observation skills are also important to supplement assessment information with that which the patient will not necessarily be able to tell the nurses.

Who assesses the patient and takes the nursing history? The nurse who has acquired the necessary skills is the nurse who can assess and take a nursing history. Both learners and qualified nurses can, and indeed must, be taught these skills. It is inappropriate for the most junior or inexperienced nurses to take a nursing history or assess patients unless they are closely supervised by a senior, more skilled nurse. If unskilled nurses take nursing histories, the information is often incomplete. The junior nurse also does not have the experience and knowledge to interpret the information accurately. Communication and observation skills must be taught, practised and reinforced as they are highly complex skills. They are no less important or complex than other nursing skills and should be regarded with the same importance. It is unlikely, for example, that a ward sister would allow a very junior nurse to do a complex tracheostomy dressing or change an underwater seal drain until she had developed a certain amount of expertise in these tasks. Assessment skills should be given equal importance when deciding who is to take a nursing history or assess a patient.

Teaching these skills and reinforcing them is essential for both learners and qualified nurses: how these skills may be taught and reinforced will be discussed in Chapter 11.

Other sources of information Until now we have concentrated on the information which is obtained from the patient, whether it is from the nursing history or by observing him. But additional information, or in some cases all the information, might come from other sources. Firstly, the nurse's own knowledge provides a source of information from which to assess patients: this includes knowledge of disease processes, anatomy and physiology, people's reactions to stress and anxiety and the effect of illness on the body's systems.

Secondly, there is expert knowledge which the nurse can seek in order to provide information which she lacks. Such information could come from the patient's medical notes, from more knowledgeable nursing, medical and paramedical colleagues or from reference books and other published material.

Thirdly, information about a patient can come from those who know him well, such as family and friends. Such sources are particularly important if the patient is too ill or otherwise unable to give the information himself.

Naturally, not all of these sources have to be tapped for every patient but whenever and wherever possible the nurse should be encouraged to seek additional information and when she has done so the information should be welcomed and used by senior members of staff. Effort should not go unrewarded for, if it does, it is less likely that the effort will continue.

Interpreting the Information

Once all the information is collected – through nursing history, observation and from other sources – the information must then be used. It is an invasion of privacy to gather personal information and not use it for planning and giving nursing care: *if it is not going to be used, it should not have been obtained in the first place*.

After gathering information about a patient, the nurse should re-read it all and try to relate the items to each other in order to build up a picture of the patient's condition. Again, this is a skill that requires teaching, practice and reinforcement, and the nurse who is unskilled or inexperienced at it should be supervised. The supervising senior nurse should, when interpreting the information herself, discuss and explain to the inexperienced nurse what the various items of information tell her about the patient, how important these are, and how she arrives at the interpretation.

One of our earliest experience with inaccurate interpretation of assessment information occurred when a junior nurse was left to take a nursing history with no supervision. She learned from the patient that he only slept for 4 or 5 hours per night and always awoke at about 4.30 in the morning. The nurse's response to this information was to ask the house officer to prescribe some sleeping tablets. Fortunately, the ward sister was given the information about that patient's sleep pattern and went to check it with him. She discovered that this had been the patient's normal sleep pattern for years, that he was quite happy to leave things as they were and wanted no sleeping tablets.

Interpreting information is a skill which must be used to ensure that the right conclusions are drawn from all the assessment information. It is the accurate interpretation of information that identifies those problems patients have which can be alleviated through appropriately planned nursing care.

Summary

Assessment is a complex activity which requires many skills in order to be carried out with the patient's best interest in mind. Collecting information and interpreting it are each components of the process of assessing patients. A nurse has to acquire many skills in order to assess the needs of her patients accurately. Even more important, she must understand what she is assessing and why. This can only be done when each ward, or hospital or district begins its implementation of care planning by first identifying its beliefs and values about people, society, health, illness and nursing (which will be discussed further in Chapter 11). Beliefs and values in these five areas lead to an understanding of what it is that is being assessed in the patient and why it is being done. Without explicit beliefs upon which to base assessment, the nursing history becomes merely a piece of paper to be filled in.

References

Henderson V (1960) *Basic Principles of Nursing Care*. Geneva: ICN.
Maslow A (1970) *Motivation and Personality*. New York: Harper Row
Norton D, McLaren R & Exton-Smith A (1975) *An Investigation of Geriatric Nursing Problems in Hospital*. Edinburgh: Churchill Livingstone
Roper N, Logan W & Tierney A (1980) *The Elements of Nursing*. Edinburgh: Churchill Livingstone

Chapter 5

Nursing Diagnosis

When all the assessment information has been gathered and has been interpreted, nursing diagnoses can be made. In the first edition of this book, we used the phrase 'nursing problem'. We found that many nurses experience difficulty in understanding what a nursing problem is and the difference between a 'nursing need' and a 'nursing problem', with the result that the two were often used (incorrectly) interchangeably.

All human beings have needs – whether they are expressed as Maslow described them, or Henderson, or Roper. 'Problems' arise when needs are unmet. One of the reasons why many care plans are so wordy and contain a great deal of unused information is that nurses have, in many instances, been documenting needs rather than problems. If a particular need is being met, there is no problem; if a problem exists, it is because a particular need is not being met. In other words, needs are basic to all people and are individual to each person, and problems are the concern of nurses.

What is a nursing diagnosis?

Use of the term 'nursing diagnosis' eases the widespread difficulty that people have in distinguishing between a need and a problem. The word 'diagnosis' is a familiar one to all nurses in the context of the patient's medical diagnosis, for a diagnosis is the term used by doctors to describe what it is that is wrong with a patient that requires medical intervention. When nurses discern that a patient has a problem that requires *nursing* intervention and describe and define exactly what is wrong with him, they are making a *nursing diagnosis.*

A nursing diagnosis is made from the interpretation of information which has been obtained by assessing a patient. A nursing diagnosis is a statement of something of concern to the patient or the nurse or to both. It is any difficulty – or problem – which the patient experiences or might possibly experience as a result of his illness, which can be helped, solved or prevented by nursing intervention. The nursing diagnosis is the *reason* why any nursing care needs to be given.

Not all disabilities indicate a need for nursing intervention, because they do not necessarily cause problems for the patient which require nursing care. Equally, not all people with the same disease or disability will have the same nursing problems. Often a patient has adapted to his illness or disability so that no nursing intervention is necessary because no problem exists for that patient. For example, if a patient has lost the use of his right hand but has learned to carry out his daily living activities and meet his own needs to his satisfaction by using his left hand, there is no need for nursing intervention because his needs are being met and no problem can be identified.

A nursing diagnosis consists of a statement of the problem written clearly and concisely and includes all the factors relating to that problem. If a nursing diagnosis, eg. pain, is related to a specific medical diagnosis or known physiological problem, there is no reason why this medical reason should not be included as the reason for the nursing diagnosis (see (Fig 6). From Figure 6 we can see that merely identifying the nursing diagnosis may not provide a complete picture of all the factors relating to the problem.

1	Chest pain caused by angina. She is sweating, has a tachycardia and says she is in pain
2	Anxiety caused by hospitalisation and not really understanding why she has been admitted. She is over-talkative and is constantly wringing her hands

Fig 6 Statement of a patient's nursing problem (an elderly woman with angina)

Writing a nursing diagnosis

A full statement of a nursing diagnosis should contain the following:
- identification of the patient's problem (eg. pain)
- identification of the cause of the problem, if known (eg. angina)
- identification of how the patient is behaving in relation to the problem (eg. sweating, tachycardia, says she is in pain).

We must remember constantly, too, that the nursing diagnosis must be one that can be helped, solved, prevented or ameliorated by *nursing* intervention. By including the cause of the problem and the way the patient is behaving we become more aware of the cause/effect relationship between problems and behaviour and we have a means by which we can begin to monitor our nursing care and measure its effectiveness (see Chapter 8).

A nursing problem or diagnosis can be caused by a physiological disorder, a psychological problem or a social or economic difficulty. Identifying the cause of the problem is important because the same problem (eg. pain) can have a number of different causes. Chest pain, for example, might be caused by angina (as in Figure 6), but it also might be caused by chest infection, trauma, surgery, shingles or cancer. By knowing the cause or reason for the problem, nurses are able to plan the appropriate approach to their nursing care.

If we also identify how the patient behaves, eg. sweating, tachycardia, etc., we are then highlighting what we have observed about the patient with a particular problem. This enables nurses to know what they should be looking for in the future to see if the care they are giving is improving that patient's condition. It gives us a focus by which we can examine the effectiveness of our care – is he less breathless? is her pulse slowing down? is she moving about a bit more? Identifying patient behaviour for each problem is the beginning of planning for evaluation.

Listing nursing diagnoses – deciding priorities

Nursing diagnoses should, as far as possible, be listed in order of priority. Problems arise for nurses because it is often difficult to know which of two (or more) diagnoses has a higher priority than the other. Wherever possible, the priority of the problems should be decided by the patient. Obviously, in a life-threatening situation a senior nurse would decide priorities of care. Another problem with listing priorities is that these often change and what is a high priority on one day is often a lower priority on another day. Many of our present care plan formats do not allow for priorities to change because the problems are written down in the order that they occur rather than in the order of their importance. One solution is to use a care plan format which allows for each nursing diagnosis to be identified on a separate sheet of paper, with the appropriate nursing actions for that problem, as well as its day-to-day progress, on the same single page. If pages are then kept in a ring-binder the order of the pages will be determined by the day-to-day priorities of that patient. An example of this type of format can be found in Appendix 7.

To establish priorities, nurses may wish to turn again to Maslow's hierarchy. Acute physiological problems may be listed first, followed by long-term or possible problems. But again, some problems may be given a high priority even if they are not immediate and acute. Possible pressure sores could be a nursing diagnosis which is made on admission. It may only be listed as a possible problem but if the patient is elderly, thin, incontinent, immobile and confused, this possible problem then becomes one which has a high priority. In this instance we can use as an assessment tool the Norton Scale (see Chapter 4) to help to determine the priority of the nursing diagnosis.

In writing nursing diagnoses, nurses sometimes create problems for a patient which really do not exist merely because they do not know what to write down, or they assume that because a patient has a certain illness, he will automatically have certain problems. The problems or diagnoses which are identified must be perceived as problems or possible problems by the patient as well as by the nurses. Make sure that there is shared perception in identifying problems.

DATE	NO	NURSING DIAGNOSES	
12.1.86	3	Possible pressure sores due to poor skin — because of arthritis previous radiotherapy, general immobility.	Health

Fig 7

Adding and deleting nursing diagnoses from the Care Plan

When using the single-sheet care plan which is most common-ly used by hospitals which have implemented a care planning system (see Figure 7), nursing problems are added at the end of the Care Plan as they arise. To delete diagnoses a line is put through the problem when it no longer exists and the date on which the problem become obsolete is often also recorded (see Chapter 8).

All too often, however, Care Plans are rewritten on new sheets of paper as old nursing diagnoses or problems are deleted and new ones are made. This means that previous nursing problems or diagnoses are forgotten even though they may recur. If the original Care Plan has been discarded there is no record to show what nursing actions solved the problem before. Old care plans, therefore, should never be thrown away merely because they have been rewritten to keep them

.S	NURSING INSTRUCTIONS	REVIEW ON/BY	DATE RESOLVED
tact skin.	(a) Change position every 2 hours; straighten sheets; use drawsheet; 2 nurses to turn patient.	Once daily.	
	(b) Keep skin clean and dry; daily bed bath with assistance. Likes baby lotion on feet and hands.	Daily.	
	(c) Encourage nourishing diet; refer to dietitian.	14.1.86	19.1.86
	To have 2 litres of fluid a day including 3 glasses of milk.	15.1.86	19.1.86

up to date: instead, they should be filed in the patient's records for use, if necessary, in the future. To make it easy to find a previous problem if it should recur, a frontsheet or Nursing Problem Index can be added to the Care Plan where the problems can be listed as they occur with the date of the diagnosis and the date when it was resolved and deleted from the Care Plan. In this way, problems which re occur weeks, months or even years later can be referred to in order that nurses may see which nursing actions were effective in the past. An example of an index to the Care Plan may also be found in Appendices 7 (p. 155) and 8.

Those hospitals or units which use a care plan consisting of an individual sheet of paper for each problem, action and day-to-day progress will find that adding and deleting nursing diagnoses (as well as establishing priorities) is much easier. When a nursing diagnosis is no longer relevant (eg. the problem no longer exists) the sheet of paper for that problem is removed from the Care Plan and placed in the patient's permanent records. If the problem recurs, that sheet of paper is taken out of the permanent record and placed in the care plan ring-binder for that patient and continued, perhaps with updating, as part of the current Care Plan. As new nursing diagnoses are made a new sheet of paper is started for that diagnosis, with new goals, nursing actions and day to day progress recorded. Appendices 7 and 8 contain examples of this.

Summary

A nursing diagnosis is a statment of a patient's problem which has arisen out of unmet needs, whether these are physical, psychological, social, economic or spiritual. Nursing diagnoses are made after a comprehensive assessment has been carried out on admission, and further nursing diagnoses are made during the patient's stay as problems arise and nursing action is indicated. Nursing diagnoses which no longer are relevant because the problem has been solved are deleted from the Care Plan. Well-written, relevant nursing diagnoses are based on problems which are real to the patient. If a nurse, therefore, makes a nursing diagnosis (or identifies a problem) she must check with the patient to make sure that her perception of the problem matches that of the patient. By stating the cause of the problem as well as the way the patient behaves in relation to the problem, the nurse will make the care plans specific to each patient and begin to plan for evaluation of nursing action.

Chapter 6

Planning

Introduction

The next step in care planning is to decide what nursing care a patient will need: this stage is called planning. The information obtained by the nurse during the admission interview, together with her observations and assessment, will enable her to identify the patient's nursing problems: these are then included on the Care Plan with life-threatening problems listed and dealt with first, continuing, less urgent problems second, and possible problems third. Once the nursing problems are listed the nurse can then plan the necessary nursing care.

Planning includes: (Fig 7)

- setting the goal (or expected outcome) for each problem.
- deciding what nursing care will meet the stated goals and writing the appropriate instructions.
- deciding when to review or evaluate each problem to see if the goal is being achieved.

Setting the goals

Goals are set for every nursing problem (Fig 8). The problem list, therefore, is the starting point for this stage of care planning and is obtained from the nurse's

- interpretation of stated facts (received verbally when taking the nursing history)
- observation of the patient's physical condition (eg.

Patient's Nursing Diagnoses	Goals
Acute back pain	Able to sit up and move around freely. Says he has no pain.
Constipation due to enforced bed rest.	Usual, once-daily bowel action.
Lack of appetite so does not eat meals.	Chooses from menu with interest, eats meals, patient says has enjoyed them.
Deep vein thrombosis and chest infection following previous surgery.	Prevention of the complications during this admission

Fig 8   Examples of problems and goals

degree of mobility, condition of skin over pressure areas, physical signs)
- interpretation of any non-verbal information (eg. attitude, mood)
- assessment of information from other sources.

All this information is utilized by the nurse to formulate her Care Plan.

Traditionally, formal identification of patients' nursing problems was rarely carried out but is becoming more usual. It is an approach which can be learned and nurses' ability to identify problems and become proficient in this skill improves with practice and experience.

Whenever or wherever a problem has been defined, a goal then needs to be set, in writing, which specifies the solution (or alleviation) it is hoped will be achieved. When this is done, all the nurses, no matter which span of duty they are working, will understand what the prescribed nursing care is expected to achieve. Furthermore, the patient can also have the same knowledge and so become more involved in his own care. Goal-setting also means that nurses can evaluate the effectiveness of their actions by comparing the result with the goal, thereby identifying whether it has been successfully achieved. Without a goal for each nursing problem, nursing care cannot be evaluated, so there is a risk that care that is ineffective (or less effective) than it should be will be continued. To be measurable, goals have to be stated in quantifiable terms, that is, written as a behavioural response of the patient, a verbal response, an observation or assessment by the nurse, or as a physiological measurement (Fig 9).

GOAL		TYPE OF RESPONSE	
No pain	as shown by	patient sitting up and talking	(behavioural)
		patient says his pain has gone	(verbal)
		colour normal	(observational)
		pulse now 88 beats per minutes	(physiological)

Fig 9 Types of responses for goals

The need for patient-centred goals

Goals should be patient-centred. They should be written in terms of what the patient will be able to do when the problem is solved and not what the nurse will do. Goals should be stated in as precise terms as possible so that they are not open to different interpretations by different nurses. To establish the goals relating to a problem the nurse must decide, firstly, what leads her to recognize that the patient has a problem, and secondly, how she would expect the patient to respond, or what she might expect to see which will convince her that the problem has been solved. The information on which the nurse's decision is made and goals are formulated, will come from three main sources:

    – what the patient tells the nurse about his symptoms
    – how the patient behaves or acts
    – clinical observations of physical signs by the nurse.

Finally, goals should be positive, that is, they should be stated wherever possible in terms of how the patient will respond or behave rather than how he will not. The intervention selected by the nurse should, if practicable, actively involve the patient. A good start in goal-setting is to find out from the patient what he hopes the outcome of any problem will be; his nursing care

DATE	NO	NURSING DIAGNOSES	
16.1.86	1	Dehydration due to inadequate fluid intake, as seen by: decreased urinary output; concentrated urine; dry, dehydrated skin; constipation	(a) Adequa 3000 n
			(b) Moist
			(c) Urina 2000 m SG 10
			(d) Daily

Fig 10

then becomes meaningful rather than an unrelated series of actions. Nurse and patient working in co-operation in this way make the care more effective.

Deciding upon nursing instructions to reach the goals

Nursing instructions are a list of actions which the nurse prescribes in order to achieve the stated goal: these instructions should always be written. Nursing instructions will be aimed at anticipating a possible problem and preventing it from becoming an actual problem. The action or instruction prescribed is specific to that patient and problem. Senior nurses use their knowledge, experience and expertise to decide what to prescribe but junior or inexperienced nurses will obviously need the help of their seniors to decide which actions are appropriate. The nurse must select that action which will best meet the patient's need. On some Care Plans

ALS	NURSING INSTRUCTIONS	REVIEW ON/BY	DATE RESOLVED
dration – take a day.	Fluids to be given so: 1500 mL : 0800 – 1600 1000 mL : 1600 – 2200 500 mL : 2200 – 0800 Offer drinks hourly, of tea, lemon, water. DOES NOT LIKE COFFEE	Daily 1400 2000 0700	
and tongue.	Clean teeth twice daily. Give mouthwashes 4 hourly. Apply Vaseline to lips after mouth care.	Daily	
put of day; o.	Observe and record output. report if less than 1000 mL. Test urine daily for SG: report if abnormal.	Daily	30.1.86
vel action.	Add bran to breakfast cereal; give fruit for dessert; give aperients as prescribed. Record bowel action.	Daily	30.1.86

the nurse may list several possible nursing actions for each problem; this is useful since it makes the nurse aware that there may be more than just *one* action to reach the goal, and also ensures that an alternative is readily available.

Nursing instructions must

- be based upon sound, scientific principles.
- be specific and clear so that no matter which nurse is carrying out the care, she will interpret each instruction in the same way.
- be realistic in terms of the nursing time and skill available to perform the care and
- prescribe care which will achieve the stated goal.

The nursing actions which are most likely to succeed will be based on sound principles, be realistic, work towards an established goal, and be planned with, and explained to, the patient so that he understands not only that something is being done but also why it is being done. Obviously, new ideas should, and must, be tried out – nursing care should be innovative. As long as the proposed nursing procedure is safe there is no reason why it should not be tried, provided that it is evaluated to see if (a) it reaches its goal (b) whether it does so more, or less, effectively that the action it replaces.

Instructions must be specific and explicit   The importance of specificity must be stressed, since this ensures that the patient receives the intended care which the nurse prescribed. Research (Lelean 1974; Hunt 1979) has shown that if instructions are too generalized they will be interpreted in many different ways. Consequently, one nurse's interpretation of such an instruction, eg. 'mobilize' or 'up and about', may be totally different from another nurse's interpretation of the instruction, and from that of the nurse who gave it.

For example, 'encourage fluids' is an instruction which is used frequently. What does it mean? It certainly does not indicate to a nurse how much fluid to give a patient, when to give it, what sort of fluids he needs, how often to give the fluids or in what way they should be given. The result is that the fluid intake of the patient often varies greatly from one day to the next. When the instruction is specific (Fig 10) the patient's intake fluctuates much less.

In many cases the nurse prescribes nursing care which falls entirely within her own sphere of responsibility. However, there will be times when this is not so, when she has to obtain instructions from, or in consultation with, other members of the health care team. Again, these instructions should be precise and detailed enough to ensure they are implemented as intended.

When should the progress of a patient's nursing problem be reviewed or evaluated?

In order that the effectiveness of nursing care can be measured, nurses should state *at the same time as they give the instructions* how soon the nursing care should be reviewed in order to assess whether it is achieving the stated goal. The time limits set for reviewing a goal will vary – what is important is that such time limits are specific to each goal and, furthermore, that they are realistic (Fig 11).

PATIENT'S NURSING PROBLEM	GOALS	REVIEW ON/BY
14.3.80		
Pain from laparotomy incision as seen by:		
–raised pulse	–pulse down to within 70–90 beats/minute	30 minutes
–sweating	–patient no longer sweating	2-hourly
–restlessness	–quiet and peaceful	2-hourly
–patient complaining of pain	–patient says he is pain free	30 minutes & 3¾ hours after injection

Fig 11 Nursing Care Plan – time limits for reviewing goals

With precise time limits such as those illustrated, all nurses work to the same time scale. In the case of an analgesic given to relieve pain, the nurse has decided to wait to see if the drug is acting and, if so, to reassess after 3 3/4 hours to see whether the pain is relieved until the next dose is due. If at either of those times the goal has not been reached, the nurse would then take appropriate action. This may mean informing the medical staff that the analgesia is not having the desired effect, or implementing some nursing care already prescribed for this problem.

By the setting of a specific date or time for the evaluation of nursing actions, all nurses will know not only what the goals are but the anticipated time for their achievement. This ensures that failure of any nursing action to meet the desired goals will be noted, the need for a change will be recognized and the necessary change made.

Summary

Planning begins with the patient's nursing problems. When these have been listed goals can then be set and instructions given for the nursing care to meet these goals. It is important, too, to establish the time limits for reviewing the effect the nursing care has had in solving the problem. Such planning may appear too detailed and cumbersome but its advantage is that every nurse will know exactly what should be done and what the nursing care should achieve, and this makes the extra effort worthwhile.

References

Hunt J (1979) A comparative study to determine the most effective method of communicating nursing instructions. Final Report. The London Hospital. (unpublished).

Lelean S (1974) *Ready for Report, Nurse?* London: Royal College of Nursing

Chapter 7

Implementation

We hope that it is fairly obvious by now that the stages in planning care do not exist in isolation from one another. Each stage overlaps the next. This is especially true when discussing nursing instructions which come into both the planning and the implementation phases. In the former they are written in the Care Plan, in the latter they are carried out. If the implementation of nursing instructions is to be successful the following points should be investigated:
- how the instructions are communicated
- when to carry out the different instructions
- co-ordinating all aspects of care
- actually giving the care
- responsibility and accountability in nursing care.

How are the instructions communicated?

If patients are to receive to care they need, instructions must be passed on correctly from nurse to nurse. One way of ensuring successful communication (see Chapter 6) is to make the instructions specific enough so that no matter who is giving the care (or following the instruction) the interpretation of that instruction will be the same. Another way of ensuring good communication of instructions is to be sure that all instructions are *written down* as well as given verbally. Using a Care Plan means that the instructions are written down and by using a problem-orientated Care Plan each instruction is related to its specific patient nursing problem.

Different wards or units develop their own Care Plan format

to suit their own needs. Within a hospital or district, however, some standardization will be necessary to facilitate the transfers of patients and the use of the Care Plan by the nurses. Whatever the format, the Care Plan becomes the major tool for communicating instructions, and provides a permanent record of these instructions to which all nurses can refer. Such a Care Plan contains all the information necessary for nursing care: thus it saves time and effort in ward handover reports because it maximizes the *useful* information and reduces the amount of *useless* information relayed from one nurse to the next.

Communicating instructions successfully

For instructions to be communicated successfully, the following criteria are suggested:
- the instructions should follow a logical step-by-step approach by relating nursing instructions to the patient problems which they are trying to meet.
- the Care Plan format should allow enough room for the nursing instructions to include all the necessary information.
- day-to-day progress notes should be written on a separate part of the Care Plan in close proximity to the nursing instructions. Each problem should be reported on separately.
- the format should allow for the addition of continuation sheets.
- all nurses should be able to see at a glance not only the short-range plans for patient care, but the long-range plans as well.

'But it will take too much time!'

Although it is necessary to spend some time on writing the initial Care Plans, time is saved in the long run by reducing the amount of information recorded elsewhere, decreasing or eliminating repetition and removing misunderstanding and confusion. Keeping the Care Plan up to date does not take a great deal of time because changes are made only when instructions change: if there is no change in nursing instructions on a particular day, there will be no change in the Care Plan. Progress notes have more meaning and are less repetitive because only the active problems are evaluated and reported on and all the meaningless phrases traditionally found in present Kardex systems are left out. Instructions like 'four-hourly turns' which are often repeated day after day in the Kardex need not be written in the progress notes because they are permanently written in the Care Plan.

Communicating the Care Plan Successfully

The use of a written Care Plan improves verbal communication because handover reporting has greater meaning – facts and progress are reported on rather than vague generalizations. A common Kardex notation in the traditional system would go something like this: 'Mrs Smith had a good day. Up and about. Specimen of urine NAD'. This entry really tells us nothing about the actual progress Mrs Smith is making, why her urine is being tested and what her individual nursing problems are or what the goals for her care might be. A Care Plan with problem-centred progress notes enables reporting to relate to what is actually happening to the patient regarding the progress of each of her problems and to the goals for which each nurse must strive. Many nurses, especially junior learners, do not fully understand why they carry out many aspects of nursing care. They are just told that Mrs Smith needs something done but not why it is needed. Problem-centred care planning and progress notes evaluating nursing care provide a system of prescribing nursing care which records the why of the care and allows experienced nurses to share their vast wealth of knowledge and skill with learners and the inexperienced.

Problem-centred Care Plans lend themselves to other forms of verbal communication such as nursing rounds and nursing care conferences. A nursing round involves Sister or staff nurse using, for example, the afternoon handover time to go round with the learners to each patient in the ward. Progress can be reported upon at this time and future care can be planned. The patient can participate in his care planning and the round provides a good time for him to ask questions and be given any necessary information and explanations. Obviously, there will at some time be information which may need to be discussed by the nursing staff out of the hearing of the patient (such as with the patient who for some reason has not been told his diagnosis) but aside from this, progress and planning can be discussed on a nursing ward round.

A nursing care conference is a time set aside by the ward nurses to discuss in depth the care, treatment, planning and progress of one patient. This is a good time for progress to be monitored and for the nursing care to be evaluated to see if goals have been met. This is also a good time to discuss alternative methods of giving nursing care if one particular technique is not working as expected. Priorities in the care for that patient can also be discussed, as well as future planning and nursing management. Other health care professionals can come to a nursing care conference and offer suggestions about the care of that patient, and this improves communication within the whole health care team.

Where to keep the Care Plan

It has hitherto been usual to keep nursing records away from patients, and often from learners as well. Frequently, the Kardex was kept in Sister's office and written only by the Sister or nurse in charge. With the development of care planning and the emphasis on patient allocation, this centralization is no longer appropriate and is found less often. Nursing records are now usually kept where all members of the nursing team can have access to them, eg. at the nurse's station. Also, where patient allocation or primary nursing is practised the records of the patients of each nurse are kept separately so that there may be three or four folders or Kardex holders. More recently in some hospitals the nursing records are kept at the patient's bedside, usually in a holder at the foot of the bed. Despite some nurses' anxiety about other patients or the relatives reading the records, our experience has shown that this does not happen.

Who updates the Care Plan?

The updating of the permanent problem list, goals and nursing instructions is left to the Ward Sister's discretion. She may choose to do this herself or she can delegate it to her staff nurses or learners if she feels they are capable. Any nurse designated as a primary nurse will need to possess the qualifications and experience necessary to fulfil that role. This is one aspect of the use of Care Plans which must be left to the individual ward sister to decide.

How to co-ordinate care

In implementing a Care Plan, the nursing care needed by one patient needs to be co-ordinated with other factors such as tests and investigations being carried out on that day for that patient, treatment being given to that patient by other health care professionals, doctors' rounds, the needs of the other patients and the number of nurses on duty. The emphasis is on making care individual to the patient which means that traditional ward routines need to be re-examined.

Traditionally, the nurses try to get all 'the work' (that is, all baths, bed-making, dressings, etc.) completed by 12.00 midday. If nursing care is to be matched with the individual needs of patients, this traditional ward routine must be abandoned. For example, if Mrs Smith is to have an X-ray at 10.00 in the morning, she should decide whether or not she would like to have her bath before the examination or afterwards. If she chooses to have it afterwards, the nurses will plan to bath her in the afternoon. The same is true for other aspects of care. If the same Mrs Smith has to drink 3 litres of fluid orally in 24 hours the nurses must take the X-ray appointment into account. It is ludicrous to plan that 1500 ml of that total be given by her morning nurse because Mrs Smith will be in the X-ray department for most of the morning. Furthermore, the afternoon nurse will know that she must make a special effort to get Mrs Smith to drink a lot during the afternoon and evening.

Priorities, for nurse or patient, can be discussed during the handover report. Other health care professionals should have access to the patient's Care Plan so they have an overall idea of the patient's total needs. The Care Plan thus co-ordinates the patient's nursing needs with the treatment being given by physiotherapists, occupational therapists and other specialists. With improved communication with these other professionals, the co-ordination between nursing and other care will be improved.

Giving the care

The concepts of task allocation, team nursing, patient allocation and primary nursing have already been introduced in Chapter 1 and will be explained in Chapter 9. Individualized care planning requires that a patient allocation or primary nursing system be used. This ensures continuity of care. The patient's nurse decided when each aspect of care is to be given and how to go about giving that care. It does not mean that she must work alone and that no one can help her to carry out care: on the contrary, there will be aspects of care such as bed-making, and lifting and turning patients, which are best performed by two nurses. Patient allocation and primary nursing mean that one nurse is *responsible* and accountable for that group of patients. She decides when and how to carry out care and whether or not she needs another nurse to help her. It means that other nurses, Sister and the medical staff know who to go to find out about that patient's care. It also means that the nurse is accountable for any care not given to the patient. Most important of all, the patient knows that one nurse is *his* nurse and that he can go to her for information or advice.

Summary

The implementation stage of care planning is not just carrying out the nursing instructions. Consideration must be given to who gives the instructions, how they are given and, also, to how the implementation of the instructions is recorded. Furthermore, the nursing staff have to define their areas of competence and expertise, and accept that they are responsible and accountable for the care they prescribe and give within those areas: these concepts will be discussed in Chapter 9. Written records that include both a Care Plan and progress notes are therefore essential tools for implementation.

Chapter 8

Evaluation

Introduction and definition

Evaluation is the last phase of nursing care planning and is essential for deciding if the care has been effective, that is, if the goals have been met. It is a continuing process that assesses and measures the quality, suitability and degree of success of both the planned nursing care and the care that is given. It is, therefore, both an end and a beginning.

The three components of evaluation

In evaluation three components can be studied: structure, process and outcome. *Structure* includes factors like the number and grade of nurses on duty, the type of ward, the nursing workload and the degree of patient dependency. *Process* includes factors such as the content of the plan and the nursing care given or recorded as having been given. *Outcome* includes the results of care in terms either of identifiable changes in the patient's condition directly attributable to the nursing care, or of comparing the expected outcome (the goal) with the actual outcome.

The functions of evaluation

All three components can be studied, firstly, to evaluate the care given to a particular patient and, secondly, to evaluate the Care Plan itself.

CARE PLAN				
DISCHARGE GOALS			**DISCHARGE PLANN** Tick those needed	

DISCHARGE GOALS
_____
_____
_____
_____
_____
_____

Social services
Community nursing
TTA's and teaching
Out patients' appt.
Transport
Other _____

DATE	NO	NURSING DIAGNOSES	
14.1.86	1	Pressure sore 3×2 cm on sacrum due to lack of mobility.	1 Sor Sm by fur m
			2 N

Fig 12

As the last phase of the nursing process, evaluation has three major functions:

   to determine whether the goals have been met;

   to provide the information for reassessment of the patient's needs.

   to discover which nursing actions are most consistently effective in solving a particular nursing problem.

1 Determining whether the nursing goals have been met   It is not easy to measure the effectiveness of nursing care, but it can be done, however, for an individual patient by looking at whether or not the nursing goals for that patient have been achieved. For this comparison to be possible the goals have to be stated in quantifiable terms (so that they can be measured) and be realistic. To be measurable, each goal must be written either as a behavioural response of the patient, a verbal response, a specific observation or assessment by the nurse or as a physiological measurement.

	OUTCOMES/RESULTS OF NURSING CARE		
d	1. Pressure sore on sacrum healed by 24·1·86 but skin surface still very fragile.		

s	NURSING INSTRUCTIONS	REVIEW ON/BY	DATE RESOLVED
uld be		16·1·86	16·1·86
wo days			
a			
n smaller			
s.		18·1·86	18·1·86
ure sore.		24·1·86	24·1·86

The time or date when any nursing action has to be evaluated is inserted in the Care Plan for that specific problem as it is written. It may be soon, eg. observing the effect of an analgesic after 30 minutes, delayed, eg. evaluating the teaching of a mentally sub-normal child to dress himself at the end of one month, or regular, eg. daily reporting on a pressure sore. The important fact is that the nurse predicts when she expects the goal to be achieved, thereby making evaluation possible.

The evaluation itself is a written statement by the nurse of the patient's response to her nursing care, ie. it is a statement of what has actually happened. This outcome statement is included on the Care Plan (Fig. 12). This gives the Care Plan a completeness which makes it useful for easy reference.

The outcome statement is then compared with the nurse's predictions, ie. the goal, and this comparison will show whether or not the goal has been or is in the process of being met. If a goal has not been met by the review date, the prescribed care will need to be examined and altered and the goal rewritten. This comparison between goal and outcome also shows whether or not the nursing care has been effective, provided the goal was realistic and the care appropriate. By studying the relationship of outcomes to goals during and after the patient's stay in hospital, the nurse is able to identify those behavioural and physiological changes which have occurred as a result of nursing action. This illuminates progress, or lack of it, towards the desired goals. In this way the nurse obtains the feedback she needs to learn which nursing action was most effective for that particular patient, thereby reducing the need to rely on ritualized patterns of care or on trial and error.

2 Providing information for re-assessment of the patient's needs A Care Plan is only useful and successful if it is up-to-date. Frequent revision will be necessary in the case of the acutely ill patient whose condition changes rapidly, whereas although it should be looked at frequently and changes considered, the Care Plan of a long-term patient may require comparatively little modification. The reasons for changing a Care Plan are as follows:
- a goal has been met and the patient's nursing problem is solved
- a goal has not been reached
- a new problem has been identified or an existing problem has been alleviated as a result of new data received
- the goals have been shown to be realistic

Problems that are solved or changed are not erased from the Care Plan. This retention of the original list of problems, plus all the other related information, is essential material for effective evaluation and makes the Care Plan a valuable permanent record with tremendous potential for research, audit, quality monitoring and teaching material. One method of indicating that a problem has been solved is to draw a line through it (Fig 13) in the same way that a line is drawn through a discontinued drug on some patients prescription sheets. Another is to include a 'Data Resolved' column which can then be linked by an arrow to the appropriate problem.

Evaluation of the care given to every patient will ensure that each will receive the best care possible. From the nurse's point of view she needs constantly to think about the care that she is

NURSING DIAGNOSIS		
Date noted	Nursing Problem	Date Resolved
16.1.86	Pain due to surgery	18.1.86

Fig 13 Care Plan: indicating that a nursing problem has been solved

giving and ask herself the following questions:

Do I have all the information I need?

Have I got my priorities right?

Are my goals realistic?

Have I helped the patient to understand the goals?

Are the nursing instructions being implemented as written on the Care Plan?

Were the instructions the right ones for reaching the goals?

Has the nursing care brought about a positive change in the patient's condition?

Does everyone understand, and give the same interpretation to, what I have written?

The evaluation of care, recorded as the actual outcome does not provide for a very detailed daily record, or for recording information which may be of very temporary importance, or for recording the intermediate stages in the form of continuous evaluation towards the solution of a problem. Progress notes fulfil these functions. These can be written by the nurses as necessary, since the record should be a continuing account of the patient's progress and not an end-of-shift report. Progress notes are best written in terms of individual problems and how the problems are being resolved or alleviated.

3 Matching nursing plans and actions Evaluation can also be used to record the effectiveness of nursing care in solving the nursing problems of a specific patient. This is of particular importance in two ways: firstly, when a problem has been particularly difficult to solve and has required several approaches before the right one has been identified; and secondly, when a patient has to be re-admitted either for regular treatment (eg. cytotoxic therapy), because of a deterioration in an existing condition (eg. chronic bronchitis), or for a new illness or accident. In all such instances the knowledge gained during previous admissions on the most effective way of dealing with that patient's nursing problems not only saves time, but also demonstrates to the patient that the nurses understand his particular needs.

The wider implications of evaluation

Evaluation has a wider application than simply assessing the effectiveness of the nursing care given to a particular patient, vital though this aspect is. It can also be used to evaluate the Care Plans themselves, the competence of the nurses' planning and giving of care, and the overall standard of performance.

Evaluation of the Care Plan

A Care Plan has to show evidence of a satisfactory level of knowledge and expertise: it can, therefore, be evaluated by 'experts' to determine whether it is of a satisfactory standard. Such an evaluation can be done on an individual basis, or acceptable criteria may be established with which the Care Plan in question can be compared. Evaluation of the Care Plan is essential because the care given reflects the standard of care prescribed; if the latter is low it is likely that the care the patient receives will be low. Clearly, when the nurse who prescribes by writing the Care Plan is the same nurse who gives the care, it is much easier to identify this relationship.

Evaluation of the Care Plan must consider all aspects of the plan: whether the patient's nursing problems accurately reflect the patient's needs, whether the goals are correct and, equally important, whether they are realistic, whether the nursing actions are those most appropriate for meeting the goals and can be carried out within the resources available, and whether the time allowed before evaluating the results of the care is appropriate and realistic. The two examples which follow demonstrate adequate and inadequate planning in relation to a similar problem.

ADEQUATE PLANNING

Problem	Goal	Instructions	Review on/by
Chest pain caused by myocardial infarction	No chest pain	1 Give analgesic every 4 hours, as prescribed 2 Give glyceryl trinitrate, as required 3 Ask patient whether he has pain	$\frac{1}{2}$ hour and $3\frac{1}{2}$ hours after analgesia

INADEQUATE PLANNING

Chest pain caused by myocardial infarction	No chest pain	1 Give analgesics if patient asks for them	4-hourly or drug rounds

Evaluating the nurses' knowledge

The writing of Nursing Care Plans is a very useful means of assessing a nurse's knowledge and how well she can apply knowledge and use her availability to interpret information. Identifying nursing problems from the available data, setting goals which are realistic and detailing the nursing care necessary to achieve these goals provides nurse managers and tutors with a very informative and accurate assessment of a nurse's knowledge and competence. The completion of the progress notes and of the outcome statements and the use the nurse makes of the continuing information not only augment the Sister's or Tutor's assessment of her knowledge, but also demonstrate the nurse's ability to translate the nursing instructions into practice, and this in turn can be assessed.

Evaluating standards of care

Finally, to refer back to a point mentioned at the beginning of this chapter, evaluation of Care Plans can be used to assess the standard of care. Nurses often complain that the standard of care is steadily declining, but the fact is that nurses have had no precise means of measuring acceptable standards and therefore cannot make such a judgement. One of the main reasons for this has been the lack of detailed and accurate records of the care planned for and given to the patient. The development and use of Care Plans makes it possible for individual nurses, groups of nurses, and ward sisters, nurse managers, teaching staff and researchers to look at what is happening, monitor the nursing care that patients receive, compare the care given on different wards and evaluate different approaches to the same nursing problem. All will, for the first time, be able to obtain data never before available about the day-to-day practice of nursing, which opens up tremendous opportunities for nurses to examine and research clinical nursing practice.

Summary

Evaluation may be the last phase in care planning but it is essential as all the other phases. Evaluation as described in this chapter is new to nurses, but if we are to develop *nursing*, evaluation must then become an accepted part of every nurse's practice. Care Plans will ensure that the information is recorded – the evaluation or critical examination of that information will ensure that high standards of care are set and maintained.

Section III

Care Planning within the Organization

This section contains three chapters. In Chapter 9 we examine the role of the clinical nurse and look at how each grade of nurse at the bedside can and must take part in care planning. We also explore various ways of managing patient care and of ward organization. Although the emphasis is on hospital-based situations, this chapter is also applicable to those nurses who care for patients in the community.

In Chapter 10 we examine the role of nurse managers in care planning and the assistance and support that they can give to clinical nurses. The role of nurse educators in care planning and the skills which nurses have to be taught in order to be able to plan and give individualized nursing care are described and discussed in Chapter 11.

Chapter 9

The Role of the Clinical Nurse

This chapter will explore two aspects of the roles of nurses at clinical level, whether in hospital or the community. They are:
- – trained staff as givers of direct care
- – ward sisters (or charge nurses)

Both of these groups will be considered in terms of their roles in care planning and in their relationship to learner nurses.

The care givers: trained staff

Each nurse, regardless of her seniority or level of experience, must be entirely familiar with the care planning system used in her particular setting. She must play her part in the day-to-day planning of total patient care and not just be allocated 'senior' tasks to perform. Community nurses, by the nature of the way their work is organized, have taken on this role in the past. Where learners give a high proportion of the direct nursing care, the role of the trained nurse in care planning is to supervise the assessment of patients by discussing the nursing history and observations made by students, assisting in identifying nursing diagnoses, supervising planning of care by making decisions regarding appropriate nursing care, as well as by supervising the giving of that care and then evaluating patient progress, both on a day-to-day basis and as specific nursing diagnoses require evaluation. Trained nurses must therefore be held accountable for all these activities in respect of their learners. It will be a trained nurse who takes the responsibility, by and large, for the allocation of appropriate patients to appropriate nurses and this decision will reflect both the condition and needs of the patient and the experience of the nurse. Trained nurses serve as role models for learners and as such they must be aware that the way in which they perform their roles will influence how learners will be likely to perform when they, too, are qualified. One way by which a trained nurse can demonstrate a patient-orientated approach is by her behaviour when coming on duty. Too often, trained nurses arrive on duty and immediately plunge in with tasks such as bedmaking. We suggest that every trained nurse should begin each shift by visiting the patients who have been allocated to her, and encourage learners to do the same thing. Each nurse, trained or learner, can spend a few minutes with every patient, quickly observe and assess him at that time, look at the Care Plan and make any necessary changes, and then decide what nursing care to give. If trained nurses and learners begin each shift in this way, patient care priorities will begin to be set in a more individualized, patient-centered way.

Ward organization and the trained nurse
Four ways of organizing patient care were mentioned and described briefly in Chapter 1.
Task allocation, although a fairly efficient way of 'getting the work done', has no real place in a care planning system because the emphasis is on tasks or jobs which must be finished in a predetermined space of time. Total individual patient needs cannot be met in such a system because the task, not the patient, is allocated to the nurse, who performs it as part of the ward routine or because a particular patient might require that particular task to be done for him on that particular day.
Team nursing can work in a care planning system although there is an inherent danger that each team of nurses will divide 'the work' into its component tasks. However, team nursing which then allocates appropriate patients to appropriate nurses within that team is a desirable form of organizing patient care. Each team should have a trained nurse as its leader who will take responsibility for allocating appropriate patients to nurses, supervising learners and assisting in assessment, nursing diagnosis, planning, giving and evaluating care.
Patient allocation is a way of organizing care so that specific

patients are allocated to specific nurses for a specific time span. The allocation may change from day to day or be continued over a longer time span in order to provide continuity of care. Again, community nurses have used a patient allocation system for some years. Allocating appropriate patients to nurses is a highly skilled activity. Inexperienced staff, especially learners, must be adequately supervised and parameters set for the amount of discretion allowed each nurse in making decisions about care and making changes to the Care Plan. There seems to be some confusion about who actually must give the care. One common error is to assume that if a particular patient is allocated to Nurse Jones it is Nurse Jones alone who must care for him. This is not, however, what patient allocation means. Patient allocation merely indicates who is *responsible* for ensuring that the care is carried out. Learners may, quite appropriately, be assigned to care for certain patients but there may be some aspects of that care which they cannot carry out. With guidance and supervision from trained staff, learners will gradually come to realize their capabilities and limitations – what they can do and what they must ensure is done by experienced nurses. A second common error is to assume that a nurse can ignore the needs of a patient if he has not been allocated to her. It should go almost without saying that if a nurse becomes aware that a patient is in need of attention when she knows that his own nurse is unavailable she will do what she can for that patient until his nurse returns.

Patient allocation also defines who is accountable for what happens to that patient in terms of nursing care. Accountability is about being answerable for nursing care which has been given or not given, reporting back to whoever is in charge about care and progress, and passing on all relevant nursing care information to the next shift of nurses, explaining what further care might be needed and describing the effects of nursing care upon the patient. Accountability, especially with regard to the ward sister's role, is discussed further in this chapter.

Primary nursing is a fairly new idea which is essentially a highly sophisticated form of patient allocation. Primary nursing must not be confused with *primary health care* which includes the nursing and medical care given in the community. Primary nursing is a way of allocating patients to nurses so that the same nurse assumes responsibility for the nursing care of those patients for their entire stay in hospital. Although community staff in many districts have for some years been carrying out a type of primary nursing, it is only relatively recently that any real attempt have been made to use primary nursing in hospitals.

The primary nurse admits the patients to the ward or unit and does the initial assessment, makes the initial diagnoses and begins their care plans. The primary nurse cares for her patients while she is on duty but when she goes off duty she will hand their care to another nurse – called an *associate nurse* – who will follow the plans of care she has laid down. If a patient's condition should alter, the associate nurse can and will change the Care Plan as may be necessary, but if his progress is maintained she will follow the primary nurse's original instructions for care. In short, primary nursing is similar to the way in which house officers care for the medical needs of their patients. When a house officer is off duty, an on-call house officer looks after his patients. The on-call house officer essentially follows the medical plan laid down by the patient's own doctors and only changes it in an emergency or if the patient's condition otherwise warrants it. At any one time, a nurse will be the primary nurse to some patients and an associate nurse to others.

Three further points are worth making with regard to primary nursing:

1 A patient must be aware that a particular nurse is his primary nurse. This allows a personal relationship to be built between primary nurse and patient and ensures that the patient is fully aware of who is responsible for his nursing care.

2 Primary nursing can only function effectively if there is a high percentage of trained staff in the ward or unit.

3 Learners, especially if they are junior, cannot function as primary nurses because a high degree of autonomy for decision-making, individual accountability and responsibility is inherent in this form of nursing.

In a care planning system the only methods of organizing care which effectively meet individual needs of patients are primary nursing or patient allocation. Team nursing is only appropriate if some form of patient allocation or primary nursing is practised within the teams.

The ward sister
The role of the ward sister is to coordinate activities on the ward, and the nature of her role will depend upon the way she chooses to manage her ward or unit and the nursing care within it.

The ward sister and ward organization

The role of the ward sister will depend upon the method she uses to organize nursing care. Historically, the ward sister's role has been to assign tasks and to ensure that the tasks were carried out. Senior students or staff nurses were given 'senior' tasks to perform, such as carrying the drugs keys, giving out drugs, doing dressings and accompanying doctors on their rounds. 'Junior' tasks were allocated to junior nurses and included bathing patients, pressure area care (the back round), and hourly drinks. Because of this historical role identification many of these 'junior' tasks still have relatively low status, despite being some of the most important and highly skilled nursing activities.

We believe Pembrey (1980) has shown that the ward sister's role must change from that of allocating 'junior' and 'senior' tasks to that of a manager of nursing care within a care planning system. Pembrey found that sisters have difficulty in conceptualizing their roles and argued that, in terms of managing care planning, sisters ought to be seeing their role in terms of a cycle of ward sister work which has four components:

defining the work,
prescribing the work,
delegating authority and
exacting accountability.

Each of these will be examined separately.

Defining the work   This component requires Sister to carry out a complete nursing round to gather up-to-date information about each patient. Using this information, as well as information received from the handover report and from the Care Plans. She will then have an overall picture of the care that is needed and of the dependency levels of patients and their condition. Ideally, the nursing round should take place after the handover report so that the nurses can accompany Sister, learn from her, discuss the diagnosis and nursing problems and identify priorities for each patient. A nursing round, according to Pembrey, is more than just saying hello to each patient and looking at the charts at the foot of the bed. Instead, it is a time where Sister gives each patient the opportunity to ask questions and express anxieties or worries: it involves her in sitting with the patient rather than standing over him or at the foot of the bed and talking to him first, before examining the charts or drips or drains. The nursing round is carried out to define the work and must not be a part of another task such as the drug round. Pembrey also emphasizes that the nursing round need not be a long-drawn-out or time-consuming affair, and in her research observed that those sisters who did carry out a complete nursing round managed to do so in a mean time of 20 minutes.

Prescribing the work   Once Sister has defined the work, the second component of managing nursing care concerns the verbal and written prescriptions for the nursing care which is to be carried out. The type of prescription will depend upon the seniority and expertise of the nurse and the basis for the prescription of work will be the Care Plan. Sister either assists and supervises junior students or delegates this task to a staff nurse or senior student. A senior nurse might prescribe her own actions for patients but only if Sister has delegated this authority to her (see below). Prescribing also includes allocating patients to the most appropriate nurse.

Delegating authority   Once the work has been described, Sister must then delegate authority: this means making explicitly clear to each nurse the degree of her responsibility and freedom to make decisions. Juniors will have less freedom than the more experienced nurses but decision-making includes sorting out the priorities of nursing care, deciding who might be available and appropriate to assist in the giving of nursing care and changing the prescribed care if the patient's condition warrants it. How much freedom of decision-making each nurse has will be different and must be made absolutely clear to her.

Exacting accountability In exacting accountability, the fourth component of Pembrey's cycle, the ward sister is expected to require of each nurse that she should be answerable for the care she carries out, or omits. This means that each nurse will know that she has to report back to Sister, and to the next group of nurses, on the care she has given and on the progress of each patient. If, therefore, a nurse is given authority or freedom for any kind of decision-making, supervised or not, she must also be held accountable for this use of authority. Exacting accountability may take the form of a verbal report from each nurse about each of her patients. It also will include a written record of care given and patient progress which allows the nurse to review her work, evaluate its effectiveness and provides the next group of nurses with up-to-date information on which to reassess patients and give appropriate nursing care.

Pembrey's management cycle for ward sisters describes changes needed in the role of the sister in an environment which has a high proportion of learner or untrained staff giving care. In units such as specialist hospitals or wards, and in the community, where there is a high proportion of trained staff giving nursing care, Sister may wish to move towards the more sophisticated system – primary nursing – that has been described earlier, in which each trained nurse by virtue of her qualifications and experience can make decisions about nursing care with little or no supervision, define her own work, prescribe nursing actions herself and be truly responsible and accountable to managers and patients for the care which she gives. The ward sister's role changes even more dramatically in a primary nursing situation to that of overall co-ordinator of ward activities, facilitator, teacher, resource person and clinical expert. In many settings where primary nursing is practised, Sister's carry their own case-load, acting as both primary and associate nurse.

Summary

Using Care Plans within the framework of the nursing process demands enormous changes in the roles of both qualified staff and sisters. We believe that one of the problems of successfully implementing care planning is that nurses and sisters have not been adequately prepared for or taught these new roles. The nursing profession is beginning to realize that qualified staff and sisters must be better trained for their roles, that these roles must be more clearly defined and described and that the roles of student, staff nurse and sister will be greatly determined by the way in which nursing is organized in their unit. The ward sister and the management style that she adopts will determine how both learners and trained staff give individualized nursing care and how Care Plans are used.

Reference

Pembrey S (1980) *The Ward Sister: Key to Nursing*. London: Royal College of Nursing

Chapter 10

The Role of Nurse Managers

Traditionally, the nurse-manager has been undervalued except for an idealized view of the Matron. Nurses are expected to want to remain 'by the bedside' despite the fact that research shows that, once qualified, trained nurses spend less time in direct patient care than in supervising and managing. Becoming a nurse-manager therefore is a move that is often suggested to the nurse, rather than one she chooses to make herself.

Yet management – good management – is essential to the provision of good care. It begins, of course, with the management of the care required by a single patient, and continues with the management of a group of patients and then to that of the various groups – ward, clinic, hospital, district – which make up our nursing system.

The role of the nurse manager becomes even more important when introducing innovation and managing change; indeed, it is probably a critical factor. Why this is so depends on understanding three factors – management, leadership and organizational structure – and the way these effect what is or can be achieved by the individual.

Who are they? For the purpose of this chapter, nurse-managers will be taken to include those in the Senior Nurse grade and above with responsibility for some kind of unit or speciality.

What is management?

Douglass (1984) has defined management as a process which

'consists of achieving organizational objectives through planning, organizing, directing and controlling human and physical resources and technology.

Nursing management is then seen to be the achievement of quality nursing care through the utilization of health care workers, physical resources and techniques. It is a cyclical process (in the same way as the nursing process) which includes the following stages:

assessment	– finding out what the problems are or what needs to be done.
organizing	– deciding how to do what is required.
directing	– getting things done.
evaluating	– assessing and re-defining.

Leadership   Leadership means being able to influence one or more other people to achieve specific goals. In the case of nurse leaders, the overall goal would be the provision of a high standard of nursing care. By definition, leaders require followers – they are reciprocal, complementary roles in the same way as nurses require patients or clients, mothers require children, and so on. *Effective* leadership requires followers who will willingly follow through plans and act upon decisions.

There are two types of leadership, formal and informal. Formal leaders are those individuals who are appointed to leadership posts and given official authority to act within the limits of that appointment. Informal leadership arises unpredictably and at any level in the organization. Such leadership can be extremely powerful. If the two forms are congruent, then there is no problem; if, however, informal leaders are not in tune with the goals and philosophy of the formal leaders and the organization, conflict and confusion then occur.

Authority and power   *Authority* is the legitimate right to give orders and make decisions. *Power* is the ability to bring about certain behaviours. Both management and leadership require authority and power to achieve their aims. Possession of one without the other creates numerous problems.

Leadership and management are therefore not identical, but effective nurses are those who blend the qualities of both. Such a combination is especially important when it comes to the introduction of an innovative and controversial development such as the nursing process.

Organization The organized structure within which individuals work should provide the means by which work is arranged and distributed among its members so that its goals can be reached. Nurses mostly work within the highly-organized bureaucratic structure of the National Health Service, which on occasion seems to be designed more to frustrate than facilitate the provision of good patient care. Control is imposed from the top down and the formal lines of communication are clearly defined. Two major problems at the current time are, firstly, that those lines of communication have become less clear and, secondly, that the organization has become too large and unwieldly.

Introducing care planning based on the nursing process involves change, and change is often threatening because it challenges accepted patterns of behaviour and forces us to rethink our ideas. The aim of care planning, however, is to improve patient care, and its introduction, therefore, is in line with our basic philosophy of nursing. Admitting that things can be improved does not mean that previous practices were of a poor standard, but that new knowledge is now available which can and should be used.

The overall role of the nurse manager is to ensure that this process of change is handled effectively and that the desired outcome (care planning) is brought about with the minimum amount of opposition and the maximum amount of support.

What has to be managed?

In the definition of management (p. 75) a manager is someone who utilizes staff, resources and technology. How then does this apply to the nurse manager and the introduction of care-planning?

Staff The most important group are nurses, but the nurse manager also has to work with other groups such as doctors, para-medicals, administrators and ancillary staff. As far as nurses are concerned the manager has to ensure that adequate numbers of nurses with the right qualifications and experience are available to provide quality nursing care.

A frequent criticism of the nursing process is that it is impossible to implement because of current staffing levels –

'How can I do all that writing when there is only myself (the Sister), two first-year students and one auxiliary on duty to care for 27 acute surgical patients?' The issue there is not care planning but insufficient staff and our inability to demonstrate objectively what care our patients need and why, what care they receive and the outcomes of that care, and what care we cannot provide because of lack of nursing time or skill and the results of that lack.

Care planning is neither the solution to providing quality nursing care, nor the scapegoat for care not being given. Care can only be as good as the person giving it. It is the manager's responsibility to ensure that there are sufficient staff of the right calibre to achieve care of a high standard.

Resources   Resources come in all shapes and forms: time, money, expertise and so on. The nurse manager can greatly facilitate the nurses' use of care planning by providing this kind of help. This could include such things as:
- legitimizing time spent on nurses learning about the nursing process.
- finding funds for buying books, folders, etc.
- getting 'experts' to come in to talk to her staff or to work full-time as a nursing process co-ordinator.

Technology   Managers need to be aware of current technological developments, eg. computers, word processing, etc. which can assist in providing information and support. Such things as Computer Assisted Learning (CAL), ward-based computer terminals, and so on, are going to become increasingly common. It is vital that nurse managers make sure that the potential of these for nursing is identified and appropriate use made of them.

How is it managed?

The manager's first task is to identify what needs to be done and what problems are likely to occur. Obviously, some problems and needs will be specific to her own unit or area and to her position in the organization, others will be more general. For example, in one hospital the Ward Sisters may be very enthusiastic: the manager's task is to find out how to channel and utilize that enthusiasm. Elsewhere it may be senior management that has decided care planning should be implemented although the ward staff are not keen. The needs and problems would be different.

It is now much easier for managers to obtain information on which to base their decision making. Many health districts, hospitals and units have introduced care planning so there is a considerable body of knowledge available about practical matters. A considerable literature exists, too, about the underlying concepts and theory.

The nurse manager should make herself familiar with this literature and the experience of other units before proceeding with her own developments. Knowledge is power. The nurse manager who knows about, and understands and is able to explain the nursing process is in a much stronger position and possesses much greater credibility than one who says she believes in it but knows very little.

Organizing – how to do what is required   Decisions on what to do depend obviously on the manager's position in the organization, the extent of her authority and power, the type of decision-making process currently in force and her own leadership skills.

It is our experience, however, that care planning only truly becomes reality if those responsible for the actual practice of it are knowledgeable about it and committed to it, and rewarded for that commitment.

The nurses (and other groups) are likely to hold one of five attitudes to care planning:
   (i) enthusiastic and knowledgeable
   (ii) enthusiastic but lacking knowledge
   (iii)superficially keen but actually antagonistic
   (iv)neutral
   (v) opposed.
Each group will require a different plan of action.

Care planning – getting it done   The skills that are most needed to implement the practice of care planning are those of leadership – of the nurse manager herself or of informal leaders. Such skills are particularly essential when dealing with those nurses who either are neutral or are opposed to care planning, because their attitudes and beliefs have to be changed.

However if some nurses will not change their practice voluntary or by persuasion, care planning may have to be imposed, ie. the manager has to use her authority. In the long term, such a solution is unsatisfactory because when supervision slackens the nurses will return to the earlier systems with which they feel comfortable and consider appropriate.

Evaluating   The main aims of the manager with regard to the nursing process are:
- understanding what it is all about
- the introduction of care planning
- maintaining the new system
- providing and monitoring quality nursing care.

The first three aims can be measured quite easily. But care planning is above all a means to an end, not an end in itself. The existence of carefully written Care Plans and well-documented nursing care are essential, for without such records we have no objective evidence on which to evaluate the care we provide and assess whether it is of a high enough standard. Care Plans therefore given us the means to do this, and should be used in this way.

Summary

The role of the nurse-manager is very important in introducing and maintaining care planning based on the nursing process. Care planning can and will happen without their support, but only as the result of efforts of particular individuals. When those individuals leave or move care planning will disappear unless the nurse-managers are committed to it.

Reference

Douglass L M (1984) *The Effective Nurse Leader and Manager.* St Louis, MO:C V Mosby

Chapter 11

The Role of Nurse Educators

Nurse educators have a new and important part to play in care planning. This can be divided into four distinct areas:-
- developing an ideology about nursing and education
- developing teaching programmes which reflect this ideology and which incorporate a problem-solving approach into the ideology and teaching programmes
- identifying the specific skills required of nurse to practice care planning and learning appropriate teaching methods to teach these
- having a direct clinical involvement as part of their teaching role

Developing an ideology

In Chapter 4 – assessment – we discussed the need to develop a statement of beliefs and values about man, society, health, illness and nursing in order to determine how we assess patients before planning the care they need. This same statement of values and beliefs must be the foundation of teaching programmes in basic and post-basic nurse education. In addition, teachers must determine what they value and believe about education in order to determine what their roles and functions are, as well as the roles of students. An educational ideology also helps to clarify what the teacher values in terms of course content, priorities in teaching and teaching methods. It is still common for teachers to speak about believing in nursing models and individualized nursing care when their teaching programmes still reflect medical models and disease-related teaching. This is not to say that diseases, anatomy and physiology are not important. What it does mean is that if we say we believe in a nursing model or models, then we must

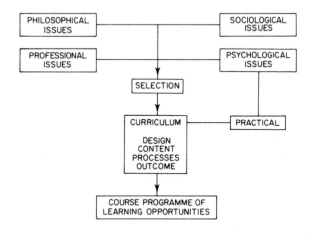

Fig 14

start with nursing models and fit in diseases, anatomy and physiology around these models. We believe that clinicians and teachers must work towards a shared ideology which is reflected in the care which is given and the nursing which is taught. By sharing a statement of beliefs and values, what is taught in the school will match up with what is practised in the clinical setting.

Docking (1981) has modified a model of curriculum from Lawton (1973) to explain the relation between ideology and curriculum development. Figure 14 shows how an ideology is determined by exploring philosophical issues, psychological issues, sociological issues and professional issues to reach an ideological statement. This statement must be amenable to practical interpretation and will be influenced by practice. What we select for our curriculum, in terms of content, teaching methods, curriculum design, outcomes and so forth will be based on this ideology. Equally, nurse educators can undertake a values clarification exercise to determine what they value and believe and then examine their present teaching programmes to see if what they are teaching matches that which they believe. If teachers believe that man is an individual who needs individualized care, does their teaching reflect this belief in individuality? If so, do teachers practice this stated belief when they teach 'the care of the patient with a myocardial infarction'? How can all patients with a myocardial infarction have the same needs?

Equally, if a school of nursing values and believes that systematic care planning – the nursing process – is a good thing, then this systematic care planning must appear as the foundation of every teaching session involving nursing care. An isolated lecture or two on the theory of the nursing process or on the stages of nursing process does not show that a school values this way of providing nursing care. We believe that the nursing process is a good thing and is not isolated or separate from nursing care – it *is* nursing care; nursing care which reflects our beliefs about man, society and health, is well thought out and based on individual information about each patient as well as a sound knowledge base of disease, and is evaluated. Because this is what we believe, it must form the foundation of our teaching programmes and of all our teaching sessions.

Developing teaching programmes which reflect our ideology

Developing teaching programmes requires the same sort of systematic thinking that is required to plan patient care. The stages of problem solving – assessment, planning, implementation and evaluation – can be used to design appropriate curricula for nursing education. Figure 15 is a model of curriculum development which uses a problem-solving approach and also begins with the ideological base mentioned in the previous section.

Curriculum planning, like care planning, requires cyclical stages:

Assessment of the curriculum is based on the same assumption as assessment in care planning. Before we can assess we must have an explicit understanding of what we feel is important to assess and what are the underlying values and beliefs about what needs to be assessed.

Planning in the curriculum must include a well-thought-out

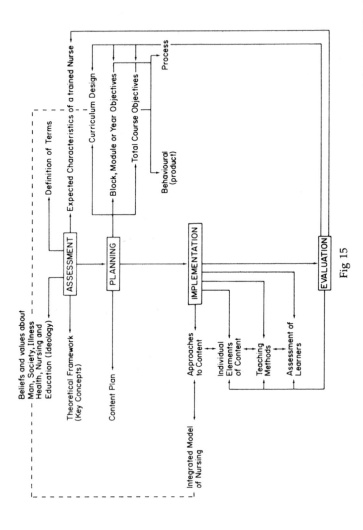

Fig 15

design with explicit objectives. As with planning nursing care, planning a rational curriculum requires direction in the form of aims, goals or objectives.

Implementation of a curriculum means putting all your planning into action – e.g. teaching. There is a relationship here between the ideology and the model of nursing chosen on which to base a teaching programme. There is also a relationship between the ideology and the teaching methods chosen. What is taught, who teaches it, when various components are taught and the structure and order of the programmes are all interwoven and are direct reflections of the ideology and the aims and objectives.

Evaluation of the curriculum involves looking back to see if aims and objectives are met and determining what changes in the programmes are required. This is identical to evaluation in care planning where nursing actions are examined to see if desired patient goals have been reached. To summarize, systematic approaches to patient care are valued. Equally, systematic approaches to nursing education are also valued. Planning nursing care begins with an ideology about man, society, health, illness and nursing. Planning a teaching programme to teach nurses to give this kind of care also requires the same or a compatible ideology as well as an ideology about what education should be about.

Identifying the skills which nurses need to practise individualized care planning

In order to assess patients, identify nursing diagnoses, plan and give appropriate nursing care and evaluate that care, a number of highly complex and sophisticated skills are involved. Assessing patients, for example, requires a wide range of communication and observation skills, including skill in interpreting information. Planning and evaluating care involves complex decision-making skills, priority-setting skills and so forth. Acting as a primary nurse involves sophisticated leadership and interpersonal skills.

Nurse educators are beginning to realize the importance of teaching these skills as well as the traditional psychomotor nursing skills, but the relative amounts of time spent in teaching care planning skills needs to be greatly increased.

One problem, however, is that nurse education programmes have traditionally been 'product-orientated' which means that teaching in the past has been geared to measureable end results such as the learning of specific facts, psychomotor skills and acceptable attitudes. But the observation, communication, leadership, interpersonal and other skills mentioned in the previous paragraph which are needed to assess patients, make nursing diagnoses, plan, give and evaluate care may not have definite, measurable end results. With these skills, rather than a pre-determined end result, the *process* of developing them at the learner's own pace is more important than a definite end result. The 'process-orientated' skills require teachers to develop appropriate 'process-orientated' teaching methods which do not require measurable behavioural objectives set by the teacher but rather will require process aims identified by the learner. These 'process-orientated' teaching methods include experiential learning, reflective teaching methods, the use of critical incidents and counselling techniques (Heath 1982), to name a few.

Clinical involvement by teachers

Clinical involvement means that the nurse teacher maintains a regular clinical commitment in some form. This may involve spending a specific time each week on a particular ward, unit or in the community. What the teacher does in this time will vary from teacher to teacher and will depend upon the needs of the ward or unit, the learners and the teacher herself. It may be a time for the teacher to exercise some of her own specialist clinical skills, it may be in patient teaching, to act as a role model, to help learners assess, make nursing diagnoses, plan, give and evaluate care or learn some of the 'process-orientated' skills required to do this more effectively. By working in the clinical area the teacher can identify areas of weakness in particular learners as well as particular strengths, can keep up to date with nursing practice, assist the ward staff by acting as a resource person for teaching information, work with clinicians to establish a common ideology and ultimately use this clinical involvement as a source of material for future teaching.

Summary

One problem with regard to care planning is that nurse teachers and practitioners are often at different stages in their understanding and use of Care Plans. Some teachers feel unable to use Care Plans as a basis for their teaching about nursing care because they have little or no practical experience of using them. Some hospitals are using Care Plans in nursing practice but their respective schools of nursing do not adequately teach learners either the theory, the practice or the skills of care planning. On the other hand, some schools of nursing teach the skills of care planning without the nurses being able to put these skills into practice when caring for patients. Problems have arisen in the past because there has been no shared ideology upon which practitioners can give care and which is also the basis for teaching programmes. What is needed is a balanced, integrated teaching programme which is based upon beliefs and values which are shared between school and service and an understanding and respect for the wide range of 'process-orientated' skills required to give individualized nursing care. There is a challenge here to post-basic, in-service and continuing education departments to provide the means by which qualified nurses can develop these skills, teaching staff can learn how to use 'process-orientated' teaching methods to teach these skills and practitioners and teachers can begin to work together on a common ideology for practice and education.

References

Docking S P (1981) *St. Bartholomew's School of Nursing SRN (RGN) Programme: Curriculum Proposal.* (unpublished)

Lawton D (1973) *Social Change, Educational Theory and Curriculum Planning.* London: Hodder & Stoughton.

Heath J (1982) Intention and practice in nursing education. *Nurse Education Today,* **2**(2), 7–9.

Marks-Maran D (1982) *An Innovative Approach to the Curriculum Development Process.* Paper presented for the Diploma in Nursing Education, Polytechnic of the South Bank. (unpublished)

Section IV

A Look at the Literature

Chapter 12

A Reading Guide

Introduction

Since the first edition of this book was published in 1980 there has been an enormous increase in the amount of literature available about all aspects of care planning. Early literature was essentially theoretical as nurses were only beginning to put Nursing Care Plans into practice. Recent literature has focused on practical application of care planning as well as introducing nursing models on which to base care planning. An increasing amount of material is also being published on nursing ideologies, concepts within nursing and how these form the basis for planning nursing care.

Because of this, the format for this reading guide is different from that of the first edition. This time we offer suggested readings about some of the more fundamental components behind care planning, beginning with ideologies and concepts and theories about nursing, continuing with a guide, albeit short, to models of nursing and then following with guides to reading on the five stages of care planning, suggested readings, on primary nursing and finishing with a section on teaching the skills required to plan nursing care.

Ideology, concepts and theories

Many nurses become confused about the definitions of these terms. *Ideology*, as already mentioned in Chapter 9, is often mistakenly called *philosophy*. Ideology is a statement (or statements) of beliefs and values about certain *concepts* related to nursing. Nursing ideology will be a statement of beliefs and values about such concepts as man, society, health, illness, to name a few.

Rines & Montag (1976) offer some very understandable definitions of the terms *theory* and *concept*. A theory is a proposed explanation which is still conjectural or not necessarily proved. A theory may be partially proved, partially unproved and is always open to question unless completely proved. A concept, however, is not a proposition like a theory: it is a general notion or idea which is formed mentally. Concepts are ideas which serve as guides and about which one can make statements. Concepts are born out of theories. Rines & Montag make the point that different theories might still be about the same concepts and that nurses must identify the concepts which are central to nursing, make statements, and possibly further theories, about each concept and base nursing practice on these. Yura & Walsh (1978) identify two concepts in the beginning of their nursing textbook – nursing process and human needs – and explore these two concepts and their relationship to each other.

Another publication which is useful – and British – is by Roper *et al* (1980). This book begins by stating values and beliefs about certain concepts which have been identified as being central to nursing, and from these beliefs and values a model of nursing is derived which forms the basis for nursing practice. We introduced Roper's model in Chapter 4 and elaborate on it below.

King (1981) and Orem (1980) also begin by identifying concepts, and theories about these concepts, but each of these takes a slightly different approach to nursing practice.

Models of nursing

A model is a pictoral representation of a theory or an idea about nursing. The function of a model is to present a scaled-down picture or diagram about the relationship between beliefs, theories and concepts about nursing. Drawing a diagram, or model, makes the ideas easier to understand. Models like that of Roper *et al* are based on theories related to human needs, but there are dimensions to this model other than identifying these basic human needs. One dimension in Roper's model is that of life span and the theory that at different periods of life between birth and death, man is able or unable to meet his own needs. Related to this dimension is a second dimension which Roper *et al* call the dependence–independence continuum. This explores the changes that people go through during their life in terms of sometimes being independent in meeting their own needs and sometimes being dependent upon others for their needs. This model of nursing enables nurses to conceptualize the process of nursing as being dependent upon each patient's ability to carry out his daily activities of living independently.

King (1981) presents a model of nursing which is different from Roper in many ways because it is not based on a human needs theory, but rather on a systems theory. Human beings are open systems and each person has his or her own *personal system* because we each have individual behaviour in relation to certain concepts such as self, perception, body image, growth, development, time and space. Individual personal systems, however, have to interact with other individual personal systems and in doing so form *interpersonal systems* which might be two personal systems interacting (called a dyad), three personal systems interacting (called a triad) and so forth. In interpersonal systems other concepts are identified such as role (eg. that of nurse or patient), interaction, communication, transactions, stress. When small groups of interpersonal systems merge and develop common interests, goals and behaviours, they are termed *social systems*. Concepts within social system include families, communities and religious groups. King believes that nursing moves within the dynamics of these systems which are constantly changing. Social forces within these systems create patient and nurse behaviour which must be fully understood in order that the nurse can understand how to deal with its fear, loneliness, anxiety and pain which happens to their patients. King's systems model also enables nurses to understand how hospital and health service organizations affect nursing.

Other models of nursing which have generated interest are adaptation models: these are based on the theory that man adapts to stressful situations, such as illness, in ways which are comfortable for him. One such model, that of Roy (1970), says that man adapts in four ways to illness; physiologically, in terms of self-concept, in his role function and in his level of dependence/independence. Each person, nurse or patient, sees the world differently. A patient may have to adapt to stressful situations like illness, but equally, the nurse has events to which she, too, must adapt (a new ward, stress, reality shock). The aim, according to Roy, is for all people to become adaptive people, eg. to cope positively with stresses and illness and to participate in their own adaptation process. Patients are helped to adapt positively to their illness and participate in their healing, and nurses also need help to become positively adaptive to the stresses of their work. Like most other nurses who have attempted to draw a picture of what nursing is, Roy begins with certain beliefs about nurses, about man, changes in the environment, decision making, response to stress. The Roy model assumes that assessment of patients in the care planning process is carried out in terms of response to illness and adaptation to their new environment, change in role function and level of dependence. Nursing care is then planned to assist the patient to adapt positely.

McFarlane & Castledine (1982) combine an adaptive model with an activities-of-living framework and patients are assessed in terms of their adaptation to their activities of living.

The most important point about using models of nursing to make a picture of what nursing care is all about is that no one model may be suitable or applicable in practice. A good understanding of those models that have already been developed will enable nurses to select those which are appropriate to any given patient. A model of nursing is a tool to clarify nurses' thinking about what their care should be and what the aim or goal for the patient is. Nurses may wish to combine elements from different models to plan nursing care.

Assessment

Assessment is, unfortunately, often used synonymously with the term 'nursing history'. But a nursing history is only one type of assessment tool and one way of assessing patients. Assessment is a continuing event while a nursing history is a once-only occurrence during a patient's stay in hospital or during his care in the community. The nursing history does, however, provide the baseline information with which to begin the patient's initial plan of care. The nursing history will reflect what nurses believe about people and what happens to them when they are ill. The content of any nursing history, therefore, will be based on our ideology as well as on our own level of experience at interviewing patients. Some nursing history sheets are highly structured, which is especially helpful to those inexperienced in formally interviewing patients, while other history sheets are relatively unstructured and are preferred by nurses who have a good deal of interviewing experience.

Examples of both structured and unstructured nursing history will be found in the Appendices 1–8. McCain (1965) and McPheteridge (1968) both outline practical aspects of nursing history-taking and how to best use the information gained. McFarlane & Castledine relate taking a nursing history to a specific model of nursing. Marriner (1982) has a particularly good chapter on assessment which includes listening skills and verbal and non-verbal cues.

But assessment is more than merely taking a nursing history at the beginning of a patient's illness. Assessment includes developing good observation skills and using other assessment tools that may be available. Castledine (1979), for example, has devised and described a way of assessing the musculoskeletal system; Norton *et al* (1975) describe the use of their now fairly-well-known scale for assessing patients' risk of developing pressure sores; Guy's Hospital (1981) provides a tool to measure confusion in patients; Smith (1980) provides an assessment sheet for psychiatric patients; and Hayward (1973) used a pain thermometer to assess patients' own perception of pain. These are only a few of the many tools available to help nurses to assess many of the nursing problems in their care plans.

Making a nursing diagnosis

Many books and articles use the term 'nursing problems' rather than nursing diagnosis and although in Chapter 5 we explain why we prefer 'nursing diagnosis', much of the literature does not use this term. McFarlane & Castledine (1982) have a particularly good chapter on identifying nursing problems which is the same thing as making nursing diagnoses and what the real difference is between a nursing diagnosis and a medical diagnosis. Carnevali (1983) also discusses how to write a nursing diagnosis. This book, however, may be quite advanced for many nurses and the American phraseology can cause confusion. For those nurses who really wish to use nursing diagnoses to their fullest extent, by relating the nature of the nursing diagnosis to the cause and severity of the problem, two books can be recommended: Gebbie & Lavin (1975) and Kim & Moritz (1982). Both these books present a classification of nursing diagnoses and very complete lists about all the components of any nursing diagnosis. Both these books are produced by an American nursing organization which aims to identify, update and teach nursing diagnoses to nurses.

Planning, and implementing the Care Plan

Any of the books about writing Care Plans will provide further information on how to write better plans. One of the easiest to read and understand, and to put into practice, is Rehman (1976), a small, pocket-sized book. Myers (1973) was one of the first American nurses to write about planning systematic nursing care and her book gives useful information about care planning and selecting appropriate nursing interventions. Saxton & Hyland (1979) is also to be recommended on the subject of planning and giving care. Grant (1975) is a readable article about Nursing Care Plans. The prologue to Yura & Walsh (1983) provides a practical case study example of planning appropriate nursing actions for specified nursing diagnoses. McFarlane & Castledine (1982) also provide useful, and British, chapters about writing a Care Plan and implementing the plan.

Evaluation

Very little has been written about the evaluation of nursing care although most of the books about care planning mentioned previously include chapters on evaluation. Walker *et al.* (1976) specifically includes documentation with good emphasis on evaluating the Care Plan and how to document the evaluation. Copp (1972) has written a series of articles about

Care Plans: Part 3 of this series particularly highlighted evaluation. Ryan (1973) also specifically examines criteria to plan and
evaluate nursing care.

Primary nursing

There is little British literature about primary nursing. Kratz
(1977) wrote of her experiences on visiting a unit in Australia
which used primary nursing as a way of organizing nursing
care. Lee (1979) discusses how primary nursing might improve
nursing care. McFarlane & Castledine (1982) discuss primary
nursing and, in particular, outline the development of primary
nursing at The Manchester Royal Infirmary. In America, Manthey (1970) was probably the most renowned advocate of
primary nursing. Her main aim was to develop a way of
organizing care which was individualized and where nurses
could assume more responsibility for fewer patients and still
provide total comprehensive nursing care. Her account is a
readable one. Ciske (1979) worked with Manthey and this
particular article discusses how primary nursing increases
accountability.

Teaching nursing process skills

There is a fair amount of literature about the relationship
between care planning and nursing education. Hollingsworth
(1979) discusses the challenge to teachers in terms of course
content and teaching methods. Ashworth & Castledine (1981)
clearly outline how the nursing process can be used in
teaching. Although there are many articles (see bibliography)
about teaching the nursing process, we would like to highlight
some of the literature which identifies specific skills required
to teach nursing process – skills which must be included in all
nurse teaching programmes. Aspinall & Tanner (1981) focus
on decision-making in their approach to teaching the nursing
process and care planning, and discuss in depth the nature of
the decision making skills required to use the nursing process.
They emphasize that an approach which concentrates on the
process (teaching methods) rather than a product (end result)
is most appropriate when teaching decision-making skills.

Grey (1983) has devised a learning package which consists of a series of planned lessons and exercises to help teachers who want to develop communication skills in their learners. The learning package, which has been produced and circulated by the DHSS includes lesson plans, overhead transparencies, audiotapes and coloured slides, all of which are designed to teach students or trained staff different communication skills such as listening, verbal and non-verbal communication, decision-making, telephone skills, setting priorities, and more.

Marson (1982) outlines the interpersonal and interactive skills required for good communication and how nursing care can be improved when nurses are specifically taught how to develop these skills. Bridge & Speight (1981) reiterate Marson's observation that nurses misunderstand what communication really means.

The ENB Learning Resources Centre, located at 55 Broomgrove Road, Sheffield S10 2NA, provides practical advice and materials for anyone involved in teaching nurses. The centre produces a newsheet called *Feedback* which provides up-to-date information about teaching communication and interpersonal skills, especially with respect to the changes needed in teaching methods to help nurses develop these skills.

Summary

This reading guide has intended to provide a sample of the literature available about care planning and has been primarily concerned with some of the wider issues related to care planning. The bibliography which follows will provide a more comprehensive list of some of the resources available for nurses to further their knowledge and understanding of care planning.

References

Ashworth P & Castledine G (1981) The way we teach nursing using the nursing process. *Medical Teacher,* **3** (3)

Aspinall M & Tanner C (1981) *Decision-Making For Patient Care: Applying the Nursing Process.* Norwalk: Appleton-Century-Crofts

Bridge W & Speight I (1981) Teaching the skills of nursing communications. *Nursing Times,* **77** (32) (Occasional Paper)

Carnevali D (1983) *Nursing Care Planning: Diagnosis and Management.* Philadelphia: Lippincott

Castledine G (1979) Nursing assessment of the musculoskeletal system. *Nursing*, 1st series, June

Ciske K (1979) Accountability: the essence of primary nursing. *American Journal Of Nursing*, **79**, (5)

Copp L (1972) Improved patient care through evaluation. *Bedside Nurse*, 5(Sept)

Gebbie K & Lavin M (1975) *Classification of Nursing Diagnoses.* St. Louis: Mosby

Grant N (1975) The nursing care plan. *Nursing Times*, 71 (27 March)

Grey J (1983) *Caring Communication.* (A teaching package of exercises and activities to teach communication skills). London: DHSS

Guy's Hospital (1981) Organic mental impairment in the elderly. *Journal of the Royal College of Physicians*, **5** (3)

Hayward J (1973) *Information: A Prescription Against Pain.* London: RCN

Hollingsworth S (1979) A challenge for nurse teachers. *Nursing Times*, **75** (30)

Kim M & Moritz D (1982) *Nursing Diagnoses* (Proceedings of the 3rd and 4th National Conferences). New York: McGraw Hill

King I (1981) *A Theory For Nursing.* New York: John Wiley

Kratz C (1979) Letter from Australia – 2: primary nursing. *Nursing Times*, **75** (42)

Lee M (1979) Towards better care: primary nursing. *Nursing Times* (**75**) (Occasional Papers)

McCain R (1965) Nursing by assessment – not intuition. *American Journal of Nursing*, **65** (4)

McFarlane J & Castledine G. (1982) *A Guide to the Practice of Nursing using the Nursing Process.* London: Mosby

McPheteridge M (1968) Nursing history: one means to personalise care. *American Journal of Nursing*, **68** (1)

Manthey M (1970) Primary nursing – a return to the concept of 'my nurse' and 'my patient'. *Nursing Forum*, **9** (1)

Marriner A (1975) *The Nursing Process: A Scientific Approach to Nursing Care.* St. Louis: Mosby

Marson S (1982) Developing skills in communication — 1 & 2: an interactive approach. *Nurse Education Today*, **2** (1 & 2)

Mayers M (1972) *A Systematic Approach to Nursing Care Plans.* Norwalk: Appleton-Century-Crofts

Norton D, McLaren R & Exton-Smith A (1975) *An Investigation of Geriatric Patients in Hospital.* Edinburgh: Churchill-Livingstone

Orem D (1980) *Nursing: Concepts of Practice.* New York: McGraw-Hill

Rehman J (1976) *Writing Patient Care Plans.* San Diego: Professional Lecture Series

Rines A & Montag M (1976) *Nursing Concepts and Nursing Care.* New York: John Wiley

Roper N, Logan W, & Tierney A (1980) *The Elements of Nursing.* Edinburgh: Churchill Livingstone

Roy C (1970) Adaptation: a basis for nursing practice. *Nursing Outlook*, **19** (4)

Ryan B J (1973) Nursing care plans: a systems approach to developing criteria for planning and evaluation. *Journal of Nursing Administration*, **3** (May/June)

Saxton D F & Hyland P (1975) *Planning and Implementing Nursing Intervention*. St. Louis: Mosby

Smith L (1980) A nursing history and data sheet (psychiatry). *Nursing Times*, **76**(13)

Walker J B et al (1976) *Dynamics of Problem-Oriented Approaches: Patient Care and Documentation*. Philadelphia: Lippincott

Yura H & Walsh M (1978) *Human Needs and The Nursing Process*. Norwalk: Appleton-Century-Crofts

Chapter 13

Bibliography

The following list is of books and journal articles recommended for reference in relation to care planning. Although fairly extensive, however, it is not intended to be comprehensive, and the reader is directed to consult *Nursing Bibliography*, a monthly publication produced by the Library of the Royal College of Nursing, for other literature relating to the subject. For books and articles published prior to the first edition of *Nursing Care Plans* the reader is referred to the comprehensive bibliography of that edition. For this new edition we have included a selection of the publications that have appeared since 1980 on care planning but only relatively few of those that appeared before that date.

The bibliography is divided into the following sections, with books and journal articles listed separately in each:

The nursing process – general
Ideologies, concepts, theories and models of nursing
Assessment
Nursing diagnoses
Care Plans and care planning
Evaluating nursing care
Primary nursing
Patient allocation
Teaching nursing process skills

The nursing process – general

BOOKS

Heath J & Law G (1982) *Nursing Process : What is it?* Sheffield:ENB
    Learning Resources Unit
Kratz C (ed) (1977) *The Nursing Process.* London: Baillière Tindall
Marriner A. (ed) (1982) *The Nursing Process: A Scientific Approach to
    Nursing Care.* St Louis: C V Mosby
Sundeen S J et al. (1981) *Nurse-Client Interaction: Implementing the
    Nursing Process.* St Louis: C V Mosby
Yura H & Walsh M (1983) *The Nursing Process: Assessing, Planning,
    Implementing, Evaluating.* New York: Appleton-Century-Crofts

ARTICLES

Bowman G (1983) The pitfalls of implementing the nursing process.
    Nursing Times, **79** (12 Jan)
Carlson S (1972) A practical approach to the nursing process. *American
    Journal of Nursing,* **72** (9)
Chiarella M (1983) Nursing process – tool or rule? *Nursing Times,* **79**
    (13 July)
Crow J (1977) The nursing process – 1: theoretical background.
    Nursing Times, **73** (16 June)
Crow J (1977) The nursing process – 2: how and why to take a nursing
    history. *Nursing Times,* **73** (23 June)
Crow J (1977) The nursing process – 3: a nursing history questionnaire
    for two patients. *Nursing Times,* **73** (30 June)
de la Cuesta C (1983) The nursing process: from development to
    implementation. *Journal of Advanced Nursing,* **8** (5)
Dickinson S (1982) The nursing process and the professional status of
    nursing. *Nursing Times,* **78** (2 June), occasional papers
Hargreaves I (1975) The nursing process: the key to individualized
    care. *Nursing Times,* **71** (28 August), occasional papers
Henderson V (1982) The nursing process: is the title right? *Journal of
    Advanced Nursing,* **7** (2)
Hurst K (1983) Nursing process: the quiet revolution. *Nursing Mirror,*
    157 (26 Oct)
Jones C (1977) The nursing process: individualized care. *Nursing
    Mirror,* **144** (13 Oct)
Kratz C (1977) The nursing process. *Nursing Times,* **73** (9 June)
Marks-Maran D (1978) Rediscovering the patient. *Nursing Times,* 74
    (30 Nov) pull-out supplement
Marks-Maran D (1979) In the process of better care. *Nursing Mirror,*
    149 (12 July)
Rumbold G (1982) The nursing process – a problem solving approach?
    Journal of Community Nursing, **5**(10)

Ideology, concepts, theories and models of nursing

BOOKS

Carnevali D (1983) *Nursing Care Planning: Diagnosis and Management.*
New York: J B Lippincott
Griffith J & Christiansen P (1982) *Nursing Process: Application of Theories, Frameworks and Models.* St Louis: C V Mosby
Kershaw B & Salvage J (1986) *Models for Nursing,* Chichester: John Wiley & Sons
King I (1981) *A Theory for Nursing.* New York: John Wiley & Sons
McFarlane J & Castledine G (1982) *A Guide to the Practice of Nursing Using the Nursing Process.* London: C V Mosby
Orem D (1980) *Nursing: Concepts of Practice.* New York: McGraw-Hill
Riehl J & Roy C (1980) *Conceptual Models for Nursing Practice.* Norwalk: Appleton-Century-Crofts
Rines A & Montag M (1976) *Nursing Concepts and Nursing Care.* New York: John Wiley & Sons
Rogers M (1970) *An Introduction to the Theoretical Basis of Nursing.* Philadelphia: F A Davis
Roper N, Logan W & Tierney A (1980) *The Elements of Nursing.* Edinburgh: Churchill Livingstone
Roy C (1976) *Introduction to Nursing – An Adaptation Model.* New Jersey: Prentice Hall
Sakalys J (1981) The meaning of health and illness, In Mitchell, *et al. Concepts Basic to Nursing.* New York: McGraw-Hill
Torres G & Yura H (1975) The meaning and functions of concepts and theories within education and nursing. *Faculty-Curriculum Development: Part III.* New York: National League for Nursing
Yura H & Walsh M (1983) *Human Needs and the Nursing Process.* Norwalk: Appleton-Century-Crofts

ARTICLES

Clark J (1982) Development of models and theories on the concept of nursing. *Journal of Advanced Nursing,* 7 (2)
Dickoff J, James P & Wiedenback E (1968) Theory in a practice discipline. *Nursing Research,* 17 (Sept/Oct); 18 (Nov/Dec)
McFarlane E (1980) Nursing theory: the comparison of four theoretical proposals. *Journal of Advanced Nursing,* 5 (1)
Payne L (1983) Health: a basic concept in nursing theory. *Journal of Advanced Nursing* 8 (5)
Roy C (1970) Adaptation: a conceptual framework for nursing. *Nursing Outlook,* 18 (3)
Roy C (1971) Adaptation: a basis for nursing practice. *Nursing Outlook,* 19 (4)
Roy C (1973) Adaptation: implications for curriculum change. *Nursing Outlook,* 21 (3)
Roy C (1975) A diagnostic classification system for nursing. *Nursing Outlook,* 23 (2)

Assessment

BOOKS

Enelow A & Swisher S (1979) *Interviewing and Patient Care*. New York: Oxford University Press

Henderson V (1960) *Basic Principles of Nursing Care*. Geneva: International Council of Nurses

Hayward J (1973) *Information: A Prescription Against Pain*. London: RCN

Maslow A (1970) *Motivation and Personality*. New York: Harper & Row

Roper N, Logan W & Tierney A (1980) *The Elements of Nursing*. Edinburgh: Churchill Livingstone

Norton D (1975) *An Investigation of Geriatric Nursing Problems in Hospital*. Edinburgh: Churchill Livingstone

Sana J & Judge R (eds) (1975) *Physical Appraisal Methods in Nursing Practice*. Boston: Little, Brown

Seedor M (1974) *The Physical Assessment: A Programmed Unit of Study for Nurses*. New York: Teacher's College Press

Watson A & Mayers M (1981) *Assessment and Documentation: Nursing Theories in Action*. Thorofare: Slack

ARTICLES

American Journal of Nursing (1974) Patient assessment: taking a patient's history – programmed instruction, *American Journal of Nursing*, **74** (2)

Boylan A (1982) Nursing at the crossroad – 1: the role of the nurse. *Nursing Times*, **78** (18 Aug)

Castledine G (1979) Nursing assessment of the musculoskeletal system. *Nursing*, June (first series), 112–114

Fry J & Majumdar B (1974) Basic physical assessment. *Canadian Nurse*, **70** (5)

Fuller D & Rosenaus J (1974) A patient assessment guide. *Nursing Outlook*, **22** (7)

Guy's Hospital (1981) Organic mental impairment in the elderly. *Journal of the Royal College of Physicians*, **5** (3)

Hefferin E & Hunter R (1975) Nursing assessment and care plan statements. *Nursing Research*, **24** (Sept/Oct)

Keithly J & Tasic P (1982) A unified approach to assessment of the surgical patient. *American Journal of Nursing*, **82** (4)

Langner S (1973) The nursing process and the interview. *Occupational Health Nursing*, **21** (12)

Lee P (1980) No half measures. *Nursing Times*, **76** (26 June)

McCain R (1965) Nursing by assessment – not intuition. *American Journal of Nursing*, **65** (4)

McPheteridge M (1968) Nursing history: one means to personalise care. *American Journal of Nursing*, **68** (1)

Mallick M (1981) Patient assessment based on dara, not intuition. *Nursing Outlook*, **29** (10)

Matheny A (1967) A guide for interviewing. *American Journal of Nursing*, **67** (10)

Norton D (1980) Assessing incontinence. *Nursing*, October (first series)

Nursing Clinics of North America (1971) Symposium on assessment as part of the nursing process. *Nursing Clinics of North America*, **6** (1)

Samy T (1983) Structured assessment. *Nursing Mirror*, **157** (23 Nov)

Smith L (1980) A nursing history and data sheet (psychiatry). *Nursing Times*, **76** (13)

Talento B & Crockett-McKeever L (1983) Improving interviewing techniques. *Nursing Outlook*, **31** (4)

Nursing diagnosis

BOOKS

Carlson J, Craft C & McGuire J (1982) *Nursing Diagnosis*. Philadelphia: W B Saunders

Carpenito L (1983) *Nursing Diagnosis: Application to Clinical Practice.* Philadelphia: Lippincott

Gordon M (1982) *Nursing Diagnosis: Process and Application*. New York: McGraw Hill

Gebbie K & Lavin M (1975) *Classification of Nursing Diagnosis*. St Louis: C V Mosby

Kim M & Moritz D (1982) *Nursing Diagnoses: Proceedings From the Third and Fourth National Conferences*. New York: McGraw Hill

ARTICLES

Advances in Nursing Science (1979) Nursing Diagnosis (entire issue devoted to this subject). *Advances in Nursing Science*, **2** (1)

Aspinall M (1976) Nursing diagnosis – the weak link. *Nursing Outlook*, **24** (7)

Bircher A (1975) On the development and classification of nursing diagnoses. *Nursing Forum*, **14** (1)

Durand M & Prince R (1966) Nursing diagnosis process and decision. *Nursing Forum*, **5** (4)

Gordon M (1976) Nursing diagnosis and the diagnostic process. *American Journal of Nursing*, **76** (8)

Gordon M, Sweeney M & McKeehan K (1980) Nursing diagnosis: look at its use in the clinical areas. *American Journal of Nursing*, **80** (4)

Hardy E (1983) The diagnostic wheel: identifying care that is unique to nursing. *Canadian Nurse*, **79** (3)

Lunney M (1982) Nursing diagnosis: refining the system. *American Journal of Nursing*, **82** (3)

Marks-Maran D (1983) Can nurses diagnose? *Nursing Times,* **79** (26 Jan)

Mundinger M & Jauron G (1975) Developing a nursing diagnosis. *Nursing Outlook,* **23** (2)

Myers N (1973) Nursing diagnosis. *Nursing Times,* **69** (20 Sept)

Price M (1980) Nursing diagnosis: making a concept come alive. *American Journal of Nursing,* **80** (4)

Roy C (1975) The impact of nursing diagnosis. *Association of Operating Room Nurses,* **21** (6)

Care plans and care planning

BOOKS

Berni R & Readey H (1978) *Problem-Oriented Medical Record Implementation.* St Louis: C V Mosby

Bower F (1982) *The Process of Planning Nursing Care: A Theoretical Model.* St Louis: C V Mosby

Hunt J (1979) *A Comparative Study to Determine the Most Effective Method of Communicating Nursing Instructions. Final Report.* The London Hospital (unpublished)

Lelean S (1974) *Ready for Report, Nurse?* London: Royal College of Nursing

Lewis L (1976) *Planning Patient Care.* Dubuque, USA: Wm Brown

Mayers M (1983) *A Systematic Approach to Nursing Care Plans.* Norwalk: Appleton-Century-Crofts

Rehman J (1976) *Writing Patient Care Plans.* San Diego; Professional Lecture Series

Saxton D & Hyland P (1979) *Planning and Implementing Nursing Intervention.* St Louis: C V Mosby

Vaughan-Wroebel B. & Henderson B. (1981) *The Problem-Oriented System in Nursing.* St Louis: C V Mosby

Vitale B et al. (1974) *A Problem-Solving Approach to Nursing Care Plans.* St Louis: C V Mosby

ARTICLES

Barnett D (1982) A series of five articles (pull-out supplements) on the implementation of care plans. *Nursing Times,* **78** (31 March, 28 April, 26 May, 23 June, 28 July)

Bendle M (1983) More reprocessing. *Journal of District Nursing,* **2** (4)

Bryant R (1980) Problem-oriented nursing care plans. *Australian Nurse,* **10** (1)

Case B & Rooney D (1982) Patient care planning strategies. *Nursing Management,* **13** (4)

Ciuca R (1972) Over the years with the nursing care plan. *Nursing Outlook,* **20** (11)

Francis M (1967) This thing called problem solving. *Journal of Nursing Education*, **6** (19 Nov)

Grant N (1975) The nursing care plan. **Nursing Times, 71** (27 Mar)

Henderson V (1973) On nursing care plans and their history. *Nursing Outlook*, **21** (6)

Little D & Carnevalli D (1967) Nursing care plans: let's be practical about them. *Nursing Forum*, **6** (1)

Little D & Carnevalli D (1971) The nursing care planning system. *Nursing Outlook*, **19** (3)

Marks-Maran D (1979) Problem-orientated nursing care plans. *Medical Record*, **20** (2)

Ryan B J (1973) Nursing care plans: a systems approach to developing criteria for planning and evaluation. *Journal of Nursing Administration*, **3** (May/June), pp 50–58

Rogers B (1981) Care planning: a comment on the Canadian experience. *Canadian Nurse*, **77** (7)

Syson-Nibbs L (1980) Progress through a planned approach. *Nursing Mirror*, **150** (14 Feb)

Evaluating nursing care

ARTICLES

Bergman R (1982) Evaluation of nursing care: could it make a difference? *International Journal of Nursing Studies*, **19** (2)

Castledine G (1983) In the best possible care. *Nursing Mirror*, **156** (11 May)

Castledine G (1982) The patient's progress. *Nursing Mirror*, **155** (20 Oct)

Copp L (1972) Improved patient care through evaluation. *Bedside Nurse*, **5** (Sept)

Farrell P & Scherer K (1983) The Delphi technique as a method for selecting criteria to evaluate nursing care. *Nursing Papers*, **15** (1)

Gamberg M (1981) Outcome charting. *Nursing Management*, **12** (10)

Goldstone L & Ball J (1983) The quality of nursing care. *Health Services Manpower Review*, **9** (3)

Hegyvary S (1979) The nursing process: the basis for evaluating the quality of nursing care. *Internamonal Nursing Review*, **26** (4)

Lillesand K & Korff S (1983) Nursing process evaluation: a quality assurance tool. *Nursing Administration Quarterly*, **7** (3)

Machray I (1980) Do it yourself evaluation. *Hospital Health Services Review*, **76** (9)

Wainwright P & Burnip S (1983) QUALPACS at Burford. *Nursing Times*, **79** (2 Feb)

Wilson-Barnett J (1981) Care evaluation: sizing up the scores. *Nursing Mirror*, **153** (26 Aug)

Primary nursing

BOOKS

Manthey M (1980) *The Practice of Primary Nursing*. Boston/Oxford: Blackwell Scientific Publications

Marram G *et al.* (1979) *Primary Nursing: A Model for Individualised Care*. St Louis: C V Mosby

ARTICLES

Anderson M (1976) Primary nursing in day to day practice. *American Journal of Nursing*, **76** (5)

Bailey K *et al.* (1981) A tool for implementing primary nursing. *Supervisor Nurse*, **12** (8)

Baskin P (1980) Primary nursing: Australia's emerging patterns. *Australian Nurse*, **9** (9)

Cavill C & Johnson J (1981) Step towards the process. *Nursing Times*, **77** (2 Dec)

Ciske K (1974) Primary nursing: an organization that promotes professional practice. *Journal of Nursing Administration*, 4 (Jan/Feb)

Ciske K (1974) Primary nursing: evaluation. *American Journal of Nursing*, **74** (8)

Ciske K (1979) Accountability: the essence of primary nursing. *American Journal of Nursing*, **79** (5)

Dawson P & Wilson N (1983) What nurses say about primary nursing. *Canadian Nurse*, **79** (6)

Jackson J (1983) The case for primary nursing. *New Zealand Nursing Journal*, **76** (4)

Lee M (1979) Towards better care: primary nursing. *Nursing Times*, **75** (51) (occasional paper)

Manthey M *et al.* (1970) Primary nursing. *Nursing Forum*, **9**

Manthey M (1973) Primary nursing is alive and well in the hospital. *American Journal of Nursing*, **73** (1)

Manthey M (1980) A theoretical framework for primary nursing. *Journal of Nursing Administration*, **10** (6)

Manthey M (1970) Primary nursing – a return to the concept of 'my nurse' and 'my patient.' *Nursing Forum*, **9** (1)

Robinson A (1974) Primary nursing at two teaching hospitals. *R N Magazine*, **47** (April)

Sellick K *et al.* (1983) Primary nursing: an evaluation of its effects on patient perception of care and staff satisfaction. *International Journal of Nursing Studies*, **20** (4)

Van Servellen G (1981) Primary nursing: variations in practice. *Journal of Nursing Administration*, **11** (9)

Patient allocation

ARTICLES

Bird K (1974) Working with patient assignment. *Australian Nurses Journal*, **3** (May)

Correy M (1976) Will patient assignment improve nursing care? *New Zealand Nursing Journal*, **69** (Feb)

Jones E (1977) A patient allocation trial. *Nursing Times*, **73** (17 March)

Jones W (1977) Management by crisis or objectives? Parts 1 & 2. *Nursing Times*, **73** (10, 17 March)

Kenny D (1973) Patient assignment. *The Lamp*, **30** (Jan)

Marks-Maran D (1978) Patient allocation v. task allocation. *Nursing Times*, **74** (25 March)

Matthews A (1975) Patient allocation: a review. *Nursing Times*, **71** (10, 17, 24, 31 July) (occasional papers)

Pembrey S (1975) From work routines to patient assignment: an experiment in ward management. *Nursing Times*, **71** (Nov)

Teaching nursing process skills

BOOKS

Aspinall M & Tanner C (1981) *Decision Making For Patient Care: Applying the Nursing Process*. New York: Appleton-Century-Crofts

Thompson B & Bridge W (1981) *Teaching Patient Care: Guidance For The Practising Nurse*. Chichester: HM & M/John Wiley & Sons

ARTICLES

Ashworth P & Castledine G (1981) The way we teach nursing using the nursing process. *Medical Teacher*, **3** (3)

Barnes D (1983) teaching communication skills to student nurses – an experience. *Nurse Education Today*, **3** (2)

Bridge W & Speight I (1981) Teaching the skills of nursing communications. *Nursing Times*, **77** (32) (occasional papers)

Briggs K (1982) Interpersonal skills training for student nurses during introductory course. *Nurse Educational Today*, **2** (1)

Briggs K & Wright B (1982) Education forum – 6: communication – a fundamental skill. *Nursing Mirror*, **155** (1 Sept)

Brown S (1981) The nursing process systems model. *Journal of Nursing Education*, **20** (6)

Carter S (1979) Teaching the nursing process: the nurse educator. *Nursing Times*, **75** (31)

Christian P & Smith L (1981) Using video tapes to teach interviewing skills. *Nurse Educator*, **6** (4)

Dick D (1983) Teaching health assessment skills: a self-instructional approach. *Journal of Nursing Education*, **22** (8)

Goble I W J (1981) Educating the professional nurse of tomorrow . . . today (a proposed framework for developing problem solving skills and research awareness in nurse learners). *Nursing Times*, **77** (23 Apr)

Gott M (1982) Theories of learning and the teaching of nursing. *Nursing Times*, **78** (21 Apr)

Grey J (1983) *Caring Communication*. (A teaching package of exercises and activities to teach communication skills). London: DHSS

Grubb M (1979) A clinical teacher's view. *Nursing Times*, **75** (23 Aug)

Heath J (1982) Intention and practice in nursing education. *Nurse Education Today*, **2** (4)

Hollingsworth S (1979) A challenge for nurse teachers. *Nursing Times*, **75** (30)

Jacoby M & Adams D (1981) Teaching assessment of client functioning. *Nursing Outlook*, **29** (4)

Kershaw B (1981) The nursing process in action – 2: Teaching and evaluating care. *Nursing Times*, **77** (24–30 June)

Lewis M (1981) The nursing process in action – 2: the teaching programme. *Nursing Times*, **77** (24–30 June)

Luker K (1979) Teaching the nursing process. *Nursing Times*, **75** (35)

McCarthy M (1981) The nursing process: application of current thinking in clinical problem-solving. *Journal of Advanced Nursing*, **6** (3)

Marson S (1982) Developing skills in communication – 1 & 2: an interactive approach. *Nurse Education Today*, **2** (1, 2)

Roy C (1979) Relating nursing theory to education: a new era. *Nurse Education*, **4** (2)

Smeltzer C (1980) Teaching the nursing process – practical method. *Journal of Nursing Education*, **19** (9)

Sparks S (1980) Teaching of interpersonal skills to nurse practitioner students. *Journal of Continuing Education in Nursing*, **11** (3)

Stewart P (1983) The nursing process: a model for teaching. *Journal of Continuing Education in Nursing*, **14** (3)

Voight J (1980) Physical assessment skills in the curriculum. *Journal of Nursing Education*, **19** (2)

Whitfield S (1983) Teaching the nurse process. *Nursing Mirror*, **156** (18 May)

Wibley S (1983) Use of role play. *Nursing Times*, **79** (22 June)

Appendices

Appendix 1a: An example of a General Acute Care Plan format.
(Reproduced by courtesy of City & Hackney Health Authority.)

PATIENT'S DETAILS	MEDICAL DETAILS	ADMISSION/DISCHARGE DETAILS
Surname _____ Title _____	Provisional diagnosis _____	Hospital number _____
Other names _____		Date(s) of admission _____
Date of birth _____ Age _____	Actual diagnosis _____	
Adress _____		Ward _____
	Operation(s) _____	CARE AT HOME
		Housing conditions _____
Telephone number _____		
Religion _____		
Religious/Cultural needs _____	Allergies _____	Community services received _____
	Relevant medical history and drug therapy _____	
Present/Previous occupation _____		Social problems due to admission of illness _____
Effect of illness on occupation _____		
	Patient's reason for admission _____	Social worker (name and date informed) _____
Hobbies/Interests _____	Patient's understanding of illness and treatment _____	DISCHARGE PLANNING
		Predicted date of discharge _____
Person to be contacted _____		Money with administrator _____
		Outpatient appointment(s) _____
Relationship _____		
Inform at night _____	Family's understanding of illness/treatment _____	Community services requested _____
Address _____		
Telephone number(s) _____		

1a (cont.)

NUTRITION	ACTIVITIES OF DAILY LIVING	BREATHING
		Smoking habits
Alcohol intake		SLEEP
ELIMINATION		
Bowel pattern		
Use of aperients		Aids to sleep
Any bowel problems		SENSES
		Vision (including aids)
Any bladder problems		
		Hearing (including aids)
Menstruation/Menopause		
		Speech (including language difficulty)
Use of contraceptives		
		Balance (co-ordination difficulty)
HYGIENE		
Description of skin/mouth condition		Pain
		EMOTIONAL STATE
Condition of teeth/dentures		
MOBILITY		
Special aids used		

1a (cont.)

Name: **Hospital Number:**   **Score on Norton Scale:**

Date	No.	Problem	Aim of Care	Nursing Action	Review Date

Date	Progress/Evaluation	Nurse's Signature	Others involved in Care Medical Investigations

Name	Age	Religion	Consultant	C.R. No.

Appendix 1b: An example of a General Acute Care Plan format.
(Reproduced by courtesy of Tower Hamlets Health Authority.)

Name:							

NURSING CARE PLAN   **TOWER HAMLETS HEALTH AUTHORITY**

Date	Patient's Problems	Goals/Outcome	Date	Date	NURSING ACTION Date	Date	Date
		A					
		Review: Evaluation:					
		B					
		Review: Evaluation:					
		C					
		Review: Evaluation:					
		D					
		Review: Evaluation:					
		E					
		Review: Evaluation:					

1b (cont.)

IDENTIFY PROBLEMS

Does the patient have difficulty with or need help to avoid a risk associated with any of the following?

Breathing	Allergy	Pain	Mobility
Eating	Elimination	Anxiety	Religion
Drinking	Investigation	Wound	Social role
Sleeping	Operation	Skin	
	Understanding		

If so, *state the problem* briefly, put the possible reason in brackets below it, in the 'Patient's Problem' column.

Then *formulate a realistic goal* for nursing action, state the goal in the space next to the problem.

List the main steps to be taken today, under today's date, in the action column.

Be precise about lengths of time (e.g. how many hours or minutes to be spent sitting in a chair), amounts of fluid (e.g. how many ml of fluid to be given each hour when awake) and frequency (e.g. how often or at what times should the action be carried out).

Review the patient's condition when writing the progress notes, are the problems still the same or are there new ones? List the nursing action each day or indicate it is to be continued by use of the arrows.

LEARNERS MUST HAVE THEIR CARE PLAN CHECKED BY A QUALIFIED NURSE.

For more detailed planning information see 'Guidance Notes for Nursing Care Planning'.

1b (cont.)

Name: _____

SUMMARY/EVALUATION OF NURSING CARE

TOWER HAMLETS HEALTH AUTHORITY

Date	Patient's Problems	Goals/Outcome	SUMMARY OF ACTION AND CURRENT STATE OF PROBLEMS (If resolved give date of resolution)	SUGGESTIONS FOR FURTHER ACTION ON TRANSFER
		A Review: Evaluation:		
		B Review: Evaluation:		
		C Review: Evaluation:		
		D Review: Evaluation:		
		E Review: Evaluation:		

Evaluation Completed By   Grade: on:

FILE COPY

1b (cont.)

INFORMATION FROM HOSPITAL TO COMMUNITY NURSING SERVICE		
Hospital	Ward	*Record No.
*Consultant	Date of Discharge	
Name		
Discharge / Home Address		
Length of anticipated stay at Discharge Address		
Special points for community staff to gain access (e.g. who holds a key or what is agreed code of knocks on door to identify nurse, deafness, slow to walk to door etc.)		
*Date of Birth	*Age	*Religion
*Marital Status	*Lives: Alone / With Spouse / With Friend or Relative	
*Next of Kin	*Relationship to Patient	
*Address		
*Telephone Number		
Information about diagnosis and/or prognosis given to patient and/or Next of Kin		
Neighbours, friends or other relatives involved in the care of the patient		
*General Practitioner		
*Address		
*Telephone Number		
Services already organised from Hospital but not included in the Nursing information overleaf		
Information Prepared By	Grade	on 198
*Information may be found in the Nursing Admission sheet		

Appendix 2a: An example of a District Nursing Care Plan format.
(Reproduced by courtesy of Hammersmith & Fulham Health Authorit

CONTINUATION SHEETS ATTACHED HERE

SUMMARY + 1ST ASSESSMENT

Date of Visit	Remarks (initial each entry)

KEY TO PROBLEM   A = ACTUAL   P = POTENTIAL
KEY TO ACTION   S = SHORT TERM   L = LONG TERM

Date Identified	Problem	Type	Objectives	Date Comme

HAMMERSMITH AND FULHAM HEALTH AUTHORITY
DISTRICT NURSING

HEALTH CENTRE/CLINIC

Reference No:

Surname:

Address: Tel. No:

Means of entry:

D.O.B:

Sex:

Next of kin:

Full name:

Address: Tel. No:

General practitioner:

Name:

Address: Tel. No:

Date of first referral to district nursing service: / /19

Nursing Action	Date Discontinued	Evaluation

2a (cont.)

HAMMERSMITH AND FULHAM HEALTH AUTHORITY
DISTRICT NURSING

1st ASSESSMENT

HEALTH CENTRE/CLINIC

REFFERED BY:

Hospital: Hospital No.:   Consultant:

Own G.P:

Other Agencies:

MEDICAL HISTORY

PAST MEDICAL HISTORY:

HISTORY OF PRESENT ILLNESS:

DIAGNOSIS:

PRESENTING SIGNS AND SYMPTOMS:

PRESENT MEDICAL TREATMENT:

DRUGS: Please complete Drug Sheet
          Wound Application/Enemas/
          Contraceptive Pill.

Signed: ....

District Nursing Sister

Date: ....

2a (cont.)

HAMMERSMITH AND FULHAM HEALTH AUTHORITY
DISTRICT NURSING SERVICE

HEALTH CENTRE/CLINIC

SOCIAL HISTORY

COMPOSITION OF FAMILY

1 Does the patient live alone?   with relatives?
  Other Tenants:

2 Number in Family?

3 What ages are they?   Under 65:   Over 65:

4 What is their health like?

5 Any help from relatives, neighbours or friends:

6 How far away do they live?

7 How often do they visit?

8 Does anyone have a key? (state who):
  (relevant if patient living alone).

9 Occupations of relatives if relevant:

10 Patients past/present occupation:

11 Patients hobbies:

12 Are there pets?

HOUSING (Delete where applicable)

1 **Accommodation:** House Flat Room Floor:
                     Own Rented Private Council
2 **Lavatory:**   Own Shared Location: Commode
3 **Bathroom:**   Own Shared Location:
4 **Water Supply:** Hot and Cold Cold Method of
                                   Heating:
5 **Heating:**   Type: Guard: Slot Meter:
6 **Ventilation:**   Type:
7 **Cooking Facilities:** Type:
8 Describe Accommodation (layout - condition - hazards - etc.)
  Sleeping Area - location - bed - electric - points (round/square)
  Rooms used by patient - suitability.

                    Signature: ....
                              District Nursing Sister

                    Date: ....

2a (cont.)

HAMMERSMITH AND FULHAM HEALTH AUTHORITY
DISTRICT NURSING SERVICE

HEALTH CENTRE/CLINIC   1st ASSESSMENT

COMMUNITY CARE DATA

AGENCIES INVOLVED — Give date and details if applicable/state if
referred by:

HEALTH VISITOR — Name :   Centre/   Tel.

Date referred   Clinic   No.

FAMILY PLANNING — CLINIC/GP

HOME HELP — Name: Days: Time:
            Duration: Date commenced:

LUNCHEON CLUB:

MEALS ON WHEELS: Days: Special diet:
                           Date commenced:

CHIROPODY: Clinic   Domiciliary:

EQUIPMENT ON LOAN:

OCCUPATIONAL THERAPIST — NAME

INCO :   LAUNDRY:

MOBILE BATHING:

DAY HOSPITAL — Treatment:
               Frequency of attendances:

DAY CENTRE ATTENDED:

HOSPITAL O P D

VOLUNTARY WORKERS:

SOCIAL CLUBS ATTENDED:

MOBILE LIBRARY:

HAIRDRESSER/BARBER:

SPIRITUAL NEEDS:

Signature:..
District Nursing Sister

Date: ....

2a (cont.)

NURSING OBSERVATIONS

CLINIC: ....

MENTAL CONDITION:	Euphoric Orientated	Cheerful Confused	Anxious Unresponsive	Distressed	Depressed
WEIGHT:	Normal	Overweight	Underweight	(according to build)	
HAIR:	Condition				

SKIN: ARMS	Hands		Nails		
LEGS	Feet		Nails		

HEARING: Good	Poor	Wearing Hearing Aid	YES NO	Satisfactory	YES NO
VISION: Good	Poor	Wears Spectacles	YES NO	Satisfactory	YES NO
SPEECH: Good	Has difficulties				

TEETH: Own	Top Bottom	Satisfactory	Dentures	Top Bottom	Satisfactory
LAVATORY:	Manages alone		Manages with help	Cannot manage	

BLADDER FUNCTION: NORMAL PATTERN:		Frequent	Nocturia	Catheter	Incontinent
BOWEL FUNCTIONS: NORMAL PATTERN: MENSTRUAL PATTERN:		Frequent	At night	Formation of Faeces	

COLOSTOMY APPLIANCE	COLOSTOMY APPLIANCE USED	ILEOSTOMY	MANAGES ALONE	WITH HELP	CANNOT MANAGE

MOBILITY: STAIRS: ADAPTATIONS IN USE:	Walks alone Manages alone	Walks with aids	Manages with help	Chair bound Cannot manage	Bed fast
PERSONAL CLOTHING:	Manages alone		Manages with help	Cannot manage	
SLEEP:	Natural		With medication		
DIET:	Normal Manages alone	Special	Manages with help	Usual meal pattern Cannot manage	

T	P	R	B/P	URINANALYSIS:

* PROTHESIS AIDS AND ADAPTATIONS REQUIRED — see supplies equipment records card.

Signed..

Date..

2a *(cont.)*

HAMMERSMITH AND FULHAM HEALTH AUTHORITY
DISTRICT NURSING SERVICE
SUPPLIES AND EQUIPMENT RECORD SHEET

Aids/Prosthesis/Adaptation	Supplied by	Delivery date	Date returned

HAMMERSMITH AND FULHAM HEALTH AUTHORITY
DISTRICT NURSING SERVICE
TREATMENT RECORD

Enter Controlled Drugs in Red

COLLECTED·BY: ....

....

....

....

NAME:

CLINIC/CENTRE:

SUPPLIED: Hospital* Consultant* GP*
  *(*Delete where applicable)*

WHERE KEPT: ....

....

....

Date	Drug/Treatment	Amount	Frequency	Review

Appendix 2b: An example of a District Nursing Care Plan format.
(Reproduced by courtesy of City & Hackney Health Authority.)

CITY AND HACKNEY HEALTH AUTHORITY - DISTRICT NURSING
NURSING HISTORY

PATIENT'S DETAILS

Surname _____ Title _____
Other names _____
Marital status _____
Date of birth _____ Age _____
Address _____
_____
Telephone number _____
Religion _____
Religious/Cultural needs _____

HOUSEHOLD DETAILS

Does patient live alone? _____
Other household members _____

Housing Conditions _____
_____

Any visiting problems _____

Person to be contacted _____
Relationship _____
Address _____
_____
Telephone numbers:-
Home _____ Work _____
Any children _____
Any other dependents _____
Other contacts _____
Address _____
_____
Telephone number _____

MEDICAL DETAILS

Diagnosis _____
_____
Operation(s) _____
_____
Allergies _____
Relevant medical history _____
_____
_____
Previous relevant hospital attendances _____
_____
Current hospital attendances _____
_____
Patient's understanding of illness _____
_____
Family's understanding of illness _____
_____

SOCIAL DETAILS

Present/previous occupation _____
Effect of illness on occupation _____
_____
Source of income _____
Who deals with income/finances _____
Hobbies/Interests _____

COMMUNITY DETAILS

Sister/Charge Nurse _____
Date of referral _____
Referred by whom _____
Reason for referral _____
G.P. _____
Address _____
Telephone number _____
Shared cared with:- _____
Twilight _____
MacMillan _____
Community psychiatric nurse _____
Other _____

COMMUNITY DISCHARGE

Date of discharge _____
Reason for discharge _____

29065 GHRJ

2b (cont.)

DRUG INFORMATION

NAME OF DRUG	DOSAGE	FREQUENCY	DATE STARTED	DATE STOPPED	SIDE EFFECTS NOTICED

COMMUNITY SERVICES

SERVICES INVOLVED	EXISTING	REQUESTED	HEALTH AUTHORITY	EQUIPMENT ON LOAN (STATE ITEMS) SOCIAL SERVICES
HEALTH VISITOR				
CLINIC NURSE				
CHIROPODIST				
PHYSIOTHERAPIST				
OCCUPATIONAL THERAPIST				
SOCIAL WORKER				
HOME HELP				
MEALS ON WHEELS				
DAY CENTRE/LUNCHEON CENTRE				
DAY HOSPITAL				
VOLUNTARY SERVICES				
BATHING SERVICE				
LAUNDRY SERVICE				
(a) HOUSEBOUND				
(b) INCONTINENT				

2b (cont.)

ACTIVITIES OF DAILY LIVING

NUTRITION

Normal meal pattern

Special diet

Alcohol intake

Cooking facilities

Who does the shopping?

Any problems with eating

ELIMINATION

Normal bowel pattern

Any aperients

Any bowel problems

any urinary problems

Special appliances

HYGIENE

Description of skin/mouth condition

MOBILITY

Type of help (including aids) required for :-

Walking

Dressing

Washing

Toiletting

Feeding

Other

BREATHING

Smoking habits

SLEEP

Normal sleep pattern

Aids to sleep

Naps during day

Any difficulties

SENSES

Vision (including aids)

Hearing (including aids)

Speech (including any language difficulty)

Balance

Co-ordination

Pain

Methods of pain relief

EMOTIONAL STATE

INITIAL ASSESSMENT

DATE	T.P.R.	B/P													NURSE'S SIGNATURE
	URINALYSIS	WEIGHT													

PROBLEM/NEED	NURSING ACTION	EVALUATION

2b (cont.)

2b (cont.)

THE CITY AND HACKNEY HEALTH AUTHORITY
COMMUNITY NURSING DIVISION

TO BE RETAINED IN PATIENT'S HOME AND COMPLETED AT EACH VISIT

NAME:

ADDRESS:

TELE. No.:

RELIGION: D.O.B

DATE COMMENCED:

DATE COMPLETED:

PERSON TO BE CONTACTED:

RELATIONSHIP:

ADDRESS:

TEL. No.:

DISTRICT NURSE

G.P.

TEL. No.:

NURSING BASE:

HEALTH VISITOR

SOCIAL WORKER

SERVICES	SUN	MON	TUES	WED	THURS	FRI	SAT
HOME HELP							
MEALS ON WHEELS							
LAUNDRY a) House-bound b) Incontinent							
DAY CENTRE							
DAY HOSPITAL							
TWILIGHT SERVICE							
OTHERS							
CHIROPODY							

2b *(cont.)*

NAME: ADDRESS: CENTRE:

DATE	No	PROBLEM	AIM OF CARE	NURSING ACTION	SIGNATURE	REVIEW DATE

Appendix 3: An example of an Obstetric Care Plan format.
(Reproduced by courtesy of City & Hackney Health Authority.)

MOTHER'S DETAILS	OBSTETRIC DETAILS	ADMISSION/TRANSFER DETAILS

MOTHER'S DETAILS

Surname

Other names

Likes to be called

Marital Status

Date of birth _____ Age

Address

Telephone number

Religion

Religious/Cultrual needs

Special dietary needs

Language difficulty

Occupation

Work plans

Person to be contacted

Relationship

Address

Telephone number(s)

Dependents in family

OBSTETRIC DETAILS

Reason for Admission(s)

Relevant Past Obstetric History

Relevant medical history and drug therapy

Emotional adjustment to pregnancy/labour/ baby

Blood Group _____ Rhesus factor

Sickle Test

Rubella Screen

Allergies

ADMISSION/TRANSFER DETAILS

Date	Time	Ward

Date of transfer to community

Date of community discharge

CARE AT HOME

Relevant housing conditions

Any problems at home due to admission

Any other problems

Social Worker/Health Visitor/Health Worker/

Interpreter contacted (date and name)

OTHER RELEVANT INFORMATION

3 (cont.)

SUMMARY OF LABOUR

_____

_____

_____

_____

_____

_____

_____

_____

Signature of student midwife _____

Countersignature of midwife _____

Date _____ Time _____

DOMESTIC ARRANGEMENTS ON TRANSFER HOME

_____

_____

_____

_____

FAMILY PLANNING ADVICE

_____

_____

Form of Contraception _____

_____

_____

_____

ASSESSMENT OF BABY

Date of delivery _____

Time of delivery _____

Weight _____

Sex _____ Name _____

Apgar Score 1 _____ 5 _____ 10 _____

Method of resuscitation _____

General condition of baby _____

Konakion given Yes/No _____ Route _____

Temperature: At birth _____ On ward _____

Cord checked _____ On ward _____

Any abnormalities/injuries _____

Feeding on labour ward _____

Plans for future care of baby _____

OTHER RELEVANT INFORMATION

_____

_____

_____

_____

_____

_____

3 (cont.)

NAME:							HOSPITAL NUMBER:

ANTENATAL CARE PLAN

GRAVIDA:	PARITY:	LMP:	EDD (by dates):	EDD (by scan):

DATE	No.	PROBLEM	AIM OF CARE	NURSING ACTION AND SIGNATURE OF MIDWIFE	DATE CHANGE RESOLVED

DATE	INVESTIGATIONS		RESULTS				STARTED	DRUGS	STOPPED
		Hb	HPL	Oestriols	Other				

3 (cont.)

NAME: _____   HOSPITAL NUMBER: _____

POSTNATAL CARE PLAN

PARITY: _____ DATE AND TIME OF DELIVERY: _____ METHOD OF FEEDING: _____ LENGTH OF STAY: _____

DATE	No.	NEED/PROBLEM	AIM OF CARE	NURSING ACTION AND SIGNATURE OF MIDWIFE	DATE CHANGE RESOLVED

LEARNING NEEDS	DATE	COMMENTS	SIGNATURE
Show Top and Tail			
Supervise Top and Tail			
Show feed			
Make feed			
Show bath			
Supervise bath			
Nursing Officer			

CHECKS	DATE	RESULT
Haemoglobin		
Blood pressure		
Guthrie Test		

Date	Progress/Evaluation	Nurse's signature

Name	Age	Religion	Consultant	Hospital Number

Appendix 4: An example of a Psychiatric Care Plan format.
(Reproduced by courtesy of City & Hackney Health Authority.)

SURNAME: _____
OTHER NAMES: _____
ADDRESS: _____

TELEPHONE NUMBER: _____
RELEVANT HOUSING CONDITIONS: _____

DATE OF BIRTH: _____ AGE: _____
PRESENT/PREVIOUS OCCUPATION: _____

FINANCIAL SUPPORT: _____

DEPENDENTS: _____

PERSON TO BE CONTACTED: _____
RELATIONSHIP: _____
ADDRESS: _____

TELEPHONE NUMBERS _____

HEIGHT: _____ WEIGHT: _____
TEMPERATURE: _____ PULSE: _____ B/P: _____
COLOUR OF EYES: _____
COLOUR OF HAIR: _____
DISTINGUISHING MARKS OR INJURIES: _____

PROVISIONAL DIAGNOSIS: _____

ACTUAL DIAGNOSIS: _____

RELEVANT PSYCHIATRIC HISTORY: _____

RELEVANT MEDICAL HISTORY: _____

RELEVANT DRUG THERAPY: _____

ALLERGIES: _____
HOBBIES/INTERESTS: _____

RELIGION: _____
RELIGIOUS/CULTURAL NEEDS: _____

COUNTRY OF ORIGIN: _____
LANGUAGE SPOKEN: _____
OTHER RELEVANT INFORMATION: _____

HOSPITAL NUMBER: _____
WARD: _____
DATE OF ADMISSION: _____
ADMITTED FROM: _____
ACCOMPANIED BY: _____
LEGAL STATUS(Date, Time, Type): _____

COMMUNITY NURSE: _____
SOCIAL WORKER (Name, Address, Telephone Number): _____

OTHER KEY WORKERS (Name, Address, Telephone Number): _____

GENERAL PRACTITIONAR (Name, Address, Telephone Number): _____

DATE OF DISCHARGE: _____
DISCHARGE ARRANGEMENTS: _____

4 (cont.)

NURSING ASSESSMENT OF MENTAL STATE		ACTIVITIES OF DAILY LIVING
General appearance:	Patient's perception of self:	Nutrition:
General behaviour:		Elimination:
	Mechanisms used in coping with stress/anxiety:	Hygiene:
Mood:		Mobility:
	Strengths of personality structure:	Breathing:
Communication and patterns of speech:		Sleep:
	Supportive environmental systems:	Senses:
Contact with reality:		
Information obtained from:	Assessment completed by:	Date:
	Counter signature of trained nurse:	

4 (cont.)

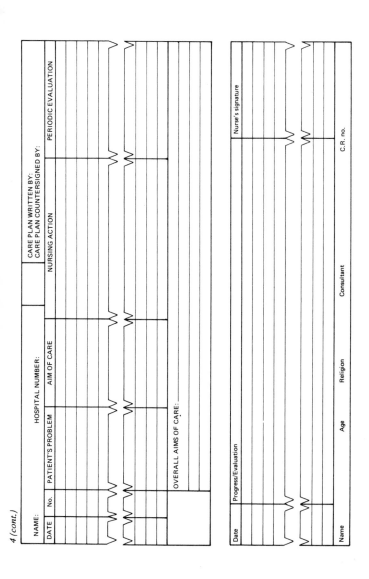

NAME:			HOSPITAL NUMBER:		CARE PLAN WRITTEN BY: CARE PLAN COUNTERSIGNED BY:	
DATE	No.	PATIENT'S PROBLEM	AIM OF CARE		NURSING ACTION	PERIODIC EVALUATION

OVERALL AIMS OF CARE:

Date	Progress/Evaluation			Nurse's signature

Name	Age	Religion	Consultant	C.R. no.

Appendix 5: An example of a Geriatric Care Plan format.
(Reproduced by courtesy of City & Hackney Health Authority.)

PATIENT'S DETAILS	MEDICAL DETAILS	HOSPITAL DETAILS
Surname _____ Title _____	Diagnosis _____	Hospital number _____
Other names _____		Date of admission _____
Likes to be known as _____		Date of discharge _____
Date of birth _____ Age _____	Operations _____	Ward _____
Address _____		SOCIAL DETAILS
		Valuables _____
	Allergies _____	
		Person dealing with financial/other affairs _____
Telephone number _____	Relevant medical history and drug therapy _____	
Religion _____		
Religious/Cultural needs _____		Long term arrangements for home _____
Previous occupation _____		Interests/Hobbies _____
Person to be contacted _____		
Relationship _____	Patient's understanding of illness and reasons for continuing care _____	Favourite TV/Radio programmes _____
Inform at night _____		
Address _____		
		Favourite music _____
Telephone number(s) _____	Family's understanding of illness and reasons for continuing care _____	
Regular visitors and how often _____		Other individual preferences _____
Help given by visitors _____		

5 (cont.)

ACTIVITIES OF DAILY LIVING

NUTRITION

Food/Drink likes _____

Food/Drink dislikes _____

Alcohol intake _____

Special diet/Food supplements _____

Any difficulties _____

ELIMINATION

Bowel pattern _____

Use of aperients _____

Any bowel problems _____

Any bladder problems _____

HYGIENE

Description of skin/mouth condition and any special care _____

Condition of teeth/dentures _____

MOBILITY

Type of help (including aids) required for: _____

Feeding _____

Toiletting _____

Washing _____

Dressing _____

Walking _____

Other _____

BREATHING

Smoking habits _____

SLEEP

Sleep pattern _____

Aids to sleep _____

Naps during day _____

Remedies if restless _____

SENSES

Vision (including aids) _____

Hearing (including aids) _____

Speech (including language difficulty) _____

Balance/Co-ordination difficulty _____

Pain _____

EMOTIONAL STATE

_____

_____

_____

_____

_____

5 (cont.)

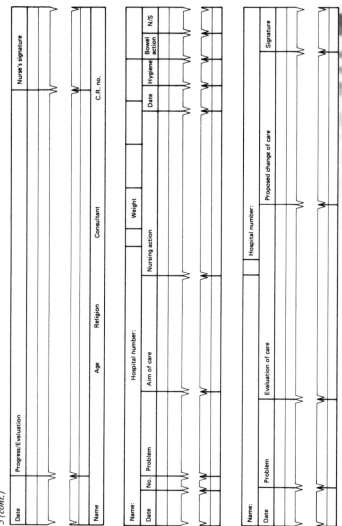

Appendix 6:   An example of a Psychogeriatric Care Plan format.
(Reproduced by courtesy of Tower Hamlets Health Authority.)

WARD
Admission History

SOCIAL INFORMATION:
Name:
Address:
Age:
Religion:
Admission status:
Next of Kin:
Address — if different:

LIVING ACCOMMODATION: Live alone:
Share with others:
Local Authority flat/house:
Local Authority home:
Sheltered flat:
Other:

DEPENDENTS:
Do you have visitors?   Yes: No:
Who calls?
How often?

Community services: Meals on wheels:
Home help:
Day centres:
Luncheon clubs:
Others:

Financial support: Pension book:
Rent book:
TV rent book:
Other:

Who is taking care of   Relative:
these?   Friend:
Hospital:

OTHER SIGNIFICANT OBSERVATIONS:

6 (cont.)

INFORMATION ABOUT ACTIVITIES FOR DAILY LIVING

DIET:	Number of meals a day: Special diet: Food preferences: Dislikes: Fluid preferences: Dislikes:
SLEEP:	Normal sleep pattern: Daytime naps: If unable to sleep — what else helps? Night sedation taken — if any:
URINARY:	Frequency: Incontinent: Dysuria: Nocturia: Normal:
BOWEL MOVEMENTS:	Daily: Other: Type of laxative: How often?
MOBILITY:	Unrestricted limited Walking: Dressing: Bathing : Eating:
HEARING:	Good: Poor: Wears aid:
VISION:	Good: Poor: Wears glasses: always: for reading:
PHYSICAL:	Health Problems:

ADDITIONAL SIGNIFICANT OBSERVATIONS:

6 (cont.)

INFORMATION ABOUT MENTAL HEALTH

GENERAL APPEARANCE: Very tidy:
                      Tidy:
                      Untidy:
                      Grubby:

HOBBIES/INTERESTS:

MOOD: Elated: Anxious:
                      Cheerful: Withdrawn:
                      Smiling: Agitated:
                      Distressed: Aggressive:
                      Miserable: Suspicious:
                      Irritable: Bland:
                      Sad: Apathetic:
                      Other:

THOUGHT CONTENT: Hallucinations:
                      Delusions:
                      Paranoid ideas:

ORIENTATION: Time:
                      Place:
                      Person:
                      Very Confused:
                      Slightly confused:
                      Slightly orientated:
                      Very orientated:

MOTOR ACTIVITY: Overactive:
                      Normal:
                      Lethargic:

SPEECH: Retarded:
                      Normal: Accelerated:

ATTITUDE TO BEING IN HOSPITAL:

ANY OTHER SIGNIFICANT OBSERVATIONS:

HISTORY OBTAINED FROM: TAKEN BY:
                                    Date:
IF NOT PATIENT   Time:
— relationship to patient:

---

6 (cont.)

Date	No.	Problems	Date Resolved	Date Implemented	No	Intervention	Date Resolved

6 (cont.)

PROGRESS NOTES

Date	Name	Signature

6 (cont.)

DISCHARGE PLAN   Ward:

                              Target date for discharge:

Name of patient:

Home Address:

Next of Kin (+ address)

Place to which patient will be discharged:

1. Has patient been told of discharge plans?
   Does he/she understand the plans?
   What is his/her reaction to the plans?

2 Have the next of kin been informed of the patient's impending discharge?
   What part are they playing in the preparations?
   What part will they play in the life of the patient after discharge?

3 Have the following referrals been (a) made (b) confirmed. (Tick where relevant.)

   Community nurses (a) (b)   Home Help   (a) (b)
   Day centre   (a) (b)   Meals-on-wheels (a) (b)
   Day hospital   (a) (b)   Laundry service (a) (b)

   Name and address of social worker:

   Has an application for Part III accommodation been made for the future?

4. Has an outpatient follow up appointment been made?
   Have TTA's been obtained?
   Has an EC10 form been completed?
   Has (a) Transport   (b) Escort home   been arranged?
   (Tick where appropriate.)
   Are his rent/pension book ready and on the ward for patient to take?

5. Comments:

Appendix 7:   An example of an Oncology Care Plan format.
           (Reproduced by courtesy of The Royal Marsden Hospital.)

PATIENT INFORMATION SHEET

Name: _____ Hospital No.: _____   Likes to be known as: _____

Address: _____ DOB: _____   Marital status: _____

_____ Religion: _____   Occupation: _____

Tel. Nos.: _____   Age: _____

G.P.:_____

Next of kin/person to contact:	1	2

Names: _____   _____

Relationship: _____   _____

Address: _____   _____

Tel. Nos.: Day – _____   _____

        Night – _____   _____

Communication/language difficulty: _____

_____

Diagnosis: _____

_____

Date of admission:	1	2	3
Reason:			
Date of discharge:			

Relevant medical information: _____

_____

_____

_____

Allergies: _____

Regular medication: _____

_____

Consultant(s): _____   House officer(s): _____

_____   _____

Registrar(s): _____   Primary nurse: _____

_____   _____

7 (cont.)

REFERRALS:		
DATE:	NAME OF PERSON/DEPT.	COMMENT

DISCHARGE INFORMATION: NB: If necessary use a problem sheet.

DATE	

7 (cont.)

NURSING ASSESSMENT		
NAME:	WARD:	HOSPITAL No.:

HEAD AND NECK

General appearance _____

Eyes/vision _____

Ears/hearing _____

Nose _____

Mouth _____

CHEST

General appearance_____

Breathing _____

_____

Smoking habits_____

ABDOMEN/PELVIS

General appearance_____

Nausea and vomiting _____

_____

Elimination _____

_____

Menstruation _____

LIMBS

General appearance _____

Mobility_____

_____

Assistance required _____

Sensation _____

_____

SKIN

General appearance _____

Pressure areas _____

Personal hygiene _____

7 (cont.)

NUTRITION

General appearance _____

Usual weight _____ loss/gain _____ % change _____

Appetite _____

Special diet _____

SLEEP

Normal pattern _____

Aids to sleep _____

PAIN — If patient has pain, use the pain assessment chart.

MENTAL/PSYCHOLOGICAL STATE

_____

_____

_____

SPIRITUAL

Religious beliefs/observances _____

Other information _____

SOCIAL: dependents, housing, other family support, etc.

_____

_____

_____

_____

_____

_____

_____

_____

_____

_____

_____

_____

_____

7 (cont.)

KNOWLEDGE OF ILLNESS

BASELINE OBSERVATIONS

Date	Urine	T	P	R	B/P	Ht	Wt	% loss % gain	Valuables	Signature

COMMUNICATION SHEET

PATIENT'S NAME:				HOSPITAL No.

NURSING PROBLEM INDEX

DATE	No.	PROBLEM/NEED	DATE RESOLVED/ CHANGED	EVALUATION

7 (cont.)

PATIENT'S NAME:		HOSPITAL No.
DATE	INVESTIGATIONS	SPECIAL INSTRUCTIONS AND COMMENTS
	TREATMENT (Radiotherapy, Chemotherapy, Surgery)	

7 (cont.)

		NURSING CARE PLAN	

PATIENT'S NAME:

HOSPITAL No.:

WARD:

DATE	No.	PATIENT PROBLEM/NEED	NURSE'S SIGNATURE
	GOAL		
	NURSING ACTION/INSTRUCTION		
DATE RESOLVED/ CHANGED	CONTINUOUS EVALUATION		

Appendix 8: An example of a Paediatric Care Plan format.
(Reproduced by courtesy of The Royal Marsden Hospital.)

CHILDREN'S DEPARTMENT — INFORMATION SHEET

DIAGNOSIS: _____ Hospital No.: _____ Primary nurse: _____

CHILD'S NAME: _____ Nickname: _____

Address: _____

Temp. Address: _____

_____

Telephone No. Home: _____ Temp. Nos.: _____

ᴐDate of Birth: _____ Religion: _____ Baptized: _____

Next of Kin: _____ Likes to be known as: _____

GP Name: _____ Telephone No.: _____

Health Visitor, Social Worker: _____

Date of admission	1	2	3
Reason			
Date of discharge			

Communication/Language difficulty:

FAMILY
1 or 2 Parent Family: _____

Siblings · Names: _____

Ages: _____

Travel: _____

Parents' comprehension of diagnosis: _____

Parents wishing to be resident: _____ Room Nos.: _____

THE CHILD
Past illness: _____

_____

Operations: _____ Varicella: _____

Allergies: _____ Measles: _____

Drugs on admission: _____

8 (cont.)

REFERRALS:		
DATE:	NAME OF PERSON/DEPT.	COMMENT

DISCHARGE INFORMATION: NB: If necessary use a problem sheet.

DATE	

8 (cont.)

**CHILDREN'S DEPARTMENT
NURSING ASSESSMENT**

THE CHILD   NAME: _____

ACTIVITIES OF LIVING

APPETITE: _____

    Likes: _____ Dislikes: _____

    _____

    Fluid preferences: _____

MOBILITY: _____

HEARING AND VISION: _____

SLEEPING: _____ Usual bedtime: _____

    Daytime sleep: _____

ELIMINATION:_____ Uses — Potty: _____ Toilet: _____

    Urinary: _____

    Bowel: _____

    _____

SOCIAL ACTIVITIES

    Hobbies/Interests: _____

    _____

    Favourite toy: _____ Toy with child? _____

    Pets: _____

    Special friends: _____

EDUCATIONAL DEVELOPMENT

    School _____

    Favourite subjects: _____

    _____

    _____

8 (cont.)

THE CHILD — NURSING ASSESSMENT

PSYCHOLOGICAL

SOCIAL

PHYSICAL APPEARANCE

8 (cont.)

KNOWLEDGE OF ILLNESS

BASELINE OBSERVATIONS

Date	Urine	T	P	R	B/P	Ht	Wt	% loss % gain	Valuables	Signature

COMMUNICATION SHEET

PATIENT'S NAME:				HOSPITAL No.

NURSING PROBLEM INDEX

DATE	No.	PROBLEM/NEED	DATE RESOLVED/ CHANGED	EVALUATION

8 (cont.)

PATIENT'S NAME:		HOSPITAL No.
DATE	INVESTIGATIONS	SPECIAL INSTRUCTIONS AND COMMENTS
	TREATMENT (Radiotherapy, Chemotherapy, Surgery)	

8 (cont.)

NURSING CARE PLAN			
PATIENT'S NAME:			
HOSPITAL No.:			
WARD:			
DATE	No.	PATIENT PROBLEM/NEED	NURSE'S SIGNATURE
	GOAL		
	NURSING ACTION/INSTRUCTION		
DATE RESOLVED/ CHANGED	CONTINUOUS EVALUATION		

Appendix 9: An example of a Short-stay Care Plan format.
(Reproduced by courtesy of The Royal Marsden Hospital.)

SHORT STAY SHEET

Consultant _____

Diagnosis _____

Past medical history_____
_____
_____
_____
_____
_____
_____
_____

History of present illness _____
_____
_____
_____
_____
_____
_____
_____

Reason for admission_____
_____
_____
_____

Information given to patients/relatives
for admission_____
_____
_____

Observation of general condition on
admission
_____
_____
_____

Signature of nurse admitting patient

Date_____

Name_____

Age_____

Address_____
_____
_____

Next of kin _____
_____

Address (if different from above) _____
_____

Telephone (1) _____

(2) _____

Admission date_____

Time_____

Accompanied by_____

From where _____

Occupation _____

Marital status_____

Will patient require transport home? _____
— If so, please book it

Transport arranged — _____

Relevant social history _____
_____
_____
_____
_____
_____

Medication on admission and how stored
_____
_____
_____

Medication ordered for return home
_____
_____

Observations on admission

Temp_____ Wgt _____

Pulse_____ Hgt _____

B/P_____ _____

Urinalysis_____ _____

9 (cont.)

Operation_____	Valuables?_____
Date:_____	How stored_____
Treatment: _____	What patient knows about his condition
_____	_____
_____	_____
Next follow up date: _____	_____
	_____

Date Patient need/problem	Nursing action/goal
1. _____	1. _____
_____	_____
_____	_____
_____	_____
_____	_____
2. _____	2. _____
_____	_____
_____	_____
_____	_____
_____	_____
3. _____	3. _____
_____	_____
_____	_____
_____	_____
_____	_____

EVALUATION/COMMENT   **Signature**

1. _____   _____
_____   _____
_____   _____
2. _____   _____
_____   _____
_____   _____
3. _____   _____
_____   _____
_____   _____

Index

165